Phonological Architecture

Oxford Studies in Biolinguistics

General editor: Cedric Boeckx, Catalan Institute for Advanced Studies (ICREA) and Center for Theoretical Linguistics at the Universitat Autònoma de Barcelona

Advisory editors:
Anna Maria Di Sciullo, Université du Québec à Montréal; Simon Fisher, The Wellcome Trust Centre for Human Genetics; W. Tecumseh Fitch, Universität Wien; Angela D. Friederici, Max Planck Institute for Human Cognitive and Brain Sciences; Andrea Moro, Vita-Salute San Raffaele University; Kazuo Okanoya, Brain Science Institute, Riken; Massimo Piattelli-Palmarini, University of Arizona; David Poeppel, New York University; Maggie Tallerman, Newcastle University

Published
The Biolinguistic Enterprise
Edited by Anna Maria Di Sciullo and Cedric Boeckx

Phonological Architecture: A Biolinguistic Perspective
By Bridget D. Samuels

The series welcomes contributions from researchers in many fields, including linguistic computation, language development, language evolution, cognitive neuroscience, and genetics. It also considers proposals which address the philosophical and conceptual foundations of the field, and is open to work informed by all theoretical persuasions.

Phonological Architecture

A Biolinguistic Perspective

BRIDGET D. SAMUELS

OXFORD
UNIVERSITY PRESS

OXFORD
UNIVERSITY PRESS

Great Clarendon Street, Oxford OX2 6DP

Oxford University Press is a department of the University of Oxford.
It furthers the University's objective of excellence in research, scholarship,
and education by publishing worldwide in

Oxford New York

Auckland Cape Town Dar es Salaam Hong Kong Karachi
Kuala Lumpur Madrid Melbourne Mexico City Nairobi
New Delhi Shanghai Taipei Toronto

With offices in

Argentina Austria Brazil Chile Czech Republic France Greece
Guatemala Hungary Italy Japan Poland Portugal Singapore
South Korea Switzerland Thailand Turkey Ukraine Vietnam

Oxford is a registered trade mark of Oxford University Press
in the UK and in certain other countries

Published in the United States
by Oxford University Press Inc., New York

British Library Cataloguing in Publication Data
Data available

Library of Congress Cataloging in Publication Data
Data available

Typeset by SPI Publisher Services, Pondicherry, India
Printed in Great Britain
on acid-free paper by
MPG Books Group, Bodmin and King's Lynn

ISBN 978–0–19–969435–8 (Hbk.)
      978–0–19–969436–5 (Pbk.)

1 3 5 7 9 10 8 6 4 2

Contents

General Preface

This series aims to shed light on the biological foundations of human language. Biolinguistics is an important new interdisciplinary field that sets out to explore the basic properties of human language and to investigate how it matures in the individual, how it is put to use in thought and communication, what brain circuits implement it, what combination of genes supports it, and how it emerged in our species. In addressing these questions the series aims to advance our understanding of the interactions of mind and brain in the production and reception of language, to discover the components of the brain that are unique to language (especially those that also seem unique to humans), and to distinguish them from those that are shared with other cognitive domains.

Advances in theoretical linguistics, genetics, developmental and comparative psychology, the evo-devo program in biology, and cognitive neuroscience have made it possible to formulate novel, testable hypotheses concerning these basic questions. Oxford Studies in Biolinguistics will contribute to the emerging synthesis among these fields by encouraging and publishing books that show the value of transdisciplinary dialogue, and which highlight the unique research opportunities such a dialogue offers.

Contributions to the series are likely to come from researchers in many fields, including linguistic computation, language development, language evolution, cognitive neuroscience, and genetics. The series welcomes work that addresses the philosophical and conceptual foundations of the field, and is open to work informed by all theoretical persuasions. We expect authors to present their arguments and findings in a manner that can be understood by scholars in every discipline on which their work has a bearing.

The present volume shows the conceptual and empirical benefits of adopting a rigorous biological orientation in the domain of phonological theory, an area that so far has received less attention within biolinguistics than syntax has. The research program delineated here is a major step forward in situating phonology in the broader cognitive, and indeed biological, sciences.

Cedric Boeckx

Acknowledgments

Like most people, I didn't have a lifelong dream of becoming a linguist, though it didn't take long—in my case, about a week into college—before I began to entertain thoughts in that direction. This book represents my attempt at answering questions about the nature of human language that first fascinated me then, and which have been nagging at me ever since. I hope, however, that I will be able to reach more than just linguists with this book. To that end, I have included a glossary, tried to explain technical concepts as they come up, and provided references to texts where more in-depth explanations can be found. However, Chapters 4 and 5 may still be daunting for those who do not have any formal background in generative syntax and phonology; Chapter 6, which examines language variation, may be more accessible. Chapters 1 and 2 are more concerned with foundational concepts and philosophy, while Chapter 3 deals mostly with animal cognition but should not require particular expertise in this area.

In thinking about the debts I've accrued on this journey, I realize that I cannot even begin to acknowledge everyone who deserves thanks here. I am struck by how lucky I've been to be at the right place at the right time for so many things. I had the good fortune to arrive at Harvard in 2002, which was fortuitous for two major reasons: first, I got my introduction to linguistics and to phonology from Bert Vaux, who has had a profound impact on me; second, Hauser, Chomsky, and Fitch's paper on the evolution of language was brand new, and being in their neighborhood, I was exposed to this transformative line of biolinguistic thought from day one. The following year, Cedric Boeckx arrived, encouraging and inspiring me to work harder; do more; think bigger. I feel so proud and so lucky to have been his student, and I have appreciated his advice and support at every stage of this particular project and so many others. I also owe a great deal to Morris Halle and Charles Reiss, who were so generous to me with their time, particularly as I was writing my dissertation, and who both contributed a great deal to how I approach and understand the issues that I address here. And when it was time for me to move on, I ended up with a truly ideal position at the University of Maryland—a place where I have been among friends and felt at home from the very beginning. I am very grateful to the linguistics faculty, especially Norbert Hornstein and Bill Idsardi, for the opportunity.

I am grateful to all my colleagues and friends who contributed both to the content of the present work and the mental state of its author. Among the Harvard group, I want to give special mention to Beste Kamali, Dennis Ott, Hiroki Narita, Julie Li Jiang, and Süleyman Ulutaş. We spent literally thousands of hours in class together during graduate school, an experience which was both humbling and inspiring. Many thanks also to the language science community at UMD, especially Ariane Rhone, Dave Kush, Eri Takahashi, Mathias Scharinger, Pedro Alcocer, Phil Monahan, So-One Hwang, and Terje Lohndal (everyone should be so lucky to have such a voracious reader and commenter for a friend). Additionally, I am particularly indebted to the students in my Fall 2010 Linguistics 419E seminar, who were the test audience for much of the following material, and to Seth Keating and Nicole Stines, who prepared the index and helped edit the manuscript. Dan Dediu's and an anonymous reviewer's thoughtful and detailed comments truly helped to strengthen the manuscript, as did Sylvie Jaffrey's careful editing, and I am grateful to each of them. I also very much appreciate the time and effort that Julia Steer at Oxford University Press put into shepherding my manuscript and me through the publication process.

Last but certainly not least, I would like to thank my family, whose love, encouragement, and generous support made this entire journey possible. This book is dedicated to them.

B. S.

May 2011
College Park, Maryland

Abbreviations and Symbols

A	Adjective
Acc	Accusative
Appl	Applicative
Asp	Aspect
C	Complementizer *or* consonant
C–I	Conceptual–Intentional
Comp	Complement
Conj	Conjunction
CP	Complementizer Phrase
D	Determiner
Dat	Dative
Dist	Distributive
DO	Direct object
DP	Determiner Phrase
DS	Deep Structure
ERP	Event-related potential
FLB	Faculty of Language—Broad Sense
FLN	Faculty of Language—Narrow Sense
Foc	Focus
Gen	Genitive
Imper	Imperative
Impf	Imperfective
Infl	Inflection
IO	Indirect object
KP	Kase Phrase
LF	Logical Form
MEG	Magnetoencephalography
MMN	Mismatch negativity
MP	Minimalist Program

N	Noun
Nom	Nominative
NP	Noun Phrase
O(bj)	Object
OOC	Out of control
(P)DbP–	(Phonological) Derivation by Phase
Perf	Perfective
PF	Phonological Form
PIC	Phase Impenetrability Condition
Pl	Plural
Pres	Present
Pst	Past
R	Resonant
Sg	Singular
Spec	Specifier
S(ubj)	Subject
S–M	Sensory–Motor
SPE	*The Sound Pattern of English* (Chomsky and Halle 1968)
SS	Surface Structure
T	Tense
Top	Topic
TP	Tense Phrase
UG	Universal Grammar
V	Verb *or* vowel
VOT	Voice Onset Time
VP	Verb Phrase
β	Beginning point (in search algorithm)
γ	Target (in search algorithm)
δ	Direction (in search algorithm)
ϕ	Phonological Phrase
σ	Syllable
Σ	String in workspace (in search algorithm)
ς	Standard (in search algorithm)
$\sqrt{\ }$	root
#	Start of a phonological string
%	End of a phonological string

1

Introduction

Over fifty years have now passed since the birth of generative linguistics, as heralded by the publication of foundational works such as Noam Chomsky's (1957) *Syntactic Structures* and his review of B. F. Skinner's *Verbal Behavior* (Chomsky 1959). These are universally hailed as two of the most influential pieces in the Cognitive Revolution, and together with works such as Eric Lenneberg's (1967) *Biological Foundations of Language*, they cemented linguistics as one of the foundational disciplines of the new science of the human mind. But today, the position of linguistics within this milieu is somewhat less certain. Neuroscience and evolutionary biology are now at a stage where they can enter a dialogue with cognitive scientists, but theoretical linguistics has some difficulty holding up its end of the conversation. David Poeppel has called this the "granularity problem": linguists and neuroscientists (and, I would also add, scientists from many other fields who could potentially find collaboration with linguists mutually beneficial) are not speaking the same language, or working at the same level of abstraction.

Enter the field of biolinguistics. As Boeckx and Grohmann (2007: 2) explain, while linguists since *Syntactic Structures* have been studying the biological foundations of language in some weak sense, "the strong sense of the term 'biolinguistics' refers to attempts to provide explicit answers to questions that necessarily require the combination of linguistic insights and insights from related disciplines (evolutionary biology, genetics, neurology, psychology, etc.)." Though the term itself is not new (see Boeckx and Grohmann 2007 for a history), interest in this approach to language has intensified greatly since the year 2000, and for the first time is being sustained with the help of the journal *Biolinguistics* and series like the one in which the present volume appears.

In order to begin to make a truly biolinguistic theory, commensurable with surrounding disciplines, there is much work to be done:

Linguists... owe a decomposition (or fractionation) of the particular linguistic domain in question... into *formal operations that are, ideally, elemental and generic.* The types of computations one might entertain, for example, include concatenation, comparison, or recursion. Generic formal operations at this level of abstraction can form the basis for more complex linguistic representation and computation.

(Poeppel 2005; emphasis his)

With this goal in mind, I endeavor in the present volume to bridge this gap by addressing consumers of the linguistic/phonological literature from other fields, as well as those who are more intimately familiar with phonology. Painted in broad strokes, the outline of this work is as follows.

First, in Chapter 2, I define the object of study with which I am primarily concerned, the computational system commonly known as phonology, and establish the methodology to be used in the remainder of the work. I characterize a research program for phonology that strives to go "beyond explanatory adequacy" (Chomsky 2004) and discuss the implications for phonology that stem from the Strong Minimalist Thesis (Chomsky 2000)—the notion that language is the optimal solution to linking the Sensory–Motor (S–M) and Conceptual–Intentional (C–I) systems—and from the idea that phonology is an "ancillary" module "doing the best it can to satisfy the problem it faces: to map to the S–M interface syntactic objects generated by computations that are 'well-designed' to satisfy C–I conditions" but unsuited to communicative purposes (Chomsky 2008).

Also in Chapter 2, I seek to circumscribe the domain to be covered by a synchronic theory of phonology by clarifying assumptions about the nature of language acquisition and sound change. Following Ohala (1981), Blevins (2004), and others, I emphasize the role of the listener in propagating sound change and maintain that the cross-linguistic distribution of sound patterns correlates, at least in large part, with the frequency of the diachronic changes that give rise to those patterns. I argue that, if the goal of synchronic phonological theory is to characterize the properties of possible phonological systems, the role of diachrony must be factored out: what is *diachronically* possible must be separated from what is *computationally* possible, which is still different from what is *learnable*. This has serious consequences for phonological theory: on this view, markedness, naturalness, ease of production, ease of perception, and other functionalist principles should be eliminated from phonology proper; these are "E-language" phenomena outside of the realm of linguistic competence, and thus not demanding of explanation in the synchronic grammar. Such a perspective has the immediate advantage of reducing the size of Universal Grammar and simplifying synchronic phonological theory.

With this done, in Chapter 3 I discuss the general properties of phonological computation and the linguistic externalization system in as theory-neutral a manner as possible, using animal cognition studies to identify which components of phonology may not be unique to humans and/or to language. I demonstrate on the basis of behavioral and physiological studies on animal cognition conducted by other researchers on primates, songbirds, and a wide variety of other species that the cognitive abilities underlying human phonological representations and operations are present in creatures other than *Homo sapiens* (even if not to the same degree) and in domains other than phonology or, indeed, language proper; this is consistent with the view of the evolution of the language faculty posited by Hauser, Chomsky, and Fitch (2002). The remainder of the work is devoted to fleshing out a theory of phonology and its interfaces which is consistent with these conclusions.

In Chapter 4, I take up the question of what *is* necessarily unique about phonology. In other words, what must the phonological module look like, if it is to interface with the infinitely recursive, species-specific combinatory engine that is (linguistic, narrow) syntax? I argue for combining the best parts of Lexical Phonology (Kiparsky 1982), Distributed Morphology (Halle and Marantz 1993), and Derivation by Phase (Chomsky 2001), creating a theory I call phonological derivation by phase or PDbP. This is in spirit a defense of the direct reference conception of the syntax–phonology interface (Kaisse 1985; Odden 1990; Cinque 1993). The basis for this theory is the notion that phonology proceeds according to a cyclic derivation regulated by the phase system. I further argue, following Marvin (2002), that this is the *direct consequence* of cyclicity (i.e. phasality) in syntax. This is the "best-case scenario" according to Chomsky (2004: 107):

Assume that all three components [syntax, semantics, & phonology] are cyclic, a very natural optimality requirement and fairly conventional. [...] In the best case, there is a single cycle only. [Phonology] is greatly simplified if it can 'forget about' what has been transferred to it at earlier phases; otherwise, the advantages of cyclic computation are lost.

Not only may this solution be computationally efficient, it also allows us to recognize the important contributions of cyclic models of phonology such as those proposed by Chomsky, Halle, and Lukoff (1956), Kean (1974), Mascaró (1976), Kiparsky (1982), and Mohanan (1982), *inter alia*.

With this model in place, I present arguments that the domains of phonological rule application, both above and below the word level, come for free when we assume Distributed Morphology and a phasal syntax. Specifically, phonological processes and operations such as linearization of looped structures get the chance to apply at each application of Spell-Out, and phonological rule application is restricted by the Phase Impenetrability Condition (Chomsky 2001). I claim that morpheme-level phases can replace Lexical

Phonology's hierarchy of strata, and that clause-level phases can replace the prosodic hierarchy. These arguments are supported with analyses of segmental and suprasegmental processes.

I then zoom in to take a closer look, in Chapter 5, at the internal components of phonology, at which point I propose a repertoire of representations and operations that are consistent with the conclusions from Chapter 3 regarding the architecture of Universal Grammar and human cognitive evolution. I first define the representations that provide a workspace for the operations I introduce later in the chapter, beginning with phonological features. Zooming out, I next discuss the organization of segmental and suprasegmental material into strings and compare phonological syllables and syntactic phrases, which have been equated by Levin (1985) and many others, with some even claiming that phrase structure was exapted from syllable structure (Carstairs-McCarthy 1999). I argue with Tallerman (2006) that these analogies are false, and provide evidence that many of the properties commonly attributed to syllabic structure can be explained as well or better without positing the existence of innate structure supporting discrete syllables in the grammar.

Three operations are formalized in Chapter 5:

- SEARCH provides a means by which two elements in a phonological string may establish a probe–goal relation. The SEARCH algorithm we adopt is a modified version of the one formulated by Mailhot and Reiss (2007), itself a formalization of the system of simultaneous rule application found in Chomsky and Halle's (1968: 344): "to apply a rule, the entire string is first scanned for segments that satisfy the environmental constraints of the rule. After all such segments have been identified in the string, the changes required by the rule are applied simultaneously."
- COPY takes a single feature value or bundle of feature values from the goal of a SEARCH application and creates a copy of these feature values on the probe. I establish a typology of possible conditions on COPY independent from the parameters of SEARCH, a program begun but not fully explored by Mailhot and Reiss (2007).
- DELETE removes an element from the derivation. We discuss the difference between deletion and 'jump links' (Raimy 2000*a*; Gagnon 2008) that mimic deletion of segments but are in fact a predicted result of SEARCH and COPY.

I illustrate the application of these operations with analyses of data from domains such as vowel harmony, reduplication, affixation, and tone spread. I argue that these three parameterized operations yield a restricted typology of possible phonological processes that can achieve the necessary empirical

coverage with fewer assumptions than previous theories and no direct constraints on representations. Picking up where Chapter 3 left off, I also discuss
possible animal counterparts to these operations.

In Chapter 6, I turn to an issue which is raised as another consequence
of the Minimalist Program (see Boeckx 2008): given that genuine variation
within narrow syntax has been eliminated, being relegated instead to the
lexicon and to morphophonology, it is imperative to understand how such
variation arises. The topic of variation brings us to revisit themes such as
underspecification and diachrony, and also leads us to consider aspects of
language acquisition such as the ambiguity of linguistic data, the nature of
induction, and arguments from the poverty of the stimulus.

Chapter 7 summarizes the present work and suggests directions for future
research.

2

A Minimalist Program
for Phonology

2.1 Introduction

Before we delve into the more technical matters that will concern us for the remainder of this work, I would first like to define the object of the present study: synchronic phonology. This chapter seeks to circumscribe the domain by laying out what I take to be the primary aims of a biolinguistic phonological theory, and one that is both "substance-free" and Minimalist in character. Since these terms mean a lot of different things to a lot of different people, I want to be clear at the outset about the usage employed here. I will discuss the implications for phonology that stem from the Strong Minimalist Thesis (Chomsky 2000), from the notion that language is the optimal solution to linking the Sensory–Motor and Conceptual–Intentional systems, and from the idea that there is an asymmetry between these two interfaces, with the latter enjoying a privileged position. I will also justify why I do *not* attempt here to account for the relative markedness of phonological processes, and introduce Evolutionary Phonology (Blevins 2004) as a theory of diachronic phonology that provides a natural companion to the synchronic theory for which I argue.

2.2 Biolinguistics and Minimalism

Since phonology does not exist in a vacuum, neither can phonological theory. The theory presented here is designed to integrate with a particular architecture of grammar, and a particular way of thinking about language as an object of scientific study, namely the biolinguistic approach. I want to introduce this way of thinking first, and then discuss its connection to phonological theory in particular. In this chapter I will not stray too far from historical and conceptual concerns, but in later chapters, and particularly in Chapter 4, I will delve into the particulars of the grammatical architecture within which I situate my theory of phonology.

The discussion in this section relies heavily on works by Cedric Boeckx (Boeckx 2006, 2010*b*), which provide a much more in-depth discussion of the historical origins and theoretical underpinnings of this way of thinking than space considerations allow me to provide here, and to the editorial by Boeckx and Grohmann (2007) in the first issue of the journal *Biolinguistics*. For those who are interested in reading more about particular syntactic topics, Bošković and Lasnik (2007) contains excerpts from many of the foundational works in Minimalist syntax, arranged thematically. There are also several good textbooks on how to do Minimalist syntax, including Lasnik, Uriagereka and Boeckx (2005) and Hornstein, Nunes and Grohmann (2005). I hope that this volume will provide a companion guide for how (and why) to do biologically informed, Minimalist phonology.

For the last half century, ever since Noam Chomsky's review of B. F. Skinner's *Verbal Behavior* (Chomsky 1959), linguists in the generative tradition have sought the answer to what has been called Plato's Problem: how do children, barring pathology, all acquire the language(s) of their surroundings—whatever those may be—in a way that seems both uniform across individuals and essentially effortless (at least compared to the difficulties adults face in acquiring a foreign language)? Chomsky put forth numerous compelling arguments that the answer to Plato's Problem lies in our human biological endowment: our species is genetically programmed to grow a language, just as we are programmed to grow arms or lungs (see also Lenneberg 1967). This laid the groundwork for biolinguistics: a science of the "language organ" or "faculty of language" that makes growing a language possible. Naturally, much of the inquiry into Plato's Problem has focused on describing the properties of Universal Grammar (UG), the initial state of the faculty of language, which make the task of language learning achievable for the human infant. Over the years, more and more structure has been attributed to UG, with the goal of reducing grammar acquisition to a manageable parameter-setting task for a child learner. Chomsky (2007) calls this the "top-down" approach to characterizing UG.

Perhaps the single most important facet of Minimalism in linguistics is that it turns the top-down approach on its head. As Chomsky (2007: 3) describes it, the Minimalist Program approaches the problem "from bottom up," seeking to determine "how little can be attributed to UG while still accounting for the variety of I-languages attained." This shift in perspective is particularly apparent in more recent Minimalist works (e.g. Chomsky 2004, 2005, 2007; Boeckx 2006, *inter alia*), but it is implicit in the Strong Minimalist Thesis, which dates back to the early 1990s. The Strong Minimalist Thesis is, as Boeckx (2010*b*) puts it, "a challenge to the linguistic community: Can it be shown that the computational system at the core of [the faculty of language] is optimally or perfectly designed to meet the demands on the systems of the mind/brain it interacts with?" This is a hard-line gamble, and one that even by Chomsky's admission is likely to be wrong. Even so, it is important to push the Strong Minimalist Thesis as far as it can go (and it has taken us quite far already) because it encourages us to *make sense* of the language faculty's properties, not in isolation, but rather within the larger picture of cognition. What's more, pursuing this line of inquiry is bound to yield new understanding of the Conceptual–Intentional and Sensory–Motor systems, because it forces us to think about the "legibility conditions" imposed on the language faculty by those other modules. It is critical to distinguish this ontological commitment from methodological minimalism (i.e. Ockham's Razor), as Martin and Uriagereka (2000) were among the first to point out. The point of linguistic Minimalism is not to make the linguist's calculations more economical (a methodological minimalism); rather, we're making a bet that *the object of our study* is simple (an ontological or metaphysical minimalism); see Narita and Fujita (2010) for further discussion. Nevertheless, ontological minimalism demands methodological minimalism, though see Fortuny and Gallego (2009) for a slightly different view. I insist that, like all other scientists, we must eliminate redundancy from our theories and adopt the simplest solutions possible, *ceteris paribus*. This is just good science, and good philosophy, as has been recognized for centuries. But the Minimalist Program goes deeper than that, imploring us to seek to go "beyond explanatory adequacy" (Chomsky 2004). A major reason for pursuing Minimalism is therefore that, in the words of Fujita (2007: 83), it is "a research program for building an evolutionarily adequate theory of UG through factorization of the language faculty to its bare minimum and a principled explanation of what is truly unique to humans and human language. The [Strong Minimalist Thesis] holds that no part of UG defies a deeper, language-independent explanation." Minimalism asks us to posit only what is a "virtual conceptual necessity" or empirically unavoidable, and to seek explanations for the latter category in the systems with which the language faculty must interface.

As is often stressed, and rightfully so, Minimalism is a *research program* in the sense of Lakatos (1970), not a theory (see discussion in Boeckx (2006), §3.3). The Strong Minimalist Thesis does not imply that any one specific view of UG or of grammatical architecture is correct. In practice, Minimalist theories are largely built on the foundations of Principles & Parameters, and on Government & Binding Theory more specifically, though there are properties that characterize Minimalist theories to the exclusion of earlier ones, such as the elimination of levels of representation (DS, SS, LF, PF).

This abandonment of the Y-/T-model inevitably leads to a new understanding of the syntax–phonology interface, which I discuss at length in Chapter 4. Despite the way Minimalism has radically reshaped our view of the interfaces, it seems odd that, as van Oostendorp and van de Weijer (2005: 3) remark, the Minimalist Program "has not been applied to phonology;" similarly, Pinker and Jackendoff (2005: 220) state that "The Minimalist Program, in Chomsky's original conception, chooses to ignore ... all the phenomena of phonology." But there is no reason why this should be. This quote summarizes one of the primary motivations behind the present work:

> For decades, generative linguists have viewed the internal grammar in terms of the interplay of two types of factors: genetic endowment, generally referred to as Universal Grammar (UG), and experience—that is, exposure to e-language. In recent years this picture has been augmented by a third type of factor: general principles of biological/physical design. This new focus tends to worry those who had been hoping for a rich and articulate UG (see Pinker & Jackendoff [2005]), but on the other hand it is fully in line with minimalist thinking. A particularly welcome effect produced by this shift of focus is that we may now reassess the issue of formal similarities and dissimilarities between syntax and phonology. For many years, the dominant view has been that syntax and phonology are fundamentally different. [...] But general principles of design may very well be active in syntax and phonology in similar ways.
>
> (van Riemsdijk 2008: 227)

Given what we now understand about syntactic architecture, investigating phonology from this shifted perspective lays the groundwork for testing and refining the arguments made by Bromberger and Halle (1989) in support of the view that phonology is fundamentally different from syntax (contra van der Hulst 2005; J. Anderson 2006). Such work allows us to focus not on the question of *whether* phonology is different, but rather *how* it is different and *why* this is the case. If Minimalist biolinguists are correct to emphasize the role of the "Third Factor" (general principles of good design) in the architecture of grammar (Chomsky 2005), then this should be a fruitful endeavor.

I also want to explore the idea advanced in many recent Minimalist writings that phonology is an "ancillary" module, and that phonological systems are "doing the best they can to satisfy the problem they face: to map to the [Sensory–Motor system] interface syntactic objects generated by computations that are 'well-designed' to satisfy [Conceptual–Intentional system] conditions" but unsuited to communicative purposes (Chomsky 2008: 136); see Chomsky (2010) on this asymmetry as well. Phonology is on this view an afterthought, an externalization system applied to an already fully functional internal language system. While some have taken this to suggest that phonology might be messy, and that we shouldn't expect to find evidence of "good design" in it, there is another perspective which suggests instead that the opposite conclusion is warranted (see also Mobbs 2008): phonology might be much *simpler* (i.e. less domain-specific) than has previously been thought, making use only of abilities that had already found applications in other cognitive domains at the time externalized language emerged. In Chapter 3, I aim to dissect phonological competence to its constituent parts and see how many of them are present in the animal kingdom—and, therefore, plausibly in our first speaking ancestors. Then, in the remaining chapters, I attempt to address the obvious next question: beyond this possible inheritance, what more is necessary? My answer, as I have previously articulated (Samuels 2009*b*, *c*, 2010*c*; Samuels *et al.* forthcoming), is simple: human narrow syntax, and very little else. This view accords with the evolutionary scenario developed by Hauser, Chomsky, and Fitch (2002) and Fitch, Hauser, and Chomsky (2005), who suggest that language may have emerged suddenly as a result of minimal genetic changes with far-reaching consequences (cf. Pinker and Jackendoff 2005 and Jackendoff and Pinker 2005, who see language as manifesting complex design). Particularly relevant is the distinction that Hauser, Chomsky, and Fitch (2002) make between the "Faculty of Language—Broad Sense" (FLB), including all the systems that are recruited for language but need not be unique to language, or to humans, and the "Faculty of Language—Narrow Sense" (FLN), which is the subset of FLB that is unique to our species and to language. At present, the leading hypothesis among proponents of this view is that FLN is very small, perhaps consisting only of some type of recursion (i.e. Merge) or lexicalization (Spelke 2003; Boeckx forthcoming *b*) and the mappings from narrow syntax to the interfaces. Pinker and Jackendoff claim that phonology constitutes a major counterexample to this hypothesis. I argue that if the theory advanced here is even close to correct, then this criticism of Hauser *et al.* is unfounded.

2.3 Galilean Phonology

In seeking to disentangle facts about an individual's grammatical computation system from a whole host of other factors that affect linguistic performance at any given time, generative linguists pursue a research program that is Galilean in character.[1] Chomsky describes the Galilean style thus:

[T]he Galilean style ... is the recognition that it is the abstract systems that you are constructing that are really the truth; the array of phenomena is some distortion of the truth because of too many factors, all sorts of things. And so, it often makes good sense

---

[1] Or Copernican, or Keplerian; see Boeckx (2006), §4.1.

to disregard phenomena and search for principles that really seem to give some deep insight into why some of them are that way, recognizing that there are others you can't pay attention to. (Chomsky 2002: 98)

While the Galilean style does not entail the Strong Minimalist Thesis per se, and indeed Chomsky wrote of a Galilean-style linguistics already in his 1980 *Rules & Representations*, it does strongly encourage ontological minimalism: the quest to go beyond explanatory adequacy. It also foregrounds the study of linguistic competence, as disentangled from interfering factors of performance (memory limitations, muscle strength, mood, barometric pressure, and so on ad infinitum). That is not to say the latter cannot or should not be studied— quite the opposite. It is just that they are outside the domain of generative grammar.

I stress that this is not meant to be a free pass to ignore difficult data, and I do not intend to use it as such. Rather, it lies behind my rejection of the "knee-jerk reaction to recalcitrant data: expansion of the computational power of the phonology" (Hale and Reiss 2008: 257). I agree strongly with the continuation of the above passage: "The best science, in our view, results when, rather than bloat theories with machinery which makes possible highly accurate data-matching, we adopt a critical attitude towards the alleged data itself. Does it truly fall within the purview of phonology as computation?" Embick (2010) calls the common criticism of this view the "Putative Loss of Generalization" argument: because we seek to explain less, we are subject to the criticism that we miss generalizations (typically concerning the correlation of phonetic facts and cross-linguistic typology). But as Embick (2010: 82) rightly notes, "not every generalization is a generalization about the grammar ... [Some] generalizations fall under the purview of diachrony, acquisition, phonetics, processing, etc., in some combination perhaps. Analyzing a generalization in these terms does not exclude it from principled explanation."

Consonant with Embick, Hale, and Reiss, I take the object of phonologists' study to be a system of abstract symbolic computation, divorced from phonetic content. This has come to be known as the "substance-free" approach. I advocate substance-free phonology as a partner to Minimalism; though it is logically independent from Minimalism and could well be correct even if the Strong Minimalist Thesis or various ways Minimalist syntax is implemented turn out to be mistaken, the substance-free view makes it possible to approach phonology from bottom-up in Chomsky's sense. The substance-free approach gets its name from Hale and Reiss (2000*a*, *b*), who argue that phonologists must stop the practice of "substance abuse," or misguidedly mixing the study of phonological form with the properties of phonetic content.[2] As summarized by Reiss (2008a: 258–9),

[Hale and Reiss (2000a, b)] conclude that the best way to gain an understanding of the computational system of phonology is to assume that the phonetic substance (say, the spectral properties of sound waves, or the physiology of articulation) that leads to the construction of phonological entities (say, feature matrices) *never* directly determines how the phonological entities are treated by the computational system. The computational system treats features as arbitrary symbols. What this means is that many of the so-called *phonological universals* (often discussed under the rubric of markedness) are in fact epiphenomena deriving from the interaction of extragrammatical factors like acoustic salience and the nature of language change. Phonology is not and should not be grounded in phonetics since the facts which phonetic grounding is meant to explain can be derived without reference to *phonology*.

In short, the goal of substance-free phonology is to determine the nature of the universal core of formal properties that underlies all human phonological systems, regardless of the phonetic substance or indeed of the modality (sound, sight, touch ...) by which they are expressed.[3] This stands in stark contrast to the practice of "phonetically grounded phonology," proponents of which maintain exactly the opposite: that phonological patterns result from articulatory and perceptual phonetic factors which should be directly encoded into the grammar (in recent years, most often as teleological constraints; see e.g. the contributions in Hayes, Kirchner, and Steriade 2004).

The debate between substance-free and grounded approaches to phonology stretches back almost a full century, with the former originating in Ferdinand de Saussure and Louis Hjelmslev's insistence on the arbitrariness of linguistic signs, and the latter in the ideas of Nikolai Trubetzkoy. The history of these divergent approaches to the present day is chronicled in Morén (2007); I will review some of it within the larger context of the formalism vs. functionalism debate later in this chapter. Within the present-day substance-free program, too, multiple different theories are being explored. As Blaho (2008) notes, there are at least five variations on substance-free phonology currently practiced. I refer the reader to §1.2 of Blaho's dissertation for a list of representative publications in these various approaches and discussion of how they differ. The core set of assumptions which all these theories (including the present work) hold in common is the following:

[2] Other cognitive scientists, such as Kaplan (1995) and Pylyshyn (2003), also caution against "the seduction of substance" in their fields (computational linguistics and vision, respectively).

[3] I readily admit, though, that "substance-free" also has its limits. That is to say, human physiology bounds the possible modalities in which language can be expressed. It is difficult to see, for example, how one might produce and perceive language using the olfactory senses.

(1)   The common basis of substance-free phonology (from Blaho 2008: 2)

- Phonology refers to the *symbolic computational system* governing the *signifiant*, i.e. the non-meaningful level of linguistic competence. Phonology is taken to be *universal*—common to all (natural human) languages and all modalities—, and *innate*. Phonological knowledge is part of UG, but phonetics is not.
- Phonological primes are substance-free, in that their phonetic interpretation is invisible to phonology, and thus does not play a role in phonological computation.
- Markedness and typological tendencies (in the sense of Greenberg (1957, 1978)) are not part of phonological competence, but rather an epiphenomenon of how extra-phonological systems such as perception and articulation work.

The theory to be presented here most closely follows arguments expressed in Hale and Reiss (2000*a*, *b*) and in subsequent individual and collaborative work by these authors. Hale and Reiss (2008) provide an excellent book-length introduction to "the phonological enterprise" as they (and I, setting aside minor disagreements) see it. I briefly summarize some arguments made in these various works below.

One of the most salient points to my mind concerns the nature of what a theory of UG, and of phonological UG in particular, should seek to explain. Hale and Reiss (2008: 3) set up this hierarchy:

(2)   ATTESTED ⊂ ATTESTABLE ⊂ HUMANLY COMPUTABLE ⊂ STATABLE

a. Attested: Cree-type grammars, English-type grammars, French-type grammars

b. Attestable: "Japanese" in 200 years, Joe's "English"

c. Humanly computable: $p \rightarrow s /\_\_ r$

d. Statable: $V \rightarrow V$: in prime numbered syllables: $paka_2nu_3tipa_5forse_7 \rightarrow paka:nu:tipa:fose:$

Clearly, the set of attested grammars is not the appropriate set of languages for us to study, if we are interested in the linguistic possibilities provided by the human genetic endowment: it is, I hope, uncontroversial that the list of attested languages does not exhaust the possibilities provided by UG. Conversely, the set of statable languages is far too large: it seems like a pretty safe bet that no grammars refer to the set of prime numbers, or the sign of the Zodiac at the time of the utterance, or whether the interlocutor owns any blue-collared shirts, etc.

The more pressing question is whether it is correct for a theory of UG to zero in on the set of attestable languages, or the humanly computable ones. In fact, it seems that many phonologists would argue that the subset relations I listed above are simply not true. One argument put forth by proponents of Optimality Theory (Prince and Smolensky 2004) is that the factorial typology generated by a free ranking of violable universal constraints represents an advantage over the "typological overkill" of rule-based theories, because the former more closely mimics the set of attested languages and makes predictions about their relative probabilities. Surely the goal of factorial typology cannot *really* be to match grammars one-to-one with attested languages; it must at least allow for the possibility that a hitherto unattested grammar could be attested at some future date. But as far as I can tell, proponents of this view collapse the distinction between attestable and humanly computable grammars. Odden (2003) highlights this issue in his review of McCarthy (2002). McCarthy (2002: 39) asks a rhetorical question: what should we do if we have a phonological theory that predicts a particular sound pattern to be possible, but "diligent research at Harvard's Widener Library failed to uncover any languages of the predicted type"? Well, although Widener Library is quite large indeed, I know from personal experience that grammars of many potentially relevant languages are housed in Tozzer Library a few blocks to the north; others are only accessible with a special appointment to visit the Archives housed in an underground warren beneath Harvard Yard. I digress, but I hope you see the point: we would be remiss in revising our phonological theory to rule out any sound patterns that are not found in Widener Library's collection. Nevertheless, revision of the theory is precisely what McCarthy suggests. As Odden (2003: 164) remarks,

A complex epistemological issue lurks behind the humour: are we constructing a model of language, or a model of what we know about language? Our sampling of language is small, and countless distinct linguistic patterns happen to be unattested today, but will become attested tomorrow or the next day.

It is clear, provided that the object of our analysis is *I-language* (i.e. UG), not E-languages, that we must account for all humanly computable grammars, even if they never arise in nature. Put more strongly, the idea "that every possible [grammar] should be instantiated by some attested language . . . is naïve, just as it is deeply naïve to expect that all logically possible permutations of genetic material in the human genome are actually attested in individual humans" (Vaux 2008: 24). Specifically with respect to phonology, this means that some properties of the typological morphospace typically attributed to formal properties of the phonological system (typically to markedness) should be explained instead by reference to properties of our perception and production systems, and to sheer accidents of history; this shifts much of the burden of explaining typological generalizations to the theory of sound change. We will discuss this issue in the final pages of this chapter.

Before turning to these issues, though, I would like to address the status of rules and constraints in synchronic phonological theory. This has been a contentious issue since the early 1990s, when Optimality Theory took the phonological community by storm. I do not intend to argue against Optimality Theory in any depth here; plenty of others have already done so, on multiple conceptual, computational, and empirical grounds.[4] It is also important to note that the question of whether phonological competence is best modeled using ordered rules or constraints (or a mixture of the two), and furthermore whether any constraints to be used should be violable or inviolable (or, again, a mixture of the two), is totally orthogonal to the question of substance-free vs. phonetically grounded phonology. For example, Reiss (2008*a*) argues for a completely rule-based, substance-free approach; Blaho (2008) argues for a substance-free Optimality Theory; Vaux (2008) argues for a substance-free (or nearly so) combination of mostly rules with some inviolable constraints; Calabrese (1995, 2005) combines inviolable constraints (which refer to substance) with repair rules.[5] It has been claimed that rules and constraints are both propositional, and therefore logically equivalent (Mohanan 2000). This would seem to make the rule vs. constraint debate moot. However, this belies the fact that rules and constraints, as employed in the phonological literature, are very different objects. I take as my starting point arguments from Reiss (2008*a*) and Ch. 8 of Hale and Reiss (2008). Take a typical constraint. It states a condition, for instance: "don't end a word with a consonant." The input string is evaluated according to a procedure that determines whether the input matches the structural description of the constraint (in this case, whether it ends with a consonant) and then maps to one of the states {YES, NO} accordingly.[6] A rule goes through the same mapping procedure but adds another step: if the result is YES, part of the input is rewritten; if the result

---

[4] To my mind, some of the most compelling critical works are Vaux (2008), Hale and Reiss (2008), and Scheer (2004, forthcoming), though my proposed framework differs from the alternatives that these authors offer in ways that will become apparent throughout the remainder of this work. Also see Narita and Fujita (2010) on the extreme difficulty of positing an evolutionary scenario for an Optimality Theoretic linguistic system.

[5] There is still another family of loosely related approaches that I am setting aside completely here: Government Phonology, Dependency Phonology, Lateral Phonology, Radical CV Phonology, and Minimalist Phonology, to name a few. However, the proposal advanced here has also been influenced by this literature, as will be discussed in the relevant places.

[6] I set aside the fact, noted by Hale and Reiss, that in practice some Optimality-Theoretic constraints are stated positively, e.g. "have an onset." This requires adding a second step to the evaluation proce-

is NO, nothing happens. There is a commonality, then, between rules and constraints: both begin with the same initial step, a mapping from an input to {YES, NO}. But rules go one step further, integrating a repair contingent on the YES output, so they are essentially functions from one representation to another. (We return to this issue, and the precise formalization of rules, in Chapter 4.)

In contrast, the violation of a constraint says to the computational system: "this representation is ill-formed." I summarize here what I take to be two of the main criticisms of constraints made by Hale and Reiss (we will see a third in the next section). First, it is impossible to incorporate every single way a representation can be ill-formed into the grammar, particularly if that grammar is supposed to be innate and universal, because a linguistic representation can be ill-formed in an infinite number of ways. That is, a grammar should be stated positively, not negatively. The second argument resonates deeply with Minimalism: even positive, inviolable constraints like "all branching is binary" are superfluous because they merely restate descriptive generalizations about the interaction of linguistic primes and structure-building operations. This highlights the inherently circular nature of constraints, which Scheer (2004: 478) illustrates with the chain of logic in this non-linguistic example:

(3) a. observation   trees grow straight up
     b. the observed facts are not   trees always grow straight up
         random
     c. they *must* be as they are   there is a constraint: GR.UP
                                         "trees *must* grow straight up"
     d. WHY do we observe   trees grow straight up because
         these facts?   GR.UP forces them to do so

The guiding principle here, which I take to be paramount, is that constraints should always have theorematic status: my goal is to uncover the deeper principles of grammar from which such generalizations arise, as emergent phenomena. Part of the substance-free view is that phonological generalizations—particularly the ones that are not exceptionless, but rather strong tendencies—emerge from properties of the para-/extra-linguistic systems with which phonology interfaces, as well as properties of UG itself. In particular, biases in the perception and production systems mean that various phonological systems (rules, constrasts, etc.) are harder than others to learn, and that over time, the more easily learnable systems gain ground on the less learnable

---

dure that maps the output Yes/No to Violation/No Violation depending on whether the constraint is positive or negative, but the arguments presented in the main text still hold.

ones. Arguments that markedness is a reflection of these phonetic biases, and therefore need not be stated in the grammar, have been articulated by Ohala (1981 et seq.) and by Blevins (2004 et seq.), among others. In the next section we discuss discuss markedness more thoroughly, and then turn to Blevins' theory, Evolutionary Phonology, more specifically.

2.4 Markedness and Evolution

As mentioned in the previous section, one of the foundational ideas that characterizes the substance-free approach to phonology is that markedness is part of performance rather than phonological competence. In other words, markedness is an e-language phenomenon rather than an i-language one, and as such it properly lies outside the realm of theories intending to model synchronic phonology as manifested in an individual language user's grammar.

Since the introduction of the concept of markedness by Prague School linguists, and in particular Jakobson and Trubetzkoy, many different ideas about what exactly it means for a particular linguistic object or construction to be 'marked' have been proposed. I refer the reader to Battistella (1996) for a comprehensive overview of the historical use of this term, but I will at least mention a few different (and not necessarily mutually-exclusive) views here.

(4)   Six roles of markedness (based on Haspelmath 2006: 41 ff.)

   a.   Prague School: Markedness is language-specific
   b.   *SPE* [Chomsky and Halle 1968, *The Sound Pattern of English*];
         (most) Optimality Theory: Markedness is innate and part of Universal Grammar
   c.   Greenberg: Markedness is purely for linguists' convenience and does not describe speakers' competence
   d.   Natural Morphology: Markedness is neither part of Universal Grammar nor particular grammars, but is explanatory (and must itself be explained by disciplines other than linguistics)
   e.   Battistella (and many others, beginning with Jakobson): Markedness is ubiquitous in human culture, not just language
   f.   Markedness is sometimes also used (by linguists) in a non-technical sense, e.g. 'marked' simply means 'unusual.'

To this we can also add a long list of diagnostics from a variety of different areas which have been used (alone or in combination) to determine which member of a particular phonological opposition is marked:

Phonetic instability, articulatory simplicity, perceptual salience, neutralization, epenthesis, assimilation, segment deletion, distribution, structural complexity, language acquisition, sound change, creole genesis, cross-language frequency, and implicational relations.   (Hume 2004: 2)

There are several problems with entertaining so many diverse definitions and diagnostics of markedness within a single discipline. The Haspelmath and Hume papers cited above are particularly illuminating with respect to this issue. Haspelmath categorizes the senses of markedness found in linguistic literature into four major types: markedness as complexity, markedness as difficulty, markedness as abnormality, and markedness as a multidimensional correlation. He makes the important point that, no matter which sense of the term one uses, markedness always *demands* rather than *provides* explanation—and it is explainable by other principles in all cases. For example, markedness as phonetic difficulty demands explanation in terms of the human articulatory and/or perceptual systems; markedness as structural complexity demands explanation in terms of the added demands that complexity makes on linguistic computation (such as taxing a limited memory capacity). So when we speak of markedness, we are really using shorthand for a number of deeper factors that are in large part extralinguistic. Moreover, as Hume has noted, markedness as currently applied in mainstream phonology seems paradoxical: on the one hand, sounds with low perceptual salience (few acoustic cues) are targeted for assimilation, by which criterion they should be considered unmarked. But on the other hand, sounds that have *high* perceptual salience are also considered unmarked on the basis of other criteria. More concretely, epenthetic segments are considered unmarked, but so are segments that have a propensity to delete (see Vaux and Samuels 2003 and discussion later in this section). Hume attempts to resolve this paradox by arguing that the criteria that supposedly diagnose markedness in all its various guises are actually characteristic of another property entirely: the predictability of the category in question. On this view, more predictable information is less salient, more often deleted, and so forth. This may well be correct, but I would still argue that predictability is itself a symptom of multiple underlying causes; Hume only pushes the problem back. Regardless of whether the cover term we use is "markedness" or "predictability," we must recognize that there are deeper principles at work.

The discussions in Chapter 7 of Hale and Reiss (2008) and §3 of Hale and Reiss (2000b) provide good summaries of the position I adopt. Hale and Reiss (2000b) quote from the beginning of *SPE*'s Ch. 9, which introduces a theory of markedness (developed more fully by Kean 1975) to address a "problem" in the earlier chapters:

The problem is that our approach to features, to rules, and to evaluation has been overly formal. Suppose, for example, that we were systematically to interchange features or to replace [αF] by [-αF] (where α is +, and F is a feature) throughout our description of English structure. There is nothing in our account of linguistic theory to indicate that the result would be the description of a system that violates certain principles governing human languages. To the extent that this is true, we have failed to formulate the principles of linguistic theory, of universal grammar, in a satisfactory manner. In particular, we have not made use of the fact that the features have intrinsic content.   (Chomsky and Halle's 1968: 400)

The addition of Chapter 9, which introduces substance in the form of markedness statements, in effect takes *SPE* from a theory of humanly computable languages to attestable ones. Hale and Reiss (2000*b*: 163) argue that "switching the feature coefficients as described [above] might lead to the description of systems that are *diachronically* impossible human languages (ones that could never arise because of the nature of language change), but not to ones that are *computationally* impossible." Practitioners of substance-free phonology take this dichotomy very seriously. From our point of view, the task undertaken in *SPE*'s ch. 9 was unnecessary and indeed fundamentally misguided; a theory of *phonological competence* should not incorporate typological patterns resulting from phonetics. Later in this section, I will describe the non-teleological theory of sound change which I believe best accords with this view.

Another problem with building markedness into UG is framed by Hale and Reiss as an argument against Optimality Theory but I think the point is a larger one. They note that if the consequence of a constraint violation is only that the resulting structure is "marked" (ill-formed in a relative, but not absolute, sense), as in Optimality Theory, and if that constraint is innate, then it is either misleading or irrelevant to a child learner:

Equipped with an [Optimality Theory]-type UG, a child born into a Standard German-speaking environment 'knows' that voiced coda obstruents are 'marked'. However, this child never needs to call upon this knowledge to evaluate voiced coda obstruents, since there are none in the ambient target language. In any case, by making use of positive evidence, the child successfully acquires a language like German. Born into an English-speaking environment, the child again knows that voiced coda obstruents are marked. However, the ambient language provides ample positive evidence that such sounds are present, and the child must override the supposed innate bias against voiced coda obstruents in order to learn English. So, this purported UG-given gift of knowledge is either irrelevant or misleading for what needs to be learned.
(Hale and Reiss 2000*a*: 173–174)

The message here is that markedness is not a particularly useful concept for language acquisition; the linguistic input is actually a far better source than a rich UG for all the information which is necessary for the child to figure out alternations or distributions which innate grammatical principles of markedness would supposedly help her to discover (see also Vaux 2009*a* for related discussion).

I would now like to discuss another case which argues against the utility and adequacy of competence-based theories of markedness, namely the process of consonant epenthesis. This is a widely attested phenomenon among the world's languages which involves the insertion of a consonant that is not found in the underlying representation of a word, such as in dialects of English which insert /r/ in phrases such as "*the pizza(r) is cold*." The arguments I present here largely follow the treatment of consonant epenthesis by Vaux and Samuels (2003).

The basic problem when faced with the facts of consonant epenthesis is to determine (*a*) what are the consonants which it is possible to insert cross-linguistically; and (*b*) why a particular language develops a process which inserts the particular consonant that it does. From the perspective of certain phonologists, consonant epenthesis "provides valuable insight into marked-ness relations" because only unmarked segments are chosen for epenthesis (de Lacy 2006: 79). In contrast, the view espoused by Vaux and Samuels (and in the present work) is that consonant epenthesis stems from the re-analysis of deletion rules and does not show anything like "emergence of the unmarked." The restrictiveness of markedness-based accounts is actually a disadvantage, because when we look at the typology of consonant epenthesis, we find that virtually anything is possible. One approach which a number of phonologists pursued in the early 1990s, and as early as Broselow (1984), was that consonant epenthesis involves the insertion of a default coronal (coronal being the least marked place), usually [t]. However, since so many counterexamples exist, this approach has largely been abandoned. More sophisticated approaches emerged with Optimality Theory: for example, Lombardi (2002) states that the glottal stop is the most frequent epenthetic consonant, and therefore must represent the least marked place. She posits a universally fixed hierarchy of markedness constraints which refer to place, intended to capture this fact:

(5)   *Dorsal, *Labial ≫ *Coronal ≫ *Pharyngeal

De Lacy (2006) takes a similar approach, positing constraints which eliminate the necessity of a fixed constraint ranking (problematic because free ranking is often taken to be a fundamental tenet of Optimality Theory) by building the hierarchy of place markedness directly into his constraints. Thus, rather than having constraints which penalize each place individually, he posits a constraint *{Dorsal} alongside *{Dorsal, Labial}, *{Dorsal, Labial,

CORONAL}, etc. The *{DORSAL, LABIAL} constraint penalizes both dorsal and labial segments, and *{DORSAL, LABIAL, CORONAL} penalizes both of these plus coronals; dorsals (the most marked place) violate more of these constraints than any other segments, labials (the second-most marked place) violate one constraint less than dorsals, and so on down the line. Lombardi and de Lacy's approaches are but two of the many markedness-based accounts to consonant epenthesis which have been proposed.

Epenthesis of a glottal stop in such a system is trivial, since it is stipulated as being quite low in markedness. And epenthesis of [t], as in the famous case of Axininca Campa /inkoma-i/ → [iŋkomati], can be achieved through inventory constraints: Axininca inserts a coronal rather than a glottal stop because its inventory lacks /ʔ/.[7] However, there are several problems with such an account. We might ask ourselves

what fact other than its propensity to get inserted reflects [ʔ]'s extreme unmarkedness? This is a harder question: the standard evidence for markedness, the implicational universals, suggest otherwise: [ʔ]'s presence in an inventory is not asymmetrically implied by the presence of all other C's, or indeed by the presence of all other members of its stricture class. [...] I conclude that there is either no constant context-free, all-purpose preference for glottal as against other stops, or, if there is a preference, it is the opposite from the one needed to predict the proper choice of epenthetic C.

(Steriade 2009: 173–4)

This is another illustration of the confusion which arises when different ostensive diagnostics for markedness yield conflicting results. As Steriade also notes, homorganic glides are more commonly epenthesized next to vowels than are glottal stops, so it is not even clear that the effort to make glottal epenthesis the unmarked case is worthwhile. But what's even worse is that many epenthetic patterns cannot be described in terms of markedness at all. Vaux and Samuels (2003; see references therein) provide a sampling:

(6) Epenthesized consonants

    t   Axininca Campa, Korean, French, Maru, Finnish
    d   a French aphasic
    n   Korean, Greek, Sanskrit, Dutch, Swiss German, Armenian, Mongolian, English
    ŋ   Buginese, Balantak
    N   Inuktitut, East Greenlandic

---

[7] Constraints which penalize segments of a particular sonority being adjacent to a vowel (e.g. *FRicV) can be used to ensure that [t] is inserted rather than other possible candidates for insertion, such as [h] and [s].

r	English, German, Kakati, Assamese, Uyghur, Basque, Japanese, Spanish
l	Bristol English, Midlands American English, Reading English, Motu, Polish, Romanian
j	Turkish, Uyghur, Faroese, Greenlandic, various Indic languages, Arabic, Portuguese, various Slavic languages
w	Guajiro, Greenlandic, Arabic, Romanian
v	Marathi, Sinhalese, Portuguese
b	Basque
ʃ	Basque
ʒ	Cretan Greek, Mani Greek, Basque
g	Mongolian, Buryat
s/z	French, Land Dayak, Dominican Spanish, child speech
x	Land Dayak
k	Maru

Cross-linguistic notions of markedness are simply not helpful for explaining this phenomenon or others like it—virtually anything is possible, though not all outcomes may be equally probable. This is a major problem for an approach such as de Lacy's, in which labials and dorsals should never be candidates for epenthesis since they are so high in the markedness hierarchy (see discussion in K. Rice 2008: 365–6). Phonological theory must be able to account for the entire range of epenthesized consonants, however idiosyncratic. Appealing to a unitary, innate notion of markedness severely hampers the flexibility required to achieve the necessary empirical coverage.

Of course, denying an explanatory role to markedness means something else must take its place in accounting for the fact that some patterns and processes are more common than others. Blevins' (2004 et seq.) Evolutionary Phonology framework provides means for filling this void. In the introduction of Blevins (2004), the working hypothesis of Evolutionary Phonology is stated very clearly (pp. 8–9; emphasis hers):

[R]ecurrent synchronic sound patterns have their origins in recurrent phonetically motivated sound change. As a result, there is no need to directly encode the frequent occurrence of these patterns in synchronic grammars themselves. Common instances of sound change give rise to commonly occurring sound patterns. Certain sound patterns are rare or unattested, because there is no common pathway of change which will result in their evolution.

S. Anderson (2009: 807) succinctly describes the implications of such an approach for the locus of explanation when it comes to phonological "universals," or strong tendencies:

Explanations of this sort do not depend on properties of the Language faculty in any essential way, and to the extent they can be generalized, deprive us of a basis for inferring properties of that faculty from phonological universals. On this view, the locus of explanation in phonology shifts from synchronic structure to diachrony, more or less as our neogrammarian ancestors told us. The regularities we find are regularities of the input data, as shaped by factors of phonetic production and perception in the operation of linguistic change ...

The substance-free approach to phonology holds that eliminating this potential source of information about UG is actually a good thing, because most "universals" in phonology are merely strong tendencies with exceptions that must be accounted for; the majority leanings are to be explained by extragrammatical pressures, not hard constraints on computation.[8] Thus, the theory of diachronic phonology must play a more active role in explaining typology. The exact implementation of both the diachronic and synchronic theories is negotiable; the former is the subject of this section, and the latter will occupy us for the rest of this work. I want to emphasize yet again that this does not mean phonetics should be abandoned or disregarded. As S. Anderson (1981: 497) succinctly puts it (emphasis his),

> it is still very much part of the business of phonologists to look for 'phonetic explanations' of phonological phenomena, but not in order to justify the traditional hope that all phenomena of interest can be exhaustively reduced in this way. Rather, just as when syntacticians look for pragmatic accounts of aspects of sentence structure, the reason is to determine what sorts of facts the linguistic system proper is *not* responsible for: to isolate the core of features whose arbitrariness from other points of view makes them a secure basis for assessing the properties of the language faculty itself.

While I question certain aspects of Evolutionary Phonology, as will soon become clear, I fully support an approach to phonological typology that emphasizes the role of extragrammatical factors over grammatical constraints. The tension between these two sources of explanation is rooted in the dialogue between formalism and functionalism that is in fact older than generative linguistics (this dialogue is, I would add, the same from which the substance-free and phonetically grounded approaches emerged). This issue has occupied several generations of linguists, at least as far back as Edward

---

[8] Though one of the arguments for Evolutionary Phonology is that so-called phonological universals typically have exceptions, I want to make clear that the presence of such exceptions is merely a *clue* that we should be looking to extragrammatical factors for an explanation of such tendencies; even exceptionless generalizations may not warrant grammatical explanations. As Hornstein and Boeckx (2009: 81) write, when we turn our attention to true "I(nternalist)-Universals," or the laws of the faculty of language, as opposed to Greenbergian "E(xternalist)-Universals," "the mere fact that every language displayed some property P does not imply that P is a universal in the I-sense. Put more paradoxically, the fact that P holds universally does not imply that P is a universal."

Sapir and Nikolai Trubetzkoy. One aspect of how the debate has manifested itself most clearly is in the way teleological explanations for phonological generalizations have been treated. Outside the realm of linguistics, teleology has come in and out of fashion at various times through the centuries: "for Aristotle, a non-teleological universe (even with respect to inanimate matter) was inconceivable ... from Darwin on, teleology is pretty much anathema, or at the very least weak-minded, romantic or obscurantist" (Lass 1980: 64). This is certainly not the case in the phonetically based phonology tradition today, nor was it the case among some circles in the pre-generative era. The Prague School was particularly amenable to teleological explanation in diachronic phonology, since in its view all language necessitated consideration from a functional perspective. Jan Baudouin de Courtenay and Otto Jespersen can be viewed as the intellectual forefathers of the functionalist movement, though it did not gain momentum until a couple of decades into the twentieth century. Roman Jakobson was one of the first linguists to develop the fledgling theory more fully, opining in a Prague Linguistic Circle paper that "the overlapping between territorially, socially or functionally distinct linguistic patterns can be fully comprehended only from a teleological point of view, since every transition from one system to another necessarily bears a linguistic function" (Jakobson 1962a: 1). He also later wrote that "quand nous considérons une mutation linguistique dans le contexte de la synchronie linguistique, nous l'introduisons dans la sphère des problèmes téléologiques" (when we consider a linguistic change in the context of synchronic linguistics, we introduce it into the sphere of teleological problems; Jakobson 1962b: 218).

Such acceptance of teleological explanation was by no means the consensus outside the Prague School, however. In other circles, the approach was met with strong criticism:

While Jakobson's propositions diverged from the practice of other linguists in all of the major respects, this was especially true in his urging a concentration on the system of distinctive sound differences to the exclusion of other phonetic facts, and in proposing a teleological, system-determined conception of linguistic change. It is by no means clear that the latter notion ever really prevailed: while historical studies came soon to be cast in terms of changes undergone by the phonological system, the role played by the system in motivating change generally in a teleological fashion was stressed more by theoreticians ... than by the mainstream of practicing historical linguists.

(S. Anderson 1985: 89)

Saussure sought to maintain a strict separation between synchrony and diachrony, a dichotomy which Jakobson rejected because it precluded the possibility of interpreting linguistic change teleologically (S. Anderson 1985: 118).

Yet Leonard Bloomfield, in stark contrast to Jakobson and Martinet, called teleology "a mentalistic pseudo-solution" that "cuts off investigation by providing a ready-made answer to any question we may ask" (Bloomfield 1970: 284).

The fundamental tenets of Evolutionary Phonology resonate with arguments made by the Neogrammarians, Jespersen, Greenberg, and particularly Baudouin de Courtenay. These founding fathers of phonology were adamant that synchronic sound systems are best understood through the changes that produce them. Blevins adopts a similar view but differs from the tradition by rejecting teleology in sound change. In Evolutionary Phonology, the only goal-directed processes that interact with pure phonological change are morphological analogy and the pressure to preserve paradigms where adhering to a regular sound change would cause paradigmatic contrasts to collapse. The elimination of teleological goals (such as ease of articulation and perceptual clarity) from the grammar is one major way in which Evolutionary Phonology differs from other theories. Adopting terminology from Newmeyer (2005), most theories on the market at present fall under the category of "atomistic functionalism": they maintain a direct link between the properties of the grammar and the functional motivations for these properties. Evolutionary Phonology, on the other hand, holds to a type of "holistic functionalism" in which the influence of functional motivations is limited to the language acquisition process and manifests itself in the patterns of linguistic change.

As I have already mentioned, Evolutionary Phonology provides a concrete theory of how to explain the relative frequencies of various sound patterns; it is the substance-free answer to factorial typology. In mainstream Optimality Theory, constraints on synchronic grammars and the cross-linguistically fixed rankings of such constraints serve to create a markedness hierarchy. The more marked a sound pattern, the rarer it will be. In contrast, Evolutionary Phonology treats markedness as an e-language concept belonging strictly to the domain of performance, not competence. Under this conception of phonology, because some sound changes are rare, the synchronic patterns created by those changes will also be rare. This has far-reaching consequences for synchronic phonological theory which are distinctly Minimalist in character: in short, pure phonology shrinks considerably.

Another reason why some sound patterns are rare according to Evolutionary Phonology is that multiple independent sound changes must occur sequentially in order for those patterns to arise. Patterns formed by common changes or sets thereof will occur at a higher frequency than patterns necessitating rarer chains of events. The status of processes such as final voicing, which are notoriously rare (to the point of being unattested, or nearly so), is critical here. The Evolutionary Phonology hypothesis is that final voicing should be computationally possible, just like final *de*voicing, but only marginally attested because of the nature of the biases in perception and production which drive phonological change. This goes directly against the statement at the beginning of *SPE* Ch. 9, quoted earlier in this chapter.

In addition to arguing for using diachronic phonology to explain the relative prevalence of synchronic patterns, Blevins also proposes a specific listener-based model of sound change. She holds that phonetically motivated sound changes fall into one (or more) of three categories in the "CCC-model" of Evolutionary Phonology: CHANGE, CHANCE, and CHOICE.

(7) Evolutionary Phonology typology of sound change (Blevins 2004: 32–3)

    a. CHANGE: The phonetic signal is misheard by the listener due to perceptual similarities of the actual utterance with the perceived utterance.

    b. CHANCE: The phonetic signal is accurately perceived by the listener but is intrinsically phonologically ambiguous, and the listener associates a phonological form with the utterance which differs from the phonological form in the speaker's grammar.

    c. CHOICE: Multiple phonetic signals representing variants of a single phonological form are accurately perceived by the listener, and due to this variation, the listener acquires a prototype or best exemplar of a phonetic category which differs from that of the speaker; and/or associates a phonological form with the set of variants which differs from the phonological form in the speaker's grammar.

The first of these, CHANGE, covers the range of cases in which a learner mishears an utterance and treats it as a token of a different but perceptually similar utterance. An example of CHANGE that Blevins gives is the sequence /anpa/, pronounced with some degree of assimilation of the nasal to the following stop, being misinterpreted as having both surface form [ampa] and underlying form /ampa/ due to the weakness of the cues indicating the place of the preconsonantal nasal.

CHANCE changes are those in which the hearer reconstructs an underlying representation of an inherently phonologically ambiguous signal which differs from the representation maintained by the speaker. A hypothetical instance of CHANCE would involve [ʔa̰ʔ] being analyzed as /ʔa/, /aʔ/, /ʔaʔ/, or /a̰/, provided this representation differs from what the speaker has in mind. Frequency guides the analysis, so less frequent sequences are less likely to be posited as underlying forms.[9] The Feature-to-Segment Mapping Principle, a property of the acquisition process which produces anti-identity (Obligatory Contour Principle) effects, also affects CHANCE:

(8) FEATURE-TO-SEGMENT MAPPING PRINCIPLE (Blevins 2004: 152)
     In the learning algorithm which allows listeners to interpret the phonetic string as a sequence of segments, a phonetic feature, F_p, whose domain overlaps with other segment-defining phonetic features is assumed to have a unique featural source $/S_F/$ in the phonological representation (where F may be a feature or feature-complex).

The Feature-to-Segment Mapping Principle disadvantages a multiple-source analysis like /ʔaʔ/ for the percept [ʔa̰ʔ]. The result of a CHANCE change driven by such reanalysis[10] is imperceptible, entailing no immediate change in pronunciation.

CHOICE, on the other hand, produces tiny shifts in pronunciation akin to those documented in the Labovian tradition. When there are multiple variants of an utterance in circulation and the hearer adopts a phonological representation or "best exemplar" that differs from the speaker's, this is an instance of CHOICE. Upon hearing [kkáta] in alternation with [kǎkáta] and [kakáta], a listener could assume underlying /kkáta/ and an epenthesis rule, rather than the speaker's underlying /kakáta/ with a vowel shortening/deletion rule.

In none of these three types of sound change does ease of articulation or ease of pronunciation directly influence the direction of change. Instead, like markedness, these are taken to be emergent properties.

While it is difficult to argue against mechanisms such as CHANCE, CHANGE, and CHOICE playing a role in sound change, it is less clear that they are the only players: explaining how these mishearings of individual words eventually explain Neogrammarian-style exceptionless sound change would not be a trivial task. It is not enough simply to say that completed sound changes undergo lexical diffusion (Blevins 2004: 260). Nor is it readily apparent that distinguishing among these particular three categories has any practical value for

[9] Language-specific constraints, which themselves must be learned, come into play here in the Evolutionary Phonology model. I do not see how, on this view, the phonologist (or the child) can determine when to posit a constraint and when doing so would be redundant restatement of a generalization which emerges from the data. As discussed earlier, I circumvent this duplication problem by eliminating such constraints entirely.
[10] Though I use the term "reanalysis" in keeping with Blevins, bear in mind that, as Faarlund (2008) points out, this is a misnomer. It might better be called simply "analysis," since (as we will discuss further in Ch. 6) the child has no access to the grammar which produced the input she receives.

the linguist since there seems little hope of ascertaining which 'C'-process(es) are responsible for producing a specific change, either in principle or in practice. There is another dichotomy emphasized in Evolutionary Phonology, the distinction between "natural" and "unnatural" or "crazy" phonology, which I feel could use clarification. On several occasions Blevins switches between discussion of unnatural rule types and unnatural sound patterns, which are quite separate matters. A strange historical development can in theory give rise to a well-behaved synchronic system, just as one or more natural phonological changes in the history of a language can produce sound patterns that seem unusual. Blevins (2004: 67) lists the following diachronic developments as potential sources of phonetically unnatural sound patterns; I recap her examples of each type of development below.

(9)   Four potential sources of phonetically unnatural sound patterns

	Original sound change	Subsequent development
a. analogy	$*XaY > XbY$	a or b extended to new environments on the basis of non-phonetic factors
b. rule inversion	$*XaY > XbY$	$b \to a/{\sim}X\_{\sim}Y$
c. rule telescoping	$*XaY > *XbY > XcY$	$a \to c/X\_Y$
d. accidental convergence	various	surface pattern is generalized

The relationship between analogy and sound change is famously expressed in what has come to be known as Sturtevant's Paradox: sound change is regular but creates irregularity in paradigms, whereas morphological (analogical) change is irregular but creates regularity in paradigms. Thus we see cases such as that of Ancient Greek, in which verb stems ending in coronal stops /t, t^h, d/ surfaced with stem-final [s] in the perfect middle, when adjacent to suffixes which began with coronal stops. This alternation between stop and fricative was subsequently extended by analogy such that first-person forms with /m/-initial suffixes also exhibited [s], and from there, to other places in the verbal paradigm (Garrett and Blevins 2009).

Earlier in this section I introduced a well-known family of rule inversion processes, namely those which (when completed) fall under the category of consonant epenthesis (see also Vaux and Samuels 2003). Perhaps the most famous of these cases is the reanalysis of coda /r/ loss as prevocalic /r/-insertion in the "non-rhotic" dialects of English, which now have /r/~/ø/ alternations involving words in which no /r/ was historically present, such as *I went to the spa* alongside *The spa[r] is closed*.

Rule telescoping occurs when a series of phonetically motivated sound changes collapse synchronically to produce a surface alternation which seems phonetically unusual. One such series of changes, discussed by Hyman (1975), resulted in the synchronic rule /p/ → [s] _ /i/ in some Bantu languages. This rule results from the Proto-Bantu sequence *$pį$ involving a superhigh vowel which triggered palatalization. The sequence of sound changes involved—all of them perfectly well-behaved from a phonetic point of view—was *$pį$ > *$p^jį$ > *$t^sį$ > $sį$ > si.

Blevins (2004: 69–70) calls it "accidental convergence" when "[i]ndependent sound changes of various sorts may result in exceptionless surface patterns which are generalized by language learners, despite their non-homogenous origins." The example she gives comes from the Northern Paman languages, which are unusual in that all their words purportedly begin with vowels and end with consonants.[11] This pattern resulted from one change that deleted word-initial consonants and one that deleted word-final vowels; the former is found in several Paman languages in the absence of apocope, and the latter is relatively common cross-linguistically but rarely co-occurs with initial-consonant loss. Accidental convergence seems to me to be simply a less prejudicial term for what phonologists since Kisseberth (1970) have called a "phonological conspiracy." One classic case of a conspiracy comes from Yokuts Yawelmani, which Kisseberth (1970: 293) describes thus:

Words may neither end nor begin with consonant clusters. Nowhere in a word may more than two consonants occur in a sequence. [...] If it were the case that these two constraints were each the result of the operation of a single rule in the grammar (as is, for example, the absence of word-final nonlow lax vowels in English, which follows from a single rule), then these constraints would be of no particular interest for general linguistic theory. But in fact there are a variety of phonological processes which, it might be said, 'conspire' to yield phonetic representations which contain no word-final clusters and no triliteral clusters.

These conspiring processes include deletion of the third consonant in a CCC sequence and epenthesis between the first two consonants in a CC# or CCC sequence. Additionally, there is in this language a syncope rule which deletes the middle vowel in the environment VC_CV; note that the structural description of this rule excludes the environments which would create the illicit #CC, CC#, or CCC clusters. The only difference between the Yawelmani case and the

---

[11] The validity of this statement has been challenged, however; see discussion of phonotactics and syllable structure in §5.3.

Paman one seems to be that the former is described in synchronic terms and the latter in diachronic ones. In both situations, we see a number of phonological changes/rules contributing to a particular synchronic state of affairs in the language. However, as the choice of the term "accidental convergence" suggests, in Evolutionary Phonology there is no unified force which drives the language down such a path.

The upshot of the discussion concerning the sources of phonetically unmotivated sound patterns in (9) is that unusual surface alternations, owing to a number of circumstances, nevertheless can have their origins in very common sound changes and/or morphophonological analogy. This intuitive distinction between phonetically motivated, "natural" rules and "crazy" or "unnatural" rules has a long history in the phonological literature. Blevins (2004: 71) writes that the "[t]hough the majority of work in phonological theory from the mid-1980s forward makes no principled distinction between natural and unnatural rule types, this contrast is central to Evolutionary Phonology." But a few pages later she opines that distinguishing between natural and unnatural sound patterns "seems unwarranted and indeed misguided" (ibid. 78). I want to stress that in the substance-free approach, there is no such thing as an "unnatural" rule or pattern from a computational point of view. This is supported by the fact that "there is no independent evidence that 'unnatural' phenomena are treated any differently by speakers vis-à-vis common phenomena" (Mielke 2008: 28), although in some cases the former have been shown to be more difficult to learn than the latter (Saffran and Thiessen 2003; Wilson 2003). The important point about "natural" and "unnatural" rules and patterns is that both exist—it is undeniable that phonological systems are full of arbitrary patterns, and the debris of historical accidents—and that whatever theory of representations and operations we adopt must be able to account for this.

Even though I am skeptical that the CCC-model provides comprehensive means for categorizing all instances of sound change, I still believe there is much from Evolutionary Phonology that should be taken to heart. The most significant consequence of adopting this type of approach to sound change is that it provides a serious alternative to (atomistic) functionalism. Building on the insights of predecessors such as Ohala (1981), Blevins provides an outline for a theory of sound change that seems plausible from a psycholinguistic standpoint while banishing markedness, ease of production, ease of perception, and other functionalist principles from phonology proper; these should be considered e-language phenomena that are not part of linguistic competence, thus not demanding of explanation in the synchronic grammar. Instead, the explanatory burden shifts onto innate biases (in perception, production, and hypothesis-formation) which we can begin to identify in the language acquisition process, keeping in mind that "the logical problem of language acquisition is the logical problem of language change" (Uriagereka 1998: 36). Such biases in acquisition can explain why certain sound patterns are more frequent than others without the redundancy of hard-wired constraints disfavoring utterances that are difficult to produce or perceive. Eliminating these functional considerations in the grammar has the immediate advantage of slimming UG and simplifying synchronic phonological theory.

Although Evolutionary Phonology makes significant strides in terms of shifting the locus of explanation concerning sound patterns to diachrony, Blevins presents the theory as an alternative to Optimality Theory as a synchronic theory. However, the Evolutionary Phonology theory of synchronic phonology is not concrete, and Blevins' belief that "most recurrent aspects of sound patterns found in the world's languages are encoded as language-specific synchronic constraints" is inconsistent with the arguments I summarized in the previous section, which support a constraint-free theory. In the chapters to follow, I present a substance-free synchronic theory which is consistent with the position that apparent constraints are epiphenomena of a simple set of phonological representations and operations, but which is still also complementary to the Evolutionary Phonology-style, non-teleological view of sound change. We will take the first step toward this goal in the next chapter, when I set out to enumerate the building blocks of phonological representations and operations.

3

Phonology in Evolutionary Perspective

3.1 Introduction

As a means of shifting the discussion from diachronic to synchronic phonology, I would like to continue our discussion of evolution, but in a somewhat different sense. In the previous section we considered how phonological patterns come into being—but this presupposes that there is a learner with a phonological system into which such patterns (rules) may be integrated. In this chapter I would like us to think about what abilities humans must have such that we are able to learn the range of attested phonological patterns. Once we identify and categorize those, I will focus heavily on a question that naturally arises from such a study: how much of human phonological computation (i.e. representations and operations) can be attributed to mechanisms present in other cognitive areas and/or other species?

Why should anyone care about whether animals have the skills that potentially underlie phonology? First and foremost, to the extent we can show that other species can do what phonological computations require, then the model of phonology under consideration gains credibility from an evolutionary/biological standpoint. As Hornstein and Boeckx (2009: 82) explain,

[I]n light of the extremely recent emergence of the language faculty, the most plausible approach is one that minimizes the role of the environment (read: the need for adaptation), by minimizing the structures that need to evolve, and by predefining the paths of adaptation, that is, by providing preadapted structures, ready to be recruited, or modified, or third factor design properties that emerge instantaneously, by the sheer force of physical laws.

Moreover, it is worth exploring the idea advanced in many recent Minimalist writings that phonology is an "ancillary" module, and that phonological systems are "doing the best they can to satisfy the problem they face: to map to the [Sensory–Motor system] interface syntactic objects generated by computations that are 'well-designed' to satisfy [Conceptual-Intentional system] conditions" but unsuited to communicative purposes (Chomsky 2008: 136). While some have taken this to suggest that phonology might be messy, and that we shouldn't expect to find evidence of "good design" in it, there is another perspective that suggests instead that the opposite conclusion is warranted (see also Mobbs 2008): even if the Conceptual–Intentional interface is more transparent than the Sensory–Motor one, phonology might nevertheless be simpler (in the sense of being less domain-specific) than has previously been thought, making use only of abilities that had already found applications in other cognitive domains at the time externalized language emerged.

This view accords with the evolutionary scenario mentioned above, which was developed by Hauser, Chomsky, and Fitch (2002) and Fitch *et al.* (2005). Hauser *et al.* suggest that language may have emerged suddenly as a result of minimal genetic changes with far-reaching consequences (cf. Pinker and Jackendoff 2005 and Jackendoff and Pinker 2005, who see language as manifesting complex design). The relation of Hauser et al.'s claims to the Minimalist Program is somewhat controversial, but at the very least, in compelling us to look for parsimonious explanations for linguistic behavior, both push us down the same path of inquiry. As Chomsky (2009: 25) puts it,

Assuming that language has general properties of other biological systems, we should be seeking three factors that enter into its growth in the individual: (1) genetic factors, the topic of UG; (2) experience, which permits variation within a fairly narrow range; (3) principles not specific to language. The third factor includes principles of efficient computation, which would be expected to be of particular significance for systems such as language. UG is the residue when third-factor effects are abstracted. The richer the residue, the harder it will be to account for the evolution of UG, evidently.

Boeckx (2010c) stresses that these three factors are not separable; rather, we must seek explanation in how the three interact, as biologists also must do with the three strands of the "triple helix," genes, organism, and environment (Lewontin 2000). But even still, whatever properties of language can be explained by interactions between ambient data and the Third Factor (or put a bit differently, by non-linguistic factors interacting with linguistic data) does not have to be explained *again* by principles of UG that are specific to language.

It is also helpful when thinking about the evolution of language in our species to maintain the distinction that Hauser, Chomsky, and Fitch (2002) make between the "Faculty of Language—Broad Sense" (FLB), including all the systems that are recruited for language but need not be unique to language, or to humans, and the "Faculty of Language—Narrow Sense" (FLN), which is the subset of FLB unique to our species and to language. At present, the leading hypothesis among proponents of this view is that FLN is very small, perhaps consisting only of the mappings from syntax to the interfaces plus some type of recursion (i.e. unbounded recursive Merge) and/or lexicalization.[1] Pinker and Jackendoff (2005: 212) claim that phonology constitutes a problematic counterexample to this hypothesis because "major characteristics of phonology are specific to language (or to language & music), [and] uniquely human."

In this chapter, I investigate the extent to which Pinker and Jackendoff's criticism is viable by examining behavioral and physiological studies on animal cognition with the goal of determining how many of the cognitive abilities necessary for the phonological representations and operations are present in creatures other than *Homo sapiens* (even if not to the same degree) and in domains other than phonology or, indeed, language proper. The conclusion I draw from the studies described in this chapter is that phonology may be entirely explainable through properties of general cognition and the Sensory–Motor system. Quite likely, no other single species has all the phonological precursors I will identify in this chapter—and clearly none of them has a syntax like ours, which precludes the possibility of a syntax/phonology interface like ours—but each of the building blocks of phonology is found *somewhere* in the animal kingdom. What I suggest, in effect, is that the operations and representations underlying phonology were exapted, or recruited from other cognitive domains for the purpose of externalizing language.[2] The rest of the present work can be seen as building on this conclusion by developing a phonological theory which takes seriously the idea that FLN is quite limited, particularly when it comes to the Sensory–Motor side.

Few authors have discussed phonology as it pertains to the FLN/FLB distinction. For example, Hauser, Chomsky, and Fitch (2002: 1573) enumerate a number of approaches to investigating a list of the Sensory–Motor system's properties shown below in (10), all of which are taken to fall outside FLN. However, none of these pertain directly to phonological computation.

---

[1] Hauser *et al.* focused on the idea that recursion might be the crucial component in FLN. However, it has proven difficult to pinpoint what is meant by recursion in the relevant sense, such that it may be unique to humans and to language. Another hypothesis to which I am sympathetic has been proposed by authors such as Spelke (2003), Ott (2009), and Boeckx (forthcoming *b*). On their view, it is not recursion but rather lexicalization—the ability to embed any concept in a lexical envelope which allows it to be recursively Merged—which arose uniquely in our species. For the purposes of the present inquiry, we may simply note that both these hypotheses exclude phonology from FLN. Speculation concerning a number of additional alternatives, still along the lines of Hauser, Chomsky, and Fitch (2002), can be found in the opening pages of Kayne (2008).

[2] On the possibility that language more generally is an exaptation, see among others Piattelli-Palmarini (1989); Uriagereka (1998); Hauser, Chomsky, and Fitch (2002); Boeckx and Piattelli-Palmarini (2005); Fitch *et al.* (2005).

(10) a. Vocal imitation and invention
Tutoring studies of songbirds, analyses of vocal dialects in whales, spontaneous imitation of artificially created sounds in dolphins

b. Neurophysiology of action-perception systems
Studies assessing whether mirror neurons, which provide a core substrate for the action-perception system, may subserve gestural and (possibly) vocal imitation

c. Discriminating the sound patterns of language
Operant conditioning studies of the prototype magnet effect in macaques and starlings

d. Constraints imposed by vocal tract anatomy
Studies of vocal tract length and formant dispersion in birds and primates

e. Biomechanics of sound production
Studies of primate vocal production, including the role of mandibular oscillations

f. Modalities of language production and perception
Cross-modal perception and sign language in humans versus unimodal communication in animals.

While everything on this list undoubtedly deserves attention, all the items focus on two problems—how auditory categories are learned and how speech is produced—which are peripheral to the core of phonological computation. The most interesting two issues from my perspective are (c) and (f), which we will discuss in this chapter and revisit in Chapter 5. These are very relevant to the question of how phonological categories are learned. And the instinct to imitate, addressed in (a) and (b), is clearly necessary to language acquisition. However, investigating neither these nor any of the other items in (10) has the potential to address how phonological objects are represented or manipulated, particularly in light of the substance-free approach to phonology, which renders questions about the articulators (e.g. (d, e)) moot since their properties are totally incidental and invisible to the phonological system.

Two papers by Yip (2006a, b) outline a more directly relevant set of research aims. Yip suggests that, if we are to understand whether "animal phonology" is possible, we should investigate whether other species are capable of:[3]

---

[3] Yip mentions two additional items which also appear on Hauser *et al.*'s list: categorical perception/perceptual magnet effects and accurate production of sounds (mimicry).

(11) a. Grouping by natural classes
  b. Grouping sounds into syllables, feet, words, phrases
  c. Calculating statistical distributions from transitional probabilities
  d. Learning arbitrary patterns of distribution
  e. Learning/producing rule-governed alternations
  f. Computing identity (total, partial, adjacent, non-adjacent).

This list can be divided roughly into three parts (with some overlap between them): (11a, b) are concerned with how representations are organized, (11c, d) are concerned with how we arrive at generalizations about the representations, and (11e, f) are concerned with the operations that are used to manipulate the representations. I would add three more areas to investigate in non-linguistic domains and non-human animals:

(12) g. Exhibiting preferences for contrast/rhythmicity
  h. Performing numerical calculations (parallel individuation and ratio comparison)
  i. Using computational operations

In the rest of this chapter, I will present evidence that a wide range of animal species are capable of all these tasks, though as I mentioned earlier, it seems to be the case that there is no single species (except ours) in which all these abilities cluster in exactly this configuration. In other words, it may be that what underlies human phonology is a unique *combination* of abilities, but the individual abilities themselves may be found in many other species—a point made long ago by Charles Hockett, though with attention focused on different features. I show (contra Yip) that there is already a substantial amount of literature demonstrating this, and that it is reasonable to conclude on this basis that no part of phonology, as conceived in the present work, is part of FLN. First, in §3.2, I discuss the role of perception in learning phonological categories.[4] In §3.3, I focus on the abilities which underlie (a, b, h)—that is, how phonological material is grouped. Next, in §3.4, I turn to (c–g), or the ability to identify and produce patterns. Finally, I delay discussion of (e, i), the abilities which have to do with symbolic computation, until §5.8, after I introduce the primitive operations SEARCH, COPY, and DELETE.

Before turning to these tasks, though, I would like to address one major concern which might be expressed about the discussion to follow. This

---

[4] I use "category" as a term which essentially means "phone": that is, neutral between "allophone" and "phoneme." This term also highlights the fact that speech sounds are perceived categorically (though they are not unique in this respect), as will be discussed in §3.2.

concern could be phrased as follows: how do we know that the animal abilities for which I provide evidence are truly comparable to the representations and operations found in human phonology, and what if these abilities are only analogous, not homologous? Admittedly, it is probably premature to answer these questions for most of the abilities we will be considering. But even if we discover that the traits under consideration are indeed analogous, that is nevertheless a significant achievement with important implications for how we understand the evolution of language. In connection with this, I would like to highlight the following statement from Hauser, Chomsky, and Fitch (2002: 1572):

Despite the crucial role of homology in comparative biology, homologous traits are not the only relevant source of evolutionary data. The convergent evolution of similar characters in two independent clades, termed 'analogies' or 'homoplasies,' can be equally revealing [(Gould 1976)]. The remarkably similar (but nonhomologous) structures of human and octopus eyes reveal the stringent constraints placed by the laws of optics and the contingencies of development on an organ capable of focusing a sharp image onto a sheet of receptors. [...] Furthermore, the discovery that remarkably conservative genetic cascades underlie the development of such analogous structures provides important insights into the ways in which developmental mechanisms can channel evolution [(Gehring 1998)]. Thus, although potentially misleading for taxonomists, analogies provide critical data about adaptation under physical and developmental constraints. Casting the comparative net more broadly, therefore, will most likely reveal larger regularities in evolution, helping to address the role of such constraints in the evolution of language.

In other words, analogs serve to highlight Third Factor principles which might be at play, and help us to identify the set of constraints which are relevant to the evolutionary history of the processes under investigation. For example, both human infants and young songbirds undergo a babbling phase in the course of the development of their vocalizations. Even though we do not want to claim that the mechanisms responsible for babbling in the two clades are homologous, nevertheless

their core components share a deeply conserved neural and developmental foundation: Most aspects of neurophysiology and development—including regulatory and structural genes, as well as neuron types and neurotransmitters—are shared among vertebrates. That such close parallels have evolved suggests the existence of important constraints on how vertebrate brains can acquire large vocabularies of complex, learned sounds. Such constraints may essentially force natural selection to come up with the same solution repeatedly when confronted with similar problems.

(Hauser, Chomsky, and Fitch 2002: 1572)

We may not know what those constraints are yet, but until we identify the homologies *and* analogies between the mechanisms which underlie human and animal cognition, we cannot even begin to tackle the interesting set of questions which arises regarding the constraints on cognitive evolution (see Bolhuis, Okanoya, and Scharff 2010 for an excellent start with respect to babbling). The present study, then, provides a place for us to begin this investigation in the domain of human phonological computation.

3.2 Categorical Perception

Let us begin by looking at the beginning of a language-learner's life. The human auditory system matures early, and many studies have shown that the youngest infants are capable of discriminating phonetic contrasts that are utilized in the various languages of the world (Werker and Tees 1984). But remarkably quickly, this power begins to wane; by 6 months of age, babies already exhibit a decline in their ability to discern vowel contrasts that are not present in their linguistic experience, and their performance degrades similarly with consonant contrasts not too long thereafter (Polka and Werker 1994). Learning a specific language with its particular subset of the possible contrasts seems to entail the loss of the ability to discriminate non-native contrasts (Eimas *et al.* 1971; Werker and Tees 1984, *inter alia*). It is commonly suggested that children are born with a full set of phonological features (see Hale and Reiss 2008 for arguments in support of this view and Mielke 2008 for the dissenting view), subsequently losing access to the ones which are not contrastive in their language. Importantly, however, the story is not so simple: it has been shown that sensitivity to the very same contrasts that are supposed to be irrevocably lost during early infancy actually remains; these contrasts are both detectable and learnable by adults under certain circumstances (such as if one becomes a phonologist). Moreover, as we will see shortly, many of these contrasts are also perceived by non-humans.

Hay (2005) investigates the retention of purportedly lost non-native categorical boundaries in adults, focusing on the difference between English and Spanish speakers' perception of the voice onset time (VOT) contrast which distinguishes /p t k/ from /b d g/. It is known from prior studies on both perception and production that the English [±voice] contrast is served by a boundary at around +30/+35 ms. VOT (short-lag vs. long-lag), while in Spanish the [±voice] contrast is between pre-voiced and short-lag, with few tokens being produced in the −30 to 0 ms. VOT range. Correspondingly, English speakers perceive a category boundary at +15/+20 ms. VOT, but Spanish speakers perceive a boundary at 0 ms. instead. The English boundary/discrimination peak coincides with the positive auditory discontinuity—a bias in the auditory system, common to humans and most mammals, which produces a non-linear mapping between acoustic inputs and the percepts they produce.[5] The +20ms. VOT boundary, to which many mammals are sensitive, appears to be the strongest case of a speech category boundary matching with an auditory discontinuity, and recent work emphasizes that discontinuities are only part of the story; experience with structured input seems to play a major role (Kluender, Lotto, and Holt 2006; Hay 2005). Auditory discontinuities seem to provide natural boundaries for speech categories (Kuhl 1993, 2000), but importantly, these are psychoacoustic biases which have nothing at all to do with human speech per se. Hay, confirming earlier work by Williams (1974) and Streeter (1976), shows that the areas of increased sensitivity corresponding to auditory discontinuities persist even in languages such as Spanish and Kikuyu, in which the discontinuities do not serve as speech category boundaries. Hay found that the same auditory discontinuities manifested in both English and Spanish speakers, but that the discrimination peaks centered on these discontinuities were of a different size and shape for the two groups of speakers when measured in both speech and non-speech perception tasks. In other words, "the underlying perceptual mechanisms that facilitated discrimination in the first place remain intact, although sensitivities may be enhanced [by language acquisition]" (Hay 2005: 103).

From a common-sense point of view, of course the raw ability to discriminate such contrasts must persist. After all, ask Hale and Kissock (1998) and Maye (2002), if discriminatory abilities take such a sharp downturn in infancy, how come early bilinguals can achieve native-like proficiency in a language to which they were not exposed during the first year of life? Further evidence comes from the fact that adults can distinguish non-native speech sounds when presented in a non-speech context. For example, Remez *et al.* (1981) found that English-speaking adults could reliably distinguish synthesized versions of [k] and [q] when they were told that the sounds they were hearing were produced by water dropping into a bucket (see also Best, Morrongiello, and Robson 1981 and Liberman 1982). These observations all support the view that there is extensive "tuning" of the perceptual system during infancy, but that the ability to distinguish contrasts that are "tuned out" remains on some level.

Across several domains, we are beginning to discover that infants are born with generic biases which become more specific during the course of

---

[5] These biases can be asymmetric; i.e. discrimination may be easier on one side of the discontinuity than the other. See Hay (2005) and references therein.

development. For instance, experiments undertaken on face perception by Pascalis, de Haan, and Nelson (2002) showed that 6-month-old human infants are as good at discriminating non-human primate faces as they are at telling apart human faces. They suggest the following (references omitted):

Our experiments support the hypothesis that the perceptual window narrows with age and that during the first year of life the face processing system is tuned to a human template. This early adjustment does not rule out the possibility that later in life individuals can learn how to discriminate a new class of stimuli on a perceptual basis. As is the case for speech perception, our evidence with face processing indicates the existence of an early tuning period that is likely dependent on experience. Although it is difficult to compare directly the tuning of speech perception with the tuning of face perception, there may be overlap between these systems. By 3 months of age infants are already relating these two types of information, as they are able to associate faces with voices. Systems for processing faces and for processing speech may thus develop in parallel, with a similar timing and a mutual influence. One possibility is that there is a general perceptuo-cognitive tuning apparatus that is not specific to a single modality and that can be described as an experience-expectant system. Alternatively, the concordance in age may simply be a developmental coincidence, thus reflecting a modality-specific, experience-dependent process.

Pascalis *et al.*'s conclusions and all the other perception studies I mention above show exactly what is to be expected if children engage in the same type of category-building across multiple domains, including speech and face perception. It seems that infants are born especially sensitive to contrasts which straddle auditory discontinuities (virtually by definition), but as they grow and are exposed to language, they undergo continuous cortical remapping which warps their perception of (speech) sound, specifically tailoring it to the input they receive. It is not the discontinuities which change—these are immutable and language-independent, being dictated purely by anatomy— but rather, the categorical perception boundaries. Category boundaries coinciding with sensory discontinuities are not only the most salient to infants but also the easiest for adults to learn, though other boundaries are also readily learnable (Hay 2005), even by language-impaired children (Wright 2006). The cortical remapping hypothesis is highly plausible because we know the human sensory cortex undergoes this type of change in a number of different circumstances: for instance, when a person is blinded or deafened, the other senses can literally take over the brain areas which formerly served the now-absent sense, and the same occurs with amputees (Ramachandran and Blakeslee 1998). Learning a musical instrument which requires very fine motor control of the fingers can cause an increase in the amount of cortex associated with the digits (Elbert *et al.* 1995). And in oscine birds who exhibit "closed-ended" song learning, we find that neurogenesis is associated with this process (see Anderson and Lightfoot 2002 §9.5.2). Birds also show the perceptual magnet effects characteristic of warping of the cortical map (Kluender *et al.* 1998). In short, the mechanism of cortical remapping is neither special to speech nor to our species—see Guenther and Gjaja (1996) for a wide variety of additional references supporting this point—but it creates a type of neural expertise which makes our processing of speech special.[6]

Neurolinguistic studies provide additional data, reinforcing the idea that learning a first language does involve a certain level of neural commitment, but that this can be (at least partially) modified into adulthood, leading to the successful acquisition of non-native contrasts. It is well known that the categorical perception of speech sounds is associated with a particular electrophysiological response. Specifically, a derived event-related potential (ERP) known as the mismatch negativity (MMN) is evoked at a latency of about 140–280ms. after stimulus presentation when a subject who has been accustomed to hearing one phoneme from his/her native language is then presented with a stimulus belonging to a different phoneme. It is also known that this MMN is significantly weaker when an acoustically different stimulus belonging to the same native phoneme is presented, or when a non-native phonemic contrast is tested.

A study undertaken by Dehaene-Lambertz, Dupoux, and Gout (2000) compared the performance of native Japanese and French speakers on the contrast between /ebzo/ and /ebuzo/. Under the hypothesis that language-specific phonotactics affect even early speech perception, since the consonant cluster in /ebzo/ is phonotactically illicit in Japanese (but not French), the Japanese group was predicted to perceive an epenthetic vowel when exposed to that stimulus, and not to exhibit a strong MMN for /ebzo/ after familiarization with /ebuzo/. Indeed, a major effect of language is exactly what Dehaene *et al.* found: the French group showed far stronger MMNs than did the Japanese. However, looking at a second ERP with 290–400ms. latency, Japanese subjects *did* show an effect of condition (i.e. different responses to /ebzo/ and /ebuzo/). Additionally, Tremblay *et al.* (1997) show that the weak MMN response to non-native contrasts can be strengthened by training: they taught native English speakers the non-native category of pre-voiced labial stops and found that after learning this new VOT boundary, the subjects generalized it to pre-voiced alveolars. This electrophysiological evidence accords with behavioral data collected by Dupoux *et al.* (1999), who also tested Japanese and French

---

[6] Nevertheless, speech does not become *entirely* special: Hay (2005) demonstrates that linguistic experience can also affect the discrimination of non-speech sounds in certain circumstances.

speakers on the perception of /VCCV/ and /VCuCV/ stimuli. They found that while French subjects were far better at discriminating these two conditions, Japanese speakers still performed significantly better than chance. While they reported hearing a medial /u/ in the /VCuCV/ condition 95 percent of the time, they reported hearing /u/ in the /VCCV/ condition 65–70 percent of the time, and in an ABX task, their error rate was 32 percent. In short, while infants' loss of ability to discriminate non-native contrasts is almost certainly associated with neurological changes, some ability to perceive non-native phonological patterns remains into adulthood, and there is evidence that some neural plasticity remains as well.[7]

What's more, there is ample evidence for category-building and abstraction in various non-linguistic domains, non-human animals, and non-infant humans. Contrary to beliefs held by early proponents of the "speech is special" hypothesis, categorical perception is not unique to speech. It has been demonstrated in humans for non-speech sounds, faces, and colors; it has also been shown that macaques, baboons, and mice perceive conspecific calls categorically (Cheney and Seyfarth 2007), and that crickets, frogs, blackbirds, sparrows, quail, finches, budgerigars, marmosets, and other animals also perform categorical labeling (see references in Hauser 1996 and Kluender, Lotto, and Holt 2006). Quite relevantly to the possibility of learned/emergent phonological categories, there is both behavioral and neurophysiological evidence for categorical perception of distinctions which we know are not innate: monkeys can be trained to distinguish categories which are novel to them, such as dogs and cats (Freedman *et al.* 2001).

Coen (2006) develops a computational model which is meant to show how warping of the cortical map leading to categorical perception of sounds could plausibly occur. His model is based on the idea that

in a notion reminiscent of a Cartesian theater—an animal can 'watch' the activity in its own motor cortex, as if it were a privileged form of *internal* perception. Then for any motor act, there are two associated perceptions—the *internal* one describing the generation of the act and the *external* one describing the self-observation of the act. The perceptual grounding framework described above can then *cross-modally ground* these internal and external perceptions with respect to one another. The power of this mechanism is that it can learn mimicry ... [It yields] an artificial system that learns to sing like a zebra finch by first listening to a real bird sing and then by learning from its own initially uninformed attempts to mimic it.   (Ibid. 19)

---

[7] Interestingly, Frey *et al.* (2008) report that a 54-year-old man who received an allogenic hand graft thirty-five years after his own hand was amputated very quickly regained normal cortical responses to tactile stimulation of the transplanted hand. So in the tactile modality, like the auditory one, neural plasticity remains to a much greater extent than has typically been assumed.

Coen demonstrates that his cross-modally grounded category-building algo-rithms can learn bird songemes, and he also successfully models the English vowel system in this way.[8] Even without priors such as the ultimate number of categories to be established, his artificial learner achieves a high degree of accuracy. Furthermore, in addition to the multimodal input produced by mimicry,[9] Coen's model can utilize input from multiple modes of external perception (in the case at hand, sight and sound). This is desirable since interplay between the senses is widespread—consider the tight relationship between olfaction and taste—but this fact is typically ignored in models of perception (see ibid. 19 for references).

Emphasizing the role of visual input in speech perception (though it is certainly not necessary for the construction of a phonological system) explains three facts that have long been known (the first two of which are discussed in Coen 2006 §2.1): first, that watching the movement of a speaker's lips can greatly aid comprehension; second, that speech sounds which are acoustically ambiguous can usually be distinguished by unambiguous visual cues; third, that visual input can affect an auditory percept, as in the famous "McGurk Effect" auditory illusion (McGurk and MacDonald 1976), in which a subject presented with (for instance) a synchronized visual /ga/ and auditory /ba/ perceives /da/.[10] Recent neurological studies corroborate this behavioral evi-dence: it has been shown that both visual and somatosensory input reaches the auditory cortical regions in macaques, and that watching lip movements produces a response in the supratemporal auditory cortex in humans (see Brosch, Selezneva, and Scheich 2005, Ghazanfar *et al.* (2005), Ghazanfar, Chandrasekaran, and Logothetis 2008, and references in Budinger and Heil 2006). Also, Weikum *et al.* (2007) have shown that visual information alone is sufficient to allow 4- to 6-month-old infants to discriminate between lan-guages.

In sum, the categories used in human speech show a great deal of overlap with categories that other animals perceive (especially mammals, given the

---

[8] The results Coen obtained are also consistent with those of de Boer (2001) and Oudeyer (2006), who model the emergence of vowel systems. These three models differ both in their aims and in the parameters they assume, yet they all do a very good job of approximating attested vowel systems. There is much more work to be done in this area—one obvious shortcoming of current research is that consonants need to be studied in addition to vowels—and I leave a detailed comparison of the existing models up to future research.

[9] Oudeyer (2006) and Guenther and Gjaja (1996) also emphasize the role of self-monitored exper-imentation ("motor babbling") in connecting auditory and articulatory representations to produce phonological categories.

[10] It is interesting to note that something similar to the McGurk Effect has been recently reported in female frogs' perception of male frogs' mating calls (Taylor *et al.* 2008).

common history of our auditory system), and we find when we look at categorical perception in domains other than language and in species other than ours that the construction, modification, and perception of speech categories appears to make use of domain-general mechanisms such as the warping of cortical maps and cross-modal perceptual grounding. One issue which arises in concert with this conclusion is whether phonological features may be learned or innate, and whether they are the building blocks of categories or emerge as properties extracted from pre-existing categories. This is an important set of questions which deserves more attention than I can give here. For now, we can certainly say that human infants are born with an auditory system which is sensitive to a variety of patterns, a subset of which are producible given the human vocal tract, and they eventually become "experts" at detecting some of these producible patterns upon repeated exposure to them. The human auditory system is largely shared with other mammals (and other, more distantly related clades), which is why many other animals can also make the category distinctions (such as VOT contrasts) utilized in our speech, as has been known since Kuhl and Miller's (1975) pioneering work on chinchillas. Brown and Sinnott (2006), reviewing a large number of animal and human discrimination studies, found that humans and non-humans perceive similar categorical boundaries for seventeen of twenty-seven tested phonemic contrasts. More recently, with single-neuron recordings from the auditory cortex of ferrets (who have hearing very similar to ours) listening to human speech, we are just beginning to understand how individual cells react to formant transitions, frication noise, and other basic properties of speech (Mesgarani *et al.* 2008). I discuss the implications of animal studies like this one in more detail in Samuels (2010*c*, forthcoming *b*). For now, I will set categories aside and move on to discuss how phonological objects, however they are constructed, are subsequently manipulated.

3.3 Grouping

To a first approximation, the difference between phonetics and phonology is that the former is the study of speech sounds (and signs), while the latter is the study of how speech sounds (again, and signs) pattern—a crucial component of the latter being how they are grouped. One might consider this broad category of grouping processes in phonology to be the best candidate for harboring a process unique to language. After all, the hypothesis put forward by Hauser, Chomsky, and Fitch (2002) takes recursion to be the central property of FLN (along with the mappings from narrow syntax to the Conceptual–Intentional and Sensory–Motor interfaces), and recursion can be described as the nesting of one object within another object of the same type: a group within a group.[11]

Anticipating Chapters 4 and 5, the theory of phonology for which I argue has fewer groupings, and consequently fewer chances for those groupings to exhibit recursion or hierarchy, than most contemporary approaches. This is true at virtually every level, from the subsegmental to the utterance: I posit no feature geometry; no subsyllabic constituency; and I maintain that phonological representations are fundamentally "flat" or "linearly hierarchical." In my view, the illusion of hierarchy is created by the pervasive processes of "chunking" (discussed in this section) and repeated concatenation (discussed in §5.8). Nobody can deny that grouping or chunking is an integral part of phonology (and there is evidence that infants use this strategy in non-linguistic domains as well; see Feigenson and Halberda 2004): features group into segments and segments group into longer strings such as syllables, morphemes, and phonological phrases.[12] Additionally, as I will discuss in §3.4, segmenting the speech stream into words, morphemes, and syllables also depends on what is essentially the converse of grouping, namely edge detection, which will be important to the discussion in §5.3.

Human beings are masters at grouping, and at making inductive generalizations. Cheney and Seyfarth (2007: 118) write that "the tendency to chunk is so pervasive that human subjects will work to discover an underlying rule even when the experimenter has—perversely—made sure there is none." This holds true across the board, not just for linguistic patterns. With respect to other species, as we saw in the previous section, many studies beginning with Kuhl and Miller (1975) show that many mammals are sensitive to acoustic parameters that are used to define phonological categories in human language. Experiments of this type provide the most direct comparanda to the groupings called natural classes (classes of segments that share a phonological feature and sometimes undergo alternations together) found in phonology.

---

[11] Some authors have argued for recursion in the higher levels of the prosodic hierarchy (e.g. at the Prosodic Word level or above). See Truckenbrodt (1995) for a representative proposal concerning recursion at the Phonological Phrase level and Itô and Mester (2007) on recursive Prosodic Words. Even if these proposals are correct (though see discussion in Ch. 4 here), the groupings in question are mapped from syntactic structure, and are therefore not created by the phonological system alone. Furthermore, this type of recursive structure is also quite different from the type found in syntax (e.g. sentential embedding) which is limited in its depth only by performance factors.

[12] After reading Ch. 4, I hope the reader will agree with me that only the first is a truly phonological concept, since phonology is a passive recipient of morphemes (i.e. morpheme-level spell-out domains) and the chunks which correspond to phonological phrases (i.e. clause-level spell-out domains). Note that the model I assume is recursive in the sense that there are two types of spell-out domain, with the potential for several morpheme-level domains within a single clause-level one. However, these domains come directly from the narrow syntax, which is totally compatible with the hypothesis that syntax is the source—but crucially *not* the exclusive domain—of all recursive structures.

Also, relevantly to the processing of tone and prosody, we know that rhesus monkeys are sensitive to pitch classes—they, like us, treat a melody which is transposed by one or two octaves as more similar to the original than one which is transposed by a different interval (Wright *et al.* 2000). They can also distinguish rising pitch contours from falling ones, which is an ability required to perceive pitch accent, lexical tone, and intonational patterns found in human speech (Brosch *et al.* 2004). However, animals are generally more sensitive to absolute pitch than they are to relative pitch; the opposite is true for humans, and both are required to process human speech (see Patel 2008).

One can also approach the question of whether animals can group sensory stimuli in ways that are relevant to phonology by investigating whether their own vocalizations contain internal structure. The organization of birdsong is particularly clear, though it is not obvious whether (and if so, how) analogies to human language should be made. Yip (2006*a*) discusses how zebra finch songs are structured, building on work by Doupe and Kuhl (1999) and others. The songs of many passerine songbirds consist of a sequence of one to three notes (or "songemes" as Coen 2006 calls them) arranged into a "syllable." The syllables, which can be up to one second in length, are organized into motifs which Yip considers to be equivalent to prosodic words but others equate with phrases. There are multiple motifs within a single song. The structure can be represented graphically as in Fig. 3.1. I use M to stand for "motif," σ for "syllable," and n for "note" (modified from Yip 2006*a*)

There are a few important differences between this birdsong structure and those found in human phonology, some of which are not apparent from the diagram. First, as Yip points out, there is no evidence for binary branching in this structure, which suggests that the combinatory mechanism used by birds

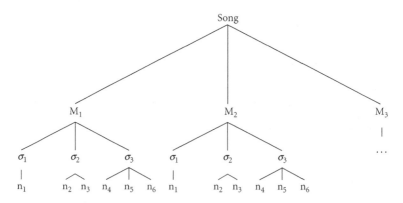

FIGURE 3.1 Structure of zebra finch song

cannot be equated with binary Merge. Second, the definition of a 'syllable' in birdsong is a series of notes/songemes bordered by silence (Williams and Staples 1992; Coen 2006). This is very unlike syllables in human language. Third, the examples from numerous species in Slater (2000) show that the motif is typically a domain of repetition (as I have represented it here); the shape of a song is $((a^x)(b^y)(c^z))^w$ with a string of syllables *a, b, c* repeated in order. This is quite reminiscent of reduplication in human morphophonology. Payne (2000) shows that virtually the same can be said of humpback whale songs, which take the shape $(a \ldots n)^w$, where the number of repeated components, *n*, can be up to around ten.

Both the birdsong and whalesong structures are what I have called "flat" or "linearly hierarchical" (in the sense of Cheney and Seyfarth 2007)—exactly what I, along with Neeleman and van de Koot (2006), argue is true of human phonology. It is interesting to note in conjunction with this observation that baboon social knowledge is of exactly this type, as Cheney and Seyfarth have described. Baboons within a single tribe (of up to about eighty individuals) obey a strict, transitive dominance hierarchy. But this hierarchy is divided by matrilines; individuals from a single matriline occupy adjacent spots in the hierarchy, with mothers, daughters, and sisters from the matriline next to one another. So an abstract representation of their linear dominance hierarchy would look something like Fig. 3.2, with each *x* representing an individual and parentheses defining matrilines.

The difference between the baboon social hierarchy and birdsong, which I translate into this sort of notation in Fig. 3.3, is merely the repetition which creates a motif (think of baboon individuals as corresponding to songemes and matrilines as corresponding to syllables). There is evidence to suggest that, as in phonology (but strikingly *unlike* narrow syntax), the amount of hierarchy capable of being represented by non-human animals is quite limited. In the wild, apes and monkeys very seldom spontaneously perform actions which are hierarchically structured with sub-goals and sub-routines, and this is true

$$(xxx)(xx)(xxxx)(xxx)(xxxxxxx)(xxx)(x)(xxxx)$$

FIGURE 3.2 Baboon matrilineal dominance hierarchy

$$\underbrace{(n_1)(n_2 n_3)(n_4 n_5 n_6)}_{\text{motif}_1} \ \underbrace{(n_1)(n_2 n_3)(n_4 n_5 n_6)}_{\text{motif}_2}$$

FIGURE 3.3 Birdsong motif structure

even when attempts are made to train them to do so.[13] Byrne (2007) notes one notable exception, namely the food processing techniques of gorillas.[14] Byrne provides a flow chart detailing a routine, complete with several decision points and optional steps, which mountain gorillas use to harvest and eat nettle leaves. This routine comprises a minimum of five steps, and Byrne reports that the routines used to process other foods are of similar complexity. Byrne further notes that "all genera of great apes acquire feeding skills that are flexible and have *syntax-like* organisation, with hierarchical structure.... Perhaps, then, the precursors of linguistic syntax should be sought in primate *manual* abilities rather than in their vocal skills" (ibid. 12; emphasis his). I concur that manual routines provide an interesting source of comparanda for the syntax of human language, broadly construed (i.e. including the syntax of phonology). Fujita (2007, 2009) has suggested along these lines the possibility that Merge evolved from an "action grammar" of the type which would underlie apes' foraging routines.[15]

Other experiments reveal that non-human primates may be limited in the complexity of their routines in interesting ways. For instance, Johnson-Pynn *et al.* (1999) used bonobos, capuchin monkeys, and chimpanzees in a study similar to one done on human children by Greenfield, Nelson, and Saltzmann (1972) (see also discussion of these two studies by Conway and Christiansen 2001). These experiments investigated how the subjects manipulated a set of three nesting cups (call them A, B, C in increasing order of size). The subjects' actions were categorized as belonging to the "pairing," "pot," or "subassembly" strategies, which exhibit varying degrees of embedding:[16]

---

[13] I am sometimes asked whether this implies animals have "a little" recursion, and what that would even mean. I view the situation as an exact parallel to the difference between humans and animals in the domain of numerical cognition; perhaps the two dichotomies are indeed manifestations of the same cognitive difference, namely that only humans have a recursive engine (Merge), as suggested by Hauser, Chomsky, and Fitch (2002). While many animals (and young human children) seem to be able to represent small numerals, only suitably mature (and, perhaps, suitably linguistic) humans go on to learn the inductive principle, which allows them to count infinitely high. See discussion later in this section and in §5.8 for more discussion and references on numeracy in animals.

[14] Interestingly, apes' food processing routines appear to be at least partially learned through imitation rather than trial-and-error, as evidenced by the techniques of young chimpanzees who have been injured by snares. Such disabled individuals do not exhibit novel techniques, which we would expect if they learned how to forage independently; instead, even the most severely affected chimps use techniques which very closely resemble those of able-bodied individuals.

[15] This possibility has also been suggested by Greenfield, Nelson, and Saltzmann (1972); Greenfield (1991, 1998). Interestingly, Greenfield (1991) considers the possibility that this type of action grammar could correspond to the combination of phonemes into words, although in other works she suggests that it is more akin to the combination of words. See Fujita (2009: 138).

[16] The situation is actually substantially more complicated than this, because the subjects need not put the cups in the nesting order. To give a couple of examples, putting cup A into cup C counts as the pairing strategy; putting cup A into cup C and then placing cup B on top counts as the pot strategy.

(13)   a. Pairing strategy: place cup B into cup C. Ignore cup A.

       b. Pot strategy: place cup B into cup C. Then place cup A into cup B.

       c. Subassembly strategy: place cup A into cup B. Then place cup B into cup C.

The pairing strategy is the simplest, requiring only a single step. This was the predominant strategy for human children up to twelve months of age, and for all the other primates—but the capuchins required watching the human model play with the cups before they produced even this kind of combination. The pot strategy requires two steps, but it is simpler than the subassembly strategy in that the latter, but not the former, requires treating the combination of cups A + B as a unit in the second step. (We might consider the construction of the A + B unit as being parallel to how complex specifiers and adjuncts are composed "in a separate derivational workspace" in the syntax; see Fujita 2007, 2009.) Human children use the pot strategy as early as 11 months (the youngest age tested) and begin to incorporate the subassembly strategy at about 20 months. In stark contrast, the non-human primates continued to prefer the pairing strategy, and when they stacked all three cups, they still relied on the pot strategy even though the experimenter demonstrated only the subassembly strategy for them. The degu, a relative of the chinchilla, has also been seen to use the pot strategy but not the subassembly one (Tokimoto and Okanoya 2004). Though we should be careful not to discount the possibility that different experimental methodologies or the laboratory context is responsible for the non-humans' performance, rather than genuine cognitive limitations, the results are consistent with the hypothesis that humans have the ability to represent deeper hierarchies than other primates (and animals outside our clade). This is what we predict if only humans are endowed with the recursive engine that allows for infinite syntactic embedding (Hauser, Chomsky, and Fitch 2002).

Many other types of experimental studies have also been used to investigate how animals group objects. It is well known that a wide variety of animals, including rhesus monkeys, have the ability to perform comparisons of analog magnitude with small numbers (<4). They can discriminate between, for instance, groups of two and three objects, and pick the group with more objects in it. As Hauser, Carey and Hauser (2000) note, such tasks require the animal to group the objects into distinct sets, then compare the cardinality of those sets. Further data come from Schusterman and Kastak (1993), who taught a California sea lion named Rio to associate arbitrary visual stimuli (cards with silhouettes of various objects printed on them). On the basis

---

I refer the reader to the original studies for explanations of each possible scenario. The differences between the strategies as I have described them in the main text suffice for present purposes.

of being taught to select card B when presented with card A, and also to select card C when presented with card B, Rio transitively learned the A–C association.[17] Rio also made symmetric associations: when presented with B, she would select A, and so forth.

We might consider the groups Rio learned to be akin to arbitrary classes such as which sounds are allophones of a particular phoneme, or which phonemes participate in a given alternation. This even comes close to the idea of a natural class, which has also been studied in animals to a certain degree, though not presented in those terms. We can think of natural classes as multiple ways of grouping the same objects into sets according to their different properties (i.e. features). Alex the parrot had this skill: he could sort objects by color, shape, or material (reported by his trainer in Smith 1999).

A recent study on Bengalese finch song (Wohlgemuth, Sober, and Brainard 2010) comes even closer to the concept of allophony which is familiar to us from human phonology: birdsong syllables seem to affect the pronunciation of their neighbors, much as (for example) vowels in English are longer when followed by a voiced consonant than a voiceless one (compare *bead* with *beat*), or /t/ is realized as a flap in words like *latter*. Moreover, the observed effect in finches appears to be neurally controlled along with the sequencing of the syllables: it is, we might (and the authors of the study do) say, a phonological effect rather than a purely phonetic one.

With respect to the ability to group objects, then, I conclude that animals— especially birds and primates in particular—are capable of everything phonology requires. They perceive (some) sounds categorically like we do; their vocalizations show linearly hierarchical groupings like ours do; they can assign objects arbitrarily to sets like we do; they can categorize objects into overlapping sets according to different attributes like we do. Their main limitations seem to be in the area of higher-degree embedding, but this is (*a*) not a property of phonology as proposed here and (*b*) an expected result if, as Hauser, Chomsky, and Fitch (2002) hypothesize, recursion is a part of FLN and therefore not shared with other species.

3.4 Patterns

The next set of abilities we will consider are those which deal with extracting patterns from a data stream and/or learning arbitrary associations. As

---

[17] See also Addessi *et al.* (2008) on transitive symbolic representation in capuchin monkeys, and Cheney and Seyfarth (2007) on transitive inference involving social hierarchy in baboons. Cheney and Seyfarth also discuss both transitive social dominance and learning of symbolic representations in pinyon jays.

I mentioned in the previous section, I view pattern-detection as the flipside of grouping: a pattern is essentially a relation between multiple groups, or different objects within the same group. Thus, the ability to assign objects to a set or an equivalence class is a prerequisite for finding any patterns in which those objects participate, so the abilities discussed in the previous section are very much relevant to this one also.

Several experimental studies on animal cognition bear on the issue of abstract pattern learning. One such study, undertaken by Hauser and Glynn (2009), tested whether tamarins could extract simple patterns ("algebraic rules") like same-different-different (ABB) or same-same-different (AAB) from a speech stream. They performed an experiment very similar to one run on infants by Marcus *et al.* (1999). The auditory stimuli in both of these studies were of the form $C_1V_1C_1V_1C_2V_2$ (the AAB condition) or $C_1V_1C_2V_2C_2V_2$ (the ABB condition), such as *li-li-wi* or *le-we-we*. The test material was novel, and either matched the habituation stimuli or mismatched. Specifically, after habituating the infants/rhesus to one of these conditions, they tested them on two novel test items: one from the same class to which they had been habituated, and a second from the other class. If subjects extracted the pattern during habituation, then they should respond more to the mismatched test trial than to the novel but matching test trial. Both infants and rhesus evidenced learning of these simple patterns; they were more likely to dishabituate to the item with the mismatched pattern.

This type of pattern-extraction ability could serve phonology in several ways, such as the learning of phonological rules or phonotactic generalizations. Heinz (2007) showed that phonotactics (restrictions on the co-occurrence of segments, such as at the beginnings or ends of words) can be captured without any exceptions if three segments at a time are taken into account, so it seems on the basis of tamarins' success in the above experiment (and Murphy, Mondragon, and Murphy 2008 showing that rats succeed in a similar task) that learning phonotactics would not be out of their range of capabilities. Furthermore, phonotactics (and all attested phonological rules) can be modeled with finite-state grammars, as has been known since Johnson (1970). If other animals can learn finite-state patterns, then in theory we would expect that they could learn any attested phonotactic restriction or phonological rule. The conclusion that animals are limited to finite-state computation is supported by van Heijningen *et al.*'s (2009) nuanced testing of finches on patterns of varying computational complexity, which casts strong suspicion on Gentner *et al.*'s (2006) claim that starlings can go beyond finite-state patterns to learn a recursive context-free rule; the interpretation of these data is still under debate (Gentner *et al.* 2010, ten Cate, van Heijningen, and Zuidema

2010). One of the most important obstacles facing a language learner/user falls into the category of pattern-extraction. This difficult task is parsing the continuous speech stream into discrete units (be they phrases, words, syllables, or segments). This speaks directly to (11b, c). Obviously, segmenting speech requires some mechanism for detecting the edges of these units. Since the 1950s, it has been recognized that one way to detect the edges of words is to track transitional probabilities, usually between syllables. If Pr(AB) is the probability of syllable B following syllable A, and P(A) is the frequency of A, then the transitional probability between A and B can be represented as:

(14) $TP(A \rightarrow B) = \frac{Pr(AB)}{Pr(A)}$

The transitional probabilities within words are typically greater than those across word boundaries, so the task of finding word boundaries reduces to finding the local minima in the transitional probabilities. Numerous experimental studies suggest that infants do in fact utilize this strategy (among others) to help them parse the speech stream, and that statistical learning is not unique to the linguistic domain but is also utilized in other areas of cognition (see references in Gambell and Yang 2005). With respect to the availability of this strategy in non-humans, various animals from tamarins to rats have been shown to be sensitive to local transitional probabilities (Toro, Trobalón, and Sebastián-Galles 2005).

While transitional probabilities between syllables are strictly local calculations (i.e. they involve adjacent units), some phonological (and syntactic) dependencies are non-adjacent. This is the case with vowel harmony, for instance, and is also relevant to languages with "templatic" morphology, such as Arabic, in which a triconsonantal root is meshed with a different group of vowels depending on the part of speech which the root instantiates in a particular context. Comparing the results obtained by Newport and Aslin (2004) and Newport *et al.* (2004) provides an interesting contrast between human and tamarin learning of such patterns. Newport *et al.* tested adult humans and cotton-top tamarins on learning artificial languages, all with three-syllable CVCVCV words, involving the three different kinds of non-adjacent dependencies:

(15)   a. *Non-adjacent syllables*: the third syllable of each word was predictable on the basis of the first, but the second syllable varied.

   b. *Non-adjacent consonants*: The second and third consonants of each word were predictable on the basis of the first, but the vowels varied.

   c. *Non-adjacent vowels*: The second and third vowels of each word were predictable on the basis of the first, but the consonants varied.

Both humans and tamarins succeeded at learning the languages tested in the non-adjacent vowel condition. Humans also succeeded at the non-adjacent consonant condition. These results are expected, at least for the humans, because both of these types of dependencies are attested in natural language (in the guises of vowel harmony and templatic morphology, as I have already noted). Tamarins failed in the non-adjacent consonant condition, though it it is suspected that they have the cognitive capability needed to create the appropriate representations; their difficulty seems to arise because they have difficulty distinguishing consonant sounds. In other words, their failure may not be due to the pattern-detection mechanism, but in the input to it. This interpretation is supported by the fact that tamarins also succeeded at establishing dependencies in the other two conditions.

From a phonological perspective, perhaps the most intriguing result is that humans failed at this non-adjacent syllable condition. Newport *et al.* (2004: 111) ask:

Why should non-adjacency—particularly syllable non-adjacency—be difficult for human listeners and relatively easy for tamarin monkeys? [... T]his is not likely to be because tamarins are in general more cognitively capable than adult humans. It must therefore be because human speech is processed in a different way by humans than by tamarins, and particularly in such a way that the computation of non-adjacent syllable regularities becomes more complex for human adults.

They go on to suggest that perhaps the syllable level is only indirectly accessible to humans because we primarily process speech in terms of segments (whereas tamarins process it in more holistic, longer chunks). Alternatively, Newport *et al.* suggest, tamarins' shorter attention span reduces the amount of speech that they process at a given time; this would restrict their hypothesis space, making the detection of the syllable pattern easier. It is not obvious to me how this explains the tamarins' pattern of performance across tasks, however.

Perhaps these results tell us that, in effect, tamarins fail to exhibit a minimality effect.[18] Let us interpret the tamarins' performance in the non-adjacent consonant condition as suggesting, as I did above, that they either (for whatever reason) ignore or simply do not perceive consonants. Then for them, the non-adjacent syllable task differs minimally from the non-adjacent vowel task in that the former involves learning a pattern which skips the middle vowel. So rather than paying attention to co-occurrences between adjacent vowels, they

---

[18] Such effects have been discussed in terms of Relativized Minimality (Rizzi 1990) or the Minimal Link Condition (Chomsky 2000, 2004) in syntax and the No Line-Crossing Constraint (Goldsmith 1976) in autosegmental phonology. In the theory proposed here, minimality in phonology (and perhaps in narrow syntax too) emerges from a directional SEARCH mechanism which traverses strings of segments (detailed in Ch. 5; see also Mailhot and Reiss (2007) and Samuels (2009a)).

have to look at co-occurences between vowels which are one away from each other. It seems likely, as Newport *et al.* also suggest, that the adjacent vs. one-away difference represents only a small increase in cognitive demand. But for us, the non-adjacent syllable condition is crucially different—and this is true no matter whether we are actually paying attention to syllables, consonants, or vowels. These categories have no import for tamarins, but for humans, they are special. The dependency we seek in this condition is between two non-adjacent elements of the same category, *which are separated by another instance of the same category*. This is a classical minimality effect: if α, β, γ are of the same category and α ≻ β ≻ γ (≻ should be read for syntax as "c-commands" and for phonology, "precedes"), then no relationship between α and γ may be established. This restriction is captured straightforwardly if linguistic dependencies (Agree, harmony, etc.) are established by means of a search procedure which scans from α segment by segment until it finds another instance of the same type (i.e. β), then stops and proceeds no further, as will be proposed in Chapter 5. If I am on the right track, then perhaps tamarins succeed where humans fail because they do not represent the portions of the stimuli which they track as all belonging to the same abstract category of "vowel" which is sufficient to trigger minimality effects for us.

A variety of other studies on primate cognition focus on the ability to learn sequences. Given that sequencing or precedence relationships are extremely important to language, particularly given the Minimalist emphasis on Merge in syntax and my parallel emphasis on linearization and the concatenation of morphemes in morphophonology, these studies are intriguing from a linguist's perspective. As Endress *et al.* (2009) emphasize, temporal sequencing underlies everything from foraging routines to structured vocalizations (i.e. the order of segments, morphemes, and words in human speech as well as notes and motifs in animal songs) and requires a specific type of memory which encodes the positions of items within the sequence. Conway and Christiansen (2001) report on a number of studies which compare primates' performances on this kind of task. In certain respects, non-human primates have abilities in this area which are comparable to those of human children: for example, when presented with an "artificial fruit" requiring four arbitrary actions to open it and thereby reveal a treat, chimpanzees and human preschoolers perform similarly; both succeed at learning the sequence.

However, another study highlights what seems to be a difference in the way humans and other primates plan and perform sequential actions. One experiment undertaken by Ohshiba (1997) tested human adults, Japanese monkeys, and a chimpanzee on the ability to learn an arbitrary pattern: they were presented with a touch screen with four different-sized colored circles on it and had to touch each one in sequence to receive a reward; the circles disappeared when touched. All the species succeeded in learning a monotonic pattern: touch the circles in order from smallest to largest or largest to smallest. They also all succeeded at learning non-monotonic patterns, though they were slower at learning them.[19] But as we will discuss later, measurements of reaction times suggest the humans and other species used different strategies in planning which circles to touch.

Rhythm, too, is a type of pattern. Rhythmicity, cyclicity, and contrast are pervasive properties of language, particularly in phonology. Everything that has been attributed to the Obligatory Contour Principle (Leben 1973)—a constraint which prohibits the adjacency of two phonological elements which are similar or identical—fits into this category. As we have already discussed, Walter (2007) argues that these effects should be described not with a constraint against repetition (see also Reiss 2008a), but as emerging from two major physical limitations: the difficulty of repeating a particular gesture in rapid succession, and the difficulty of perceiving sensory stimuli distinctly in rapid succession. These are both extremely general properties of articulatory and perceptual systems which we have no reason to expect would be unique to language or to humans. To date, perhaps the most direct cross-species tests of the perception of human speech rhythm (prosody) come from Ramus *et al.* (2000) and Tincoff *et al.* (2005). In Ramus *et al.*'s experiment, human infants and cotton-top tamarins were tested on their ability to discriminate between Dutch and Japanese sentences under a number of conditions: one in which the sentences were played forward, one in which the sentences were played backward, and one in which the sentences were synthesized such that the phonemic inventory in each language was reduced to /s a l t n j/. The results of these experiments showed that both tamarins and human newborns were able to discriminate between these two unfamiliar and prosodically different languages in the forward-speech condition, but not in the backward-speech condition. A generous interpretation of these results would suggest "at least some aspects of human speech perception may have built upon preexisting sensitivities of the primate auditory system" (Ramus *et al.* 2000: 351). However, Werker and Vouloumanos (2000) caution that we cannot conclude much about the processing mechanisms which serve these discrimination abilities; this is of

---

[19] In some situations, non-human primates fail entirely at learning non-monotonic patterns. For example, Brannon and Terrace (1998, 2000) found that while rhesus macaques who had been taught the first four steps in a monotonic pattern could spontaneously generalize to later steps, they failed to learn a four-member non-monotonic pattern even with extensive training. It is not clear what accounts for the worse performance in the Brannon and Terrace studies; there are too many differences between the paradigm they used and the one reported in the main text, including the species tested.

particular concern given that the tamarins' ability to tell Dutch and Japanese apart was reduced in the reduced phonemic inventory condition. This may indicate that tamarins rely more strongly on phonetic cues than prosodic ones. Given the apparent importance of prosody for syntactic acquisition in human children—specifically, babies seem to use prosodic information to help them set the head parameter—Kitahara (2003: 38) puts forth the idea that "cotton-top tamarins fail to discriminate languages on the basis of their prosody alone, because syntactic resources that require such prosodic-sensitive system [*sic*] might not have evolved for them." Though it is unclear how one might either support or disprove such a hypothesis, it is at the very least interesting to consider what prosody might mean for an animal which does not have the syntactic representations from which prosodic representations are built. Another example of rhythmicity in speech is the wavelike sonority profile of our utterances, which we will discuss in detail in §5.3. Permissible syllable shapes vary widely in shape across languages, yet all syllables, from CV (Fig. 3.4) to CCCVCC (Fig. 3.5), combine to yield a sonority profile roughly as in Fig. 3.6).

It has been known since the early days of phonological theory that the ability to break this wave up into periods aids with the identification of word

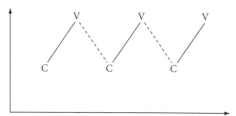

FIGURE 3.4 CV syllables

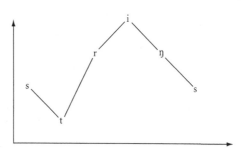

FIGURE 3.5 CCCVCC syllable

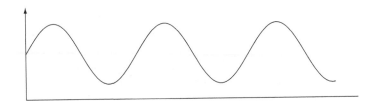

FIGURE 3.6 Sonority wave

boundaries: they tend to fall at the local minima or maxima in the wave. And as we saw earlier in this section, we already know that both human infants and tamarins are sensitive to local minima (of transitional probabilities) in speech, which I believe suggests that this is a legitimate possibility.

Animals from a wide variety of clades show preferences for rhythmicity in their vocalizations and other behaviors as well, though it is important to note that our own (non-musical) speech has no regular beat; while language does have a rhythm, it is not a primitive (see discussion in Patel 2008). Yip (2006*b*) mentions that female crickets exhibit a preference for males who produce rhythmic calls, and Taylor *et al.* (2008) discovered that female frogs prefer rhythmic vocalizations as well. Rhythmic behaviors, or the ability to keep rhythm, appear to be widespread in the animal kingdom. Gibbons produce very rhythmic "great calls," and while Yip (2006*b*: 443) dismisses this, saying that "the illusion of rhythm is probably more related to breathing patterns than cognitive organization," this should hardly disqualify the data. For example, the periodic modulation of sonority in our speech is closely connected to the opening and closing cycle of the jaw (Redford 1999; Redford, Chen, and Miikkulainen 2001), just as it is in many other vertebrates (see Fitch 2010: §10.3 and references therein), and it is widely accepted that the gradual downtrend in pitch which human utterances exhibit has to do with our breathing patterns. So for humans, too, there is at least some purely physiological component; however, the fact noted above that females of various species prefer rhythmic calls shows that at the very least, there is also a cognitive component to animals' perception of rhythmicity. Recently, a pet cockatoo named Snowball became an internet sensation for his head-bobbing, foot-stamping reaction to pop music; subsequent experimental studies confirmed that Snowball was indeed synchronizing ("entraining") to the beat of the music (Patel *et al.* 2009). A broader survey of many species undertaken by Schachner *et al.* (2009) confirmed Patel *et al.*'s findings and additionally showed that several other vocal mimicking species, including many varieties of birds as well as elephants, also entrain to music whereas none of the non-mimicking species tested did. This correlation between vocal mimicking and beat induction is suggestive that there may be an evolutionary connection between these two abilities which is certainly worthy of further study.

There are also some animals that synchronize the rhythms produced by multiple individuals. For example, frogs, insects, birds, and captive bonobos have all been shown to engage in chorusing during which they synchronize their calls; some fireflies synchronize their flashing, and crabs synchronize their claw-waving (see Merker 2000 and references therein). However, while elephants can be taught to drum with better rhythmic regularity than human adults, they do not synchronize their drumming in an ensemble (Patel and Iversen 2006).

Finally, we should note that it is extremely common for animals to exhibit "rule-governed" behavior in the wild, and in their communicative behavior in particular. Cheney and Seyfarth (2007) make the case that baboon vocalizations are rule-governed in that they are directional and dependent on social standing. That is, a baboon will make different vocalizations to a higher-ranked member of the group than she will to a lower-ranked member. By this same rubric, vervet monkey grunts and chimpanzee calls should also be considered rule-governed; a number of articles on species ranging from tree frogs to dolphins to chickadees in a recent special issue of the *Journal of Comparative Psychology* (122/3, Aug. 2008) devoted to animal vocalizations further cement this point. And as we saw in the previous section, both bird and whale songs obey certain combinatorial rules—in other words, they have some kind of syntax (in the broad sense of the term). Here the distinction made by S. Anderson (2004) and suggested in earlier work by Peter Marler is useful: plenty of animals have a "phonological" syntax to their vocalizations, but only humans have a "semantic" or "lexical" syntax which is compositional and recursive in terms of its meaning. Again, this reiterates Hauser *et al.*'s view that what is special about human language is the mapping from syntax to the interfaces (and particularly the LF interface, as Chomsky emphasizes in recent writings; see e.g. Chomsky 2004), not the externalization system.

3.5 Conclusions

I believe the studies of animal cognition and behavior which I have presented in this chapter provide ample evidence that Pinker and Jackendoff's (2005) criticism of Hauser, Chomsky, and Fitch (2002) concerning phonology is unfounded, if the list of abilities presented at the outset of this chapter are the correct set to home in on. A wide range of animal species have been shown to group objects, extract patterns from sensory input, perform sequential objects, and—as we will see more in Chapter 5—perform searches, engage in copying behaviors, and manipulate sets through concatenation. Nevertheless, another one of Pinker and Jackendoff's qualms with Hauser *et al.*—that the latter implicitly reject the popular hypothesis that "speech is special"—should also be viewed skeptically. I do not deny the wide range of studies showing that speech and non-speech doubly dissociate in a number of ways which should be familiar to all linguists, as evidenced by aphasias, amusias, Specific Language Impairment, Williams Syndrome, autism, studies of speech and non-speech perception, and so on. Pinker and Jackendoff (2005) provide numerous references pointing to this conclusion, as does Patel (2008) with regards to language and music specifically.[20]

But on the other hand, there is also a great deal of literature which shows that many species' vocalizations are processed in a different way from non-conspecific calls, or from sounds which were not produced by animals. This is true of rhesus macaques, who exhibit different neural activity—in areas including the analogs of human speech centers—and lateralization in response to conspecific calls (Gil da Costa *et al.* 2004). Perhaps we should amend the "speech is special" hypothesis: speech is special (to us), in just the same way that conspecific properties throughout the animal kingdom often are (see Belin 2006 for a review of evidence concerning processing of conspecific and non-specific calls in primates), but there is nothing special about the way human speech is externalized or perceived in and of itself.

As conceived of here, phonology thus provides no challenge to the idea that FLN is very small, perhaps consisting of just recursion and the mappings from syntax to the Conceptual–Intentional and Sensory–Motor interfaces. In the chapters to follow, I will try to keep as close as possible to the set of abilities for which we have seen evidence in animals, in order to arrive at a biologically plausible model of phonological competence consistent with the view that the human phonological system is, in short, a domain-general solution to a domain-specific problem, namely the externalization of language.

---

[20] In this area the state of the art is changing rapidly, and the presence of a language/music dissociation is still an open and interesting question. Mithen (2005) explores one interesting hypothesis advanced by Charles Darwin, namely that music/singing (re-)emerged in the human lineage prior to the emergence of compositional language (see also Fitch 2005). This could explain the complicated mixture of shared and distinct abilities and anatomy which serve music and language, discussed in great detail by Patel (2008).

4

The Syntax–Phonology Interface

4.1 Introduction

Now that I have made clear the starting assumptions upon which the theory to be developed here will rest, the next logical step is to consider how phonology is situated within the organization of the language faculty. I will therefore focus here on phonology's interfaces with syntax and morphology: in other words, the mechanism by which phonology is fed. Because any theory of the interface is necessarily dependent on the current state of affairs in syntactic theory, which is constantly in flux, this chapter is necessarily somewhat speculative. I merely attempt here to offer proof of concept for a particular type of approach, with the caveat that the details may well have to change as our understanding of syntax and the architecture of grammar progresses.[1] For this reason, I focus primarily on the logic of the arguments for the theory I present here, which I call "phonological derivation by phase" (PDbP). This theory makes it possible to combine the best parts of Lexical Phonology (Kiparsky 1982), Distributed Morphology (Halle and Marantz 1993), and Derivation by Phase (Chomsky 2001), and potentially obviates the need for prosodic domain construction in the phonology (a return to a conception of PF more like the "direct reference" theories of Kaisse 1985, Odden 1990, and Cinque 1993). The basis for this theory is the notion that phonology is cyclic and therefore inescapably derivational. I further argue, following Marvin (2002), that this is the *direct consequence* of cyclic transfer (i.e. phasality) in syntax.

---

[1] Specifically, my theory depends on the inventory of phase heads, and on the particular structures and movements involved in the constructions I analyze. At present, as I try to demonstrate throughout the chapter, research indicates that the structures I require are not ad hoc, but supported on independent syntactic and semantic grounds.

With this model in place, I present arguments that the domains of phonological rule application, both above and below the word level, come for free when we assume Distributed Morphology and a phasal syntax. Specifically, phonological processes and operations such as linearization of looped structures get the chance to apply at each application of Spell-Out (also sometimes known as Transfer; I will refine this terminology in the next section), and are limited in scope by the Phase Impenetrability Condition (Chomsky 2001). I claim that morpheme-level phases can replace Lexical Phonology's hierarchy of strata, and that clause-level phases can replace the prosodic hierarchy. These arguments are supported with analyses of segmental and suprasegmental (e.g. tone and phrasal stress assignment) processes from English, Bantu, and Korean, among others.

4.2 From Syntax to Phonology

My main goal in this chapter is to provide an account of phonological domains and cyclicity; this story is rooted in the interface between syntax and phonology, but there are many other facets of that interface also deserving of attention. Understanding syntax's interfaces is a particularly pressing issue if Minimalist syntacticians are correct to relegate to the interfaces more and more attributes of what was once thought to be narrow syntax, creating what Scheer (forthcoming) calls "the minimalist dustbin: clean syntax, dirty phonology." Making sense of the PF interface in its entirety is a massive undertaking in light of this, and one which I will not attempt at present. I will, however, try to present a plausible sketch of the various components of an articulated syntax–phonology interface before I spend the rest of this chapter discussing the properties of a selected few of these components in more detail.

The view of the interface presented here rests on two basic assumptions which are mainstream in Minimalist syntax and in Distributed Morphology. First, syntax is sensitive only to hierarchical relationships while morphology (i.e. allomorphy choice and so forth) can be sensitive to both hierarchy and linear adjacency (see e.g. Embick and Noyer 2001); phonological representations encode only linear adjacency—as we will see, hierarchy plays an important role in phonology but it does so indirectly, through procedural means only. Second, phonological features are not present in narrow syntax, but enter the derivation during the transformation from (morpho)syntax to phonology ("Late Insertion"; Halle and Marantz 1993). Conversely, only phonological features may persist in the phonological component.

Adopting these views has two immediate consequences: there must be a mechanism by which syntactic representations are linearized, and there must be a mechanism by which the features present in the narrow syntactic computation are traded for phonological ones (an operation commonly called vocabulary insertion). On the basis of examining certain empirical phenomena, we also know a bit more about the order of operations which occur on the way from syntax to phonology (see Lohndal and Samuels 2010 for a more detailed roadmap). For example, Kahnemuyipour (2004) argues that phrasal stress is assigned to the *highest* phrase within a particular domain (we will discuss this proposal in detail later); the necessity of referring to a hierarchical relation means that this must occur before linearization is completed and that information is lost.[2] Also, the well-known case of *wanna*-contraction shows that certain morphophonological processes are sensitive to traces (unpronounced copies) of syntactic movement. This phenomenon is illustrated by the fact that *who* in (16a) can be interpreted as originating from either the subject position (t_i) or from the object position (t_j)—that is to say, the question can be answered along the lines of *I want to visit Marcus* or *I want Marcus to visit*—whereas in (16b) with the reduced form *wanna*, only the reading where *who* originates from the object position (answer: *I want to visit Marcus*) is possible.

(16)   a. Who do you want (t_i) to visit (t_j)?

       b. Who do you wanna visit t_j?

We still do not fully understand the range of effects of null syntactic objects such as unpronounced products of movement, *pro*, and vocabulary items without overt content. I address some aspects of this issue in Ch. 5 of Samuels (2009*b*), and interesting empirical generalizations (some of them still in need of explanation) concerning the interplay between null elements and allomorph selection can be found in Embick (2010).

At present, one of the most detailed proposals concerning the order of operations on the way from syntax to phonology is that of Idsardi and Raimy (forthcoming). They argue that linearization should properly be subdivided into components which they term "immobilization," "spell-out," and "serialization," thus:

---

[2] Note that some information is necessarily lost when translating a hierarchical syntactic tree into a linear representation. This is an unavoidable result of projecting an object onto a lower number of dimensions, in any domain. A linear representation bears exactly the same relation to a syntactic "mobile" as a two-dimensional shadow does to a three-dimensional object.

(17)   The path from narrow syntax to PF (Idsardi and Raimy forthcoming: 2)

Module	Characteristics
Narrow syntax	hierarchy, no linear order, no phonological content
LINEARIZATION-1	= **Immobilization**
Morphosyntax	hierarchy, adjacency, no phonological content
LINEARIZATION-2	= **Spell-out**
Morphophonology	no hierarchy, directed graph, phonological content
LINEARIZATION-3	= **Serialization**
Phonology	no hierarchy, linear order, phonological string

Let us now walk through this architecture step by step; I will present some refinements as we go.

4.2.1 *Linearization-1: Immobilization*

First, in narrow syntax, only hierarchy—not linear adjacency—plays a role. Next, in the immobilization step, sisterhood is translated into adjacency, following Sproat (1985) and Embick and Noyer (2001). Consider, for example, the syntactic tree in (18). (Keep in mind that viewing a syntactic object is misleading on paper for exactly the reasons we have discussed above: a better representation would be a mobile.)

(18)

During immobilization, adjacency will be fixed such that the following relations are established (where A * B reads "A is adjacent to B"):

(19)   X * [Y * ZP]

Adjacency and hierarchical information need to be simultaneously present in order for morphological operations such as Local Dislocation to take place (Embick and Noyer 2001). Phrasal stress assignment must also take place before hierarchical information is eliminated, along with the marking for deletion of copies which will not ultimately be pronounced. This is because, as has been noted since Bresnan (1971), stress "moves with" a *wh*-word, as in the object question:

(20)   What <u>book</u> did you read ~~what book~~?

This is explained if stress is initially assigned as it usually would be (see Kahnemuyipour 2009 and Sato 2009*a* for proposals) to the lower copy of *what book* on the first derivational cycle and then carried over to the higher copy which is ultimately pronounced. Since it appears that c-command (i.e. hierarchy/dominance) is relevant to selecting which copy to pronounce (Nunes 2004), all of this must occur before the tree is completely flattened. The base-generated copy of the *wh*-phrase must be marked to receive stress and then copied higher in the tree, with the original, lower copy only subsequently being deleted.

The adjacency relations established during immobilization are not enough to determine linear order where mutually c-commanding objects such as Y and ZP are concerned. That is to say, (19) is consistent with a number of linear orders: X-Y-ZP, X-ZP-Y, Y-ZP-X, and ZP-Y-X. Following Epstein *et al.* (1998) and M. Richards (2004), I assume that in such an "overdetermined" configuration, either Y or ZP's c-command relations over its sister must be ignored; which set of relations is ignored is subject to parametric variation. This issue is discussed further in Lohndal and Samuels (2010).

4.2.2 *Linearization-2: Spell-out*

The transformation from adjacency to precedence is achieved during the spell-out step, as vocabulary insertion occurs. But, following Raimy (2000*a*, *b*), the result of spell-out is not a completely linear string: it is a directed graph which may include loops and as a result be 'non-asymmetric' (we will return to this issue shortly; see Raimy 2003 for lucid discussion of (non-)asymmetry). On this view, which I will be adopting here, each word comes specified with precedence relations which order all its elements (technically, feature bundles which we typically note in shorthand as segments), which makes sense given that order matters: *dog* does not mean the same thing as *god*. These precedence relationships are denoted by arrows or as ordered pairs, with X → Y and (X, Y) both read as "X precedes Y." In the usual case, a lexical representation consists of a linear string initiated by the symbol # and terminated by %:

(21)   /kæt/ is shorthand for: # → k → æ → t → %
        or as ordered pairs: (#, k), (k, æ), (æ, t), (t, %)

However, during spell-out, the insertion of a new precedence relationship between two terminals as they are sequentially given phonological content may create a loop (specifically here a "backward" loop) in the string. This additional precedence relationship can serve a variety of morphological functions, from making a noun plural to making a verb iterative—it is a far less exotic process than it seems at first blush, given that "regular" affixation is just a special case of this process, as we are about to see. I will later propose a mechanism by which this happens, but for now, let us keep strictly to the representational side of things. Here is an example in which one precedence relationship has been added to /kæt/:

(22)   Add (t, k): $\# \to k \to æ \to t \to \%$

In this case, the direction that /t/ precedes /k/ has been added, while the instructions that /t/ precedes % and that # precedes /k/ remain. This creates a set of precedence relations for this string that is "non-asymmetric." If precedence is to be asymmetric, then if A precedes B, the statement B precedes A can never be true. But notice that by adding the direction that /t/ (directly) precedes /k/, it is still the case (via transitivity) that /k/ precedes /t/.

Raimy argues, following Kayne's (1994) asymmetry hypothesis for syntax, that a non-asymmetric phonological representation must be made asymmetric, as all phonological output is on the surface. (Think of this as a bare output condition.) In other words, all loops must be linearized, and this is the purpose of what Idsardi and Raimy (forthcoming) call serialization.

4.2.3 *Linearization-3: Serialization*

The serialization process ensures that as many precedence relationships as possible, and in particular all the morphologically added relations, are represented in the final linear structure. Moreover, the route taken is also economical: a loop like the one in (22) is only taken once, such that the output is /kætkæt/, not /kætkætkætkæt .../. As we will see momentarily, this serialization process is in fact deterministic, even if it may not seem so on the basis of this description. For the structure in (22), the result of linearization (which indeed preserves every precedence relation) is what we would characterize as total reduplication:

(23) $\# \to k \to æ \to t \to k \to æ \to t \to \% = $ /kætkæt/

One major selling point of Raimy's approach (see in particular Raimy 2000*b*) is that it accounts for both reduplication and affixation with exactly the same mechanism. Consider now a case which differs minimally from the reduplication examples discussed above: X precedes Y, and a morpheme Z is inserted with the instructions "X precedes Z and Z precedes Y." This situation is illustrated in (24):

(24)   Add (X, Z), (Z, Y):   # $\rightarrow$ X $\rightarrow$ Y $\rightarrow$ % = XZY

Z

Unlike the example in (149), the loop in (24) is in the "forward" direction. The precedence relations of the loop force Z to come between X and Y: in other words, XY with an infix Z. Thus, infixation and reduplication are two sides of the same coin: the former derives from a forward loop and the latter derives from a backward loop. Prefixation and suffixation are the special cases which involve the addition of a forward loop between # and the first lexical segment, or between the last lexical segment and %. This predicts a high degree of parallelism between reduplication and affixation; Samuels (2010*d*) shows that this prediction is indeed borne out.[3] I will also discuss in the next chapter how templatic and subtractive morphology as well as metathesis can be described with this notation.

Next I will turn to the matter of how to *remove* loops: how to serialize. As I mentioned earlier, Raimy has pursued the idea that the linearized output is the shortest path through the looped string, as many precedence relations as possible are realized (concretely, this means taking backward loops as soon as possible), and where there are conflicts, the morphologically added links are realized instead of lexical links. Fitzpatrick (2006) formalizes the first two of these principles with a fixed ranking of Optimality Theoretic constraints which he calls Economy and Completeness, plus an additional constraint, Shortest, which ensures that, when multiple nested loops begin at the same point, the shorter one is taken first. But there is a way to get the same results without any constraints, and this is the approach I will pursue: the linearization algorithm I adopt is Idsardi and Shorey's (2007) modified version of Dijkstra's shortest path algorithm (Dijkstra 1959).

At the core of Idsardi and Shorey's approach is the idea that the set of segments represented in the precedence statements is the phonological equivalent of the numeration in syntax. While the numeration is an unordered set, the precedence statements are organized in an ordered queue. By making this distinction, the problem of of linearizing a phonological string is reduced to finding the shortest path that connects the vertices (= segments) in the

---

[3] It should be noted that Raimy is hardly the first—or the last—to unify reduplication and infixation; McCarthy (1979) and Marantz (1982) had previously argued in favor of this approach (though see Raimy 2000*a* for a criticism of the templatic copy-and-associate method they used, which prevents reduplication and affixation from being truly integrated with each other), and more recently, so have Frampton (2009) and Halle (2008).

directed graph. The algorithm always begins with the start symbol, #, and then scans the queue until it finds the highest precedence statement which begins at #. It then moves along the path specified by that statement, outputs the result, and deprioritizes the newly traversed path by moving it to the bottom of the queue. Next, starting from its new position, the algorithm again scans from the top of the queue until it finds a path which begins at its current location. This is repeated until the termination symbol, %, is reached. I illustrate a simple example of this procedure step-by-step with the word /kæt/ below.

(25)   Vertices: {#, k, æ, t, %}
       Initial queue:
       1) # → k
       2) k → æ
       3) æ→ t
       4) t → %

       Step 1 (begin at #)
       Traverse path: # → k
       Output: # → k
       New queue:
       1) k → æ
       2) æ→ t
       3) t → %
       4) # → k

       Step 2 (begin at /k/)
       Traverse path: k → æ
       Output: # → k → æ
       New queue:
       1) æ→ t
       2) t → %
       3) # → k
       4) k → æ

       Step 3 (begin at /æ/)
       Traverse path: æ→ t
       Output: # → k → æ→ t
       New queue:
       1) t → %
       2) # → k
       3) k → æ
       4) æ→ t

Step 4 (begin at /t/)
Traverse path: t → %
Output: # → k → æ→ t → %
Algorithm halts.

In this particular example, since each vertex was the starting point for only one path in the queue, the order of the statements in the queue did not actually matter; I leave it to the reader to verify that any ordering of statements would have yielded the same output. But, as we are about to see, this is not the case when there are non-asymmetric precedence statements involved. Consider what would happen if we were to add one additional precedence statement, (t, k), to the queue. If it were added in the lowest-priority position, at the bottom of the original queue, the result of running the algorithm would still be /kæt/ because the algorithm would find (t, %) first and halt as a consequence, never traversing (t, k). But if we added this new statement *above* (t, %), something quite different would happen:

(26)   Vertices: {#, k, æ, t, %}
        Initial queue:
        1) t → k
        2) # → k
        3) k → æ
        4) æ→ t
        5) t → %

        Step 1 (begin at #)
        Traverse path: # → k
        Output: # → k
        New queue:
        1) t → k
        2) k → æ
        3) æ→ t
        4) t → %
        5) # → k

        Step 2 (begin at /k/)
        Traverse path: k → æ
        Output: # → k → æ
        New queue:
        1) t → k
        2) æ→ t
        3) t → %

4) # → k
5) k → æ

Step 3 (begin at /æ/)

Traverse path: æ→ t

Output: # → k → æ→ t

New queue:

1) t → k
2) t → %
3) # → k
4) k → æ
5) æ→ t

Step 4 (begin at /t/)

Traverse path: t → k

Output: # → k → æ→ t → k

New queue:

1) t → %
2) # → k
3) k → æ
4) æ→ t
5) t → k

Step 5 (begin at /k/)

Traverse path: k → æ

Output: # → k → æ→ t → k → æ

New queue:

1) t → %
2) # → k
3) æ→ t
4) t → k
5) k → æ

Step 6 (begin at /æ/)

Traverse path: æ→ t

Output: # → k → æ→ t → k → æ→ t

New queue:

1) t → %
2) # → k
3) t → k
4) k → æ
5) æ→ t

Step 7 (begin at /t/)
Traverse path: t → %
Output: # → k → æ→ t → k → æ→ t → %
Algorithm halts.

If we stipulate that the precedence relations added by morphology are always added to the top of the queue, the result will be exactly what we desire: an asymmetric string which realizes the morphological links in preference to lexical material, and is economical. These properties result from how the algorithm operates; they do not need to be represented by constraints in the grammar.

There is another issue of linearization with which we need to grapple, namely how to account for the effects of Fitzpatrick's (2006) SHORTEST constraint. The effect of this highly ranked constraint in his system is to ensure that when there are two loops which begin at the same point, the shorter one is taken first. The primary evidence for such a constraint comes from the interaction of two types of verbal reduplication in the Salishan language Lushootseed. The way to make a verb in Lushootseed distributive is to reduplicate up through the second consonant (i.e. CVC or CC; see Broselow (1983)), and there is also a process of 'out-of-control' reduplication that copies the first VC. Let us assume along with Fitzpatrick, at least temporarily, that the loops created by both these processes are present in the representation at the same time. Then the root *bali-* "to forget" when undergoing both types of reduplication and prior to linearization would be:

(27)   # → b → a → l → i → %

On the face of it, there are two ways to linearize this string. We could take the "inner" (l, a) loop first and then the "outer" (l, b) loop, which would produce *bal-al-bali*. This is the derivation that is preferred by SHORTEST. Alternatively, we could take the outer loop first and then the inner one, yielding *bal-bal-ali*. This derivation would violate SHORTEST. It so happens that the attested form in Lushootseed is *bal-al-bali*. I am not aware of any other cases of multiple reduplication in which two loops which begin at the same point, so as far as I know, the *bal-bal-ali*-type pattern is unattested and Lushootseed stands alone in exhibiting the *bal-al-bali*-type pattern.

As I see it—lacking any evidence for a minimally differing language with forms like *bal-bal-ali*—there are two ways to obtain this result in a manner which is consistent with the theory developed here. First, one could accept that both loops are present at the same time and find some property of the serialization mechanism which guarantees that the inner loop is taken first (i.e. reduce the ostensive constraint to an emergent property of the algorithm and/or representations). This would make reduplication akin to repeat notation in music, in which the innermost of two repeats is always performed first. Alternatively, one could argue that the order of affixes entering the derivation is always distributive first, then out-of-control, and the *bal-al-bali* pattern is attributable solely to this fact. I argue in what follows that the latter view is correct—in other words, that there could easily be a language with forms like *bal-bal-ali*. The reason why Fitzpatrick argues that both loops are present in the representation at the same time is that, according to him, there are two attested hierarchical orderings of the distributive (DIST) and out-of-control (OOC) morphemes:

(28)   a. [DIST [OOC $\sqrt{root}$]]
       b. [OOC [DIST $\sqrt{root}$]]

Fitzpatrick claims that these two possibilities correspond to two distinct semantic types which he identifies. (28a) produces "semantics that could be paraphrased as something like 'many X's involved in random, ineffectual action,'" whereas with regards to (28b) "it seems that OOC has little or very subtle effects on the semantics of DIST forms" (Fitzpatrick 2006: 20). Examples of the two types are:

(29)   [DIST [OOC $\sqrt{root}$]]   [OOC [DIST $\sqrt{root}$]]

       saq'^{w} → saq'^{w}-aq'^{w}-saq'^{w} bali → bal-al-bali
       'fly' → 'many flying around'   'forget' → 'to (suddenly)
                                                     be forgetful'

       g^{w}ax → g^{w}ax^w-ax^w-g^{w}ax^w g^{w}ad → g^{w}ad-ad-g^{w}ad
       'walk' → 'a lot of walking around'   'talk' → 'talk (a lot), speak up'

I agree that there are clearly two different semantic classes here, but this does not necessarily correlate with a difference in scope between the two morphemes. It could be instead that there are two Aspect positions for the distributive, but both are lower than the out-of-control morpheme, which (following Davis *et al.* 2009 on the related language St'at'imcets) is a modal. The forms with unpredictable semantics would be "lexical distributives" with low attachment of the aspectual and semantics which must be learned. The forms with predictable semantics would result from higher attachment of the aspectual, but would still have OOC-over-DIST ordering and therefore take the same shape on the surface. From a syntactic point of view, this is a tenable conclusion: Brody and Szabolcsi (2003) and Butler (2007) have argued for iterated positions in the cartography of the TP domain; see also Travis (2010) on multiple causatives in Tagalog.

As long as DIST is lower than OOC, we have some latitude in how to cash out the derivation. One option would be to perform distributive reduplication first, then serialize, which (again taking *bali* as our example) would produce *bal-bali*, and then to perform out-of-control reduplication to this (via another cycle of spell-out and associated concatenation), yielding *bal-al-bali*. Alternatively, it is possible to get the correct ordering with only one serialization step. Provided the out-of-control morpheme is added after the distributive one, a bottom-up spell-out mechanism within a single cycle means the (l, a) link added by OOC will be added to the queue later and therefore will be closer to the top than the (l, b) link added by DIST.[4] A single run-through of the serialization algorithm will give the desired result. Independently, anticipating discussion of cyclicity in the sections to follow, we might prefer the latter option over the former one considering that we are dealing with TP-domain elements here, so no new cycle is expected between DIST and OOC.

This raises another question, namely whether serialization always applies immediately after concatenation upon spell-out creates a loop, or whether any phonological processes can apply while the representation is non-asymmetrical. In Samuels (2009*b*) I argue at length that serialization must precede phonological rules on a given cycle, contra Raimy (2000*a, b*) and Reiss and Simpson (2009). I will not recap the empirical evidence from 'backcopying' effects (certain interactions between reduplication and phonological rules) for this here, but I would like to note that, if we are adopting Idsardi and Raimy's view that serialization is not part of the phonological module but rather part of the process by which spelled-out material is *transformed into* phonological objects, then it is inconsistent for any truly phonological processes to apply before serialization.

What I have sketched above is the basic order of operations at the syntax/phonology interface. In the remainder of this chapter, I discuss the timing and scope of these operations. In other words, I will be addressing issues such as which terminals undergo spell-out when, and how many objects are serialized at a time. To make a long story short: everything—in narrow syntax, at the interface, in phonology proper, and, for that matter, in the semantic component—occurs cyclically from the bottom up and the inside out, one phase at a time. Now let me elaborate on what I mean by this.

---

[4] Idsardi and Shorey (2007) argue that new links are not always added to the top of the queue: suffixhood is the property of being "in competition with" the segment that is linked to %, and therefore, to target the existing statement (x, %) for deprioritization. See Samuels (2009*b*), §4.3.6 for arguments against this approach.

4.3 Phonological Derivation by Phase

Throughout the generative era, several "inside-out" cyclic models of phonology have been proposed. The first of these was Chomsky, Halle, and Lukoff (1956), which introduced the phonological cycle. Indeed, unlike phonological rules and features, the cycle is a genuinely new concept from the generative era which originated in phonology, only later being adopted in syntax by Chomsky (1965). The phonological cycle formed a crucial component of Chomsky and Halle's (1968) and Bresnan (1971), later being implemented as the "strict cycle" of Kean (1974) and Mascaró (1976).[5] The tradition of Lexical Phonology (and Morphology) begun by Kiparsky (1982) and Mohanan (1982) developed the idea of cyclicity further, building on Pesetsky (1979). Lexical Phonology classifies morphemes into a number of ordered strata or levels, each of which constitutes a domain associated with a set of phonological rules, plus a final set of "post-lexical," "non-cyclic" rules.[6] (We will discuss the differences between lexical/cyclic and post-lexical/non-cyclic rules in §4.3.3.) Since the late 1980s, Lexical Phonology has come under heavy criticism, with Gussmann (1988) even proclaiming the "death knell" of Lexical Phonology with the advent of the first published book on the subject, Mohanan (1986). I will evaluate a number of these criticisms in the remainder of this chapter. However, we should note at this juncture that Gussman's report of Lexical Phonology's death proved premature, as research in this vein has continued, with numerous studies making headway towards defining the lexical strata in various languages, and more theoretical debates over issues such as the typology of cyclic vs. non-cyclic and lexical vs. post-lexical rules as well as the correct characterization of principles such as the Strict Cycle Condition. Lexical Phonology has also yielded two Optimality Theoretic frameworks, the LPM-OT of Kiparsky (2000) and the Stratal OT of Bermúdez-Otero (forthcoming).

Recently, a new movement in phonological theory has emerged, attempting to combine the insights of Lexical Phonology with Distributed Morphology (Halle and Marantz 1993) and the concept of 'derivation by phase' in syntax, developed by Chomsky (2001, 2008). The theory presented here, which I call phonological derivation by phase (PDbP), falls under this umbrella, as it takes as a starting point the conceptual argument laid out in the foundational work by Marvin (2002: 74): "If we think of levels in the lexicon as levels of syntactic

---

[5] Scheer (forthcoming) provides a book-length history of cyclicity and conceptions of syntax/morphology/phonology interactions; a brief history is also provided in Samuels (forthcoming *a*). See Freidin (1999), Lasnik (2006) for a history of the cycle's various incarnations in syntax.

[6] I will make reference to numerous Lexical Phonology concepts in this chapter; for a proper introduction, see the works cited above, the papers in Kaisse and Hargus (1993), or McMahon (2000).

attachment of affixes, we can actually say that Lexical Phonology suggests that phonological rules are limited by syntactic domains, possibly phases."

From a Minimalist standpoint, a model of grammar which, like this one, has synchronous cycles across the various modules is highly desirable.[7] Indeed, it is the "best-case scenario" according to Chomsky (2004: 107):

Assume that all three components [narrow syntax (NS), semantics (Σ), & phonology (Φ)] are cyclic, a very natural optimality requirement and fairly conventional. In the worst case, the three cycles are independent; the best case is that there is a single cycle only. Assume that to be true. Then Φ and Σ apply to units constructed by NS, and the three components of the derivation of <PHON, SEM> proceed cyclically in parallel. [...] When a phase is transferred to Φ, it is converted to PHON. Φ proceeds in parallel with the NS derivation. Φ is greatly simplified if it can 'forget about' what has been transferred to it at earlier phases; otherwise, the advantages of cyclic computation are lost.

Not only may this solution be computationally efficient, it also allows us to recognize the important contributions of cyclic models of phonology such as the ones noted at the beginning of this section. For instance, all attempts to account for phonological opacity effects (i.e. counterbleeding and counter-feeding interactions of the attested types) in a monostratal theory suffer from serious empirical or technical problems (see Vaux 2008 and references therein for discussion). Furthermore, the model proposed here relies on a cycle that is not proprietary to phonology. This insulates the approach from one family of recurring criticisms of Lexical Phonology, that its levels were poorly motivated and allowed to proliferate in an unconstrained manner (see e.g. Itô and Mester 2003). In PDbP, by contrast, evidence for the cycle should come from syntax and semantics in addition to (morpho)phonology. There can be no ad hoc stipulation of cycles/levels if a phonological analysis must be responsible to such external evidence; conversely, phonological phenomena should be able to provide evidence which bears on syntactic analysis.

Let us now turn to the question of what form such a model should take, from the phonological point of view. I take as my guide this quote from Cole (1995: 108):

A theory of phonology that can account for the phenomena attributed to cyclicity must include (1) a subtheory of domains which can construct domains on the basis of morphological structure, though not necessarily isomorphic to that structure, within

---

[7] There is a growing body of literature which argues that phases are required (follow from virtual conceptual necessity) to regulate syntax's interfaces with the semantic and phonological components. It is beyond the scope of the present work to discuss the implications of derivation by phase for syntax and interpretation, but see, for instance, Boeckx (2008) on how phases facilitate "wild-type" or "free" Merge and a conjunctivist semantics of the type proposed by Pietroski (2005 et seq.).

which certain phonological rules may apply; (2) a condition ... which restricts certain rules from applying in monomorphemic environments; and (3) a mechanism for modeling the interaction that can occur between rules applying in cyclic domains and those applying in the larger domains defined by word and phrase structure.

In the text to follow, I describe how PDbP achieves each of these three desiderata.

4.3.1 *Phases*

Before going any further, I should clarify how the basic phase architecture works. Consider a syntactic tree like this:

(30)

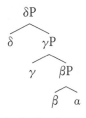

This is a static picture of a syntactic derivation at a particular point in time. Let's follow that derivation step by step. When a tree is assembled, elements are merged in the syntax two at a time, from the bottom of the tree to the top.[8] The first stage in the construction of (30), then, is a syntactic object β merging with another syntactic object α. This creates a set, $\{\beta, \alpha\}$. Depending on certain properties (which we may set aside for present purposes), either β or α will "project," that is, one of them will be selected as the head of the phrase under construction. We represent this state of affairs as $\{\beta \{\beta, \alpha\}\}$. (In (30), merely for convenience, I label the new projection as βP, i.e. a β Phrase.) The derivation proceeds in this fashion, creating $\{\gamma \{\beta \{\beta, \alpha\}\}\}$, and so forth.

At certain points, the derivation is punctuated by the introduction of an element which bears the property of being a "phase head." The factors that decide what is and what isn't a phase head are still subject to much speculation and debate, but they are not directly relevant to us. What is crucial is that phase heads initiate what is commonly called Transfer,[9] sending a chunk of the completed derivation to the semantic and phonological systems. Specifically,

---

[8] For justification, see Chomsky (2008), which grounds binary Merge and the requirement that Merge be "to the edge" in basic principles of computational efficiency.

[9] Transfer on the PF side is also sometimes called spell-out, not to be confused with spell-out in the more specialized sense of Idsardi and Raimy (forthcoming). Idsardi and Raimy's spell-out or LINEARIZATION-2 is one process which occurs at the point which many linguists would loosely call "at Transfer," "at PF," or "at spell-out." I will continue to use "transfer" as a blanket term and reserve "spell-out" for LINEARIZATION-2 associated with vocabulary insertion.

the complement of a phase head is the chunk that gets transferred, at the point when another phase head enters the derivation. The crucial fact which can be leveraged for this purpose is that cyclic transfer enforces a particular kind of cyclic opacity which has the potential to govern the locality of operations in syntax, phonology, morphology, and semantics. This is formalized in the Phase Impenetrability Condition:

(31)   PHASE IMPENETRABILITY CONDITON (Chomsky 2001)[10]
        For [ZP Z ...[HP α [H YP]]]: The domain of H is not accessible to operations at ZP, but only H and its edge.

Let us now assume for illustrative purposes that each of α, β, γ, δ in (30) are all phase heads. Then the steps of the derivation yielding that are:

(32)   Derivation of (30)

    a. Merge (β, α): α accessible to β.

    b. Merge (γ, βP): β accessible to γ. α transferred.

    c. Merge (δ, γP): γ accessible to δ. βP transferred.

However, in syntax the situation is virtually never like this, with a sequence α, β, γ, δ all phase heads, and all simplex (non-branching, terminal) nodes. Typically (or perhaps even necessarily; see Richards forthcoming and Boeckx 2010*a*), phase heads and non-phase heads alternate with one another, so the chunks being transferred are larger than depicted in (32). Let's consider a more realistic situation in (33) below. Assume that only γ and ε are phase heads (if you prefer to think more concretely, pretend that γ = *v* and ε = C):

(33)

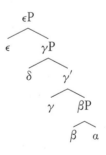

---

[10] There are two versions of the Phase Impenetrability Condition, the original from Chomsky (2000) (sometimes called PIC_1) and the newer version presented here, from Chomsky (2001) (PIC_2). One difference between the two formulations is crucial for morphophonology: under the original formulation, transfer is triggered immediately by the introduction of the phase edge of α, whereas for Chomsky (2001), the search space of α is expanded, allowing α and β to be accessible to one another for the purposes of syntactic and morphophonological operations.

The derivation will proceed thus:

(34)   a. Merge (β, α): α accessible to β.

   b. Merge (γ, βP): β, α accessible to γ.

   c. Merge (δ, γ'): γ accessible to δ.

   d. Merge (ϵ, γP): δ, γ accessible to ϵ. βP transferred.

Here are some general properties which can be seen by inspecting (33)–(34): a phase head's complement (such as βP in (33)) is accessible only to the phase head (γ) and any non-branching specifiers within the same phrase (δ). A phase head (γ) is accessible up to the next c-commanding phase head (ϵ). A complex specifier or adjunct forms its own spell-out domain (Uriagereka 1999); it is 'constructed in a separate workspace' from the rest of the structure. In the discussion to follow, I assume that Uriagereka's conception of Multiple Spell-Out (i.e. complex specifiers and adjuncts are transferred to phonology alone) and Chomsky's phase framework are compatible. One means for accomplishing this is suggested in recent proposals by Narita (2009*b*) and Boeckx (2008), who argue that only simplex syntactic objects can undergo Merge: complex objects introduced on a left branch must therefore be reduced to simplex objects before they can be integrated with the main derivational spine. This is achieved by the transfer of all but the head of the mergee. That is to say, complex specifiers and adjuncts must be headed by phase heads.[11]

One important clarification is necessary in order to enable us to make broader use of the Phase Impenetrability Condition. In narrow syntax, "accessible to operations" essentially means eligible for movement (i.e. Internal Merge or Re-Merge), and able to participate in Agree. For phonological purposes, I will move forward under the assumption that an "accessible" string of phonology can be operated upon by phonological rules (we will specify this further in the next chapter to mean accessible to the primitive operations SEARCH, COPY, and DELETE). Now let us assume that phase impenetrability holds in phonology, so each phonological string becomes inaccessible subsequent to the transfer of another string to the phonological component. This is the fundamental assumption upon which the analyses of stress assignment proposed in Marvin (2002) rest, and upon which I will build in the remainder of this chapter.

By preventing "reaching back too far" into the derivation, the Phase Impenetrability Condition derives the effects previously attributed to the deletion of

---

[11] Note that Newell (2008), in her discussion of the phase as a phonological domain, also makes the assumption that Uriagereka-style and Chomsky-style spell-out domains can be simultaneously entertained.

morpheme boundaries ("bracket erasure") at the end of every cycle (Siegel 1974; Mohanan 1982), opacifying the results of earlier ones. Put differently, chunks which are accessible to each other in the syntax undergo morphological and phonological operations together. Phase architecture represents a continuation of the interactionist system pioneered by Pesetsky (1979) and the Lexical Phonology tradition following it: word-building operations and phonological rules interleave, and the Phase Impenetrability Condition prevents modifying previous cycles after they are built. It should also be noted that there is some overlap implied here: for instance, in (34), in step (b) we see that γ is accessible to βP, whereas in steps (c–d), γ remains accessible throughout the construction of ϵP, but access to βP is prohibited. So there can be processes (be they syntactic, morphological, semantic, or phonological) which are contingent on the simultaneous presence of βP and γ in the derivation and there can be other processes which are contingent on the simultaneous presence of ϵP and γ in the derivation, but the Phase Impenetrability Condition prevents any processes from acting upon βP and ϵP simultaneously. I will expand on this shortly.

First, if we are going to pursue this type of theory, we must identify what is a phase head, and therefore what is a spell-out domain. This is an actively evolving area of syntactic theory, but the assumptions I will make here are fairly mainstream. Chomsky (2001 et seq.) takes C and transitive v to be phase heads; Legate (2003), Marvin (2002), Marantz (2008), and others argue that v must be a phase head in unaccusative and passive constructions as well. Crucially, T is not a phase head. Svenonius (2004), Bošković (2005), and Ott (2008), among others, argue for D as a phase head, and I will discuss this possibility later in the chapter. McGinnis (2001) adds the High Applicative (ApplH) to this list. Other questions remain open, such as whether P is also a phase head (see Abels 2003). It is my hope that the present work will open the door for phonological effects to shed some light on these unresolved matters, but for the time being, I will limit the examples used for illustrative purposes here to the less controversial cases.

Phasal domains are also identifiable within words. Parallel to v, Marantz (2001) and Arad (2003) establish $\{n, a\}$ as phase heads. In Distributed Morphology terms, following Marantz (1997), these elements are the categorial heads to which a-categorial roots must merge, and derivational affixes also belong to these classes. Arad (2003) put forth evidence for this conclusion based on apparent locality constraints on denominal and deadjectival verb meanings. For example, in Georgian the root $\sqrt{cx}$ can make a number of root derivatives as in (35):

(35)   Root formations of $\sqrt{cx}$ (Arad 2003: 774)
    a.   acxobs   'to bake', v
    b.   namcxvari   'cake'; literally, participle of *bake*
    c.   sicxe   'fever', n
    d.   cxeli   'hot', adj

This illustrates that the root $\sqrt{cx}$ can entertain a number of different, idiosyncratic interpretations depending on the affix with which it is merged. However, once the adjective *cxeli* 'hot' is derived, the only deadjectival verb that can be made from this word is *acxelebs* 'to heat,' which is predictable and dependent in meaning on the adjective. The same case can be made with denominal verbs in Hebrew: while the root $\sqrt{sgr}$ can make several root-derived verbs and nouns with varying meanings, as shown in (36), the only verb that can be made from the noun *misgeret* 'frame' is the verb *misger* which predictably means "to frame."[12]

(36)   Root formations of $\sqrt{sgr}$ (Arad 2003: 746)
    a.   sagar   'to close', v
    b.   hisgir   'to extradite', v
    c.   histager   'to cocoon onseself', v
    d.   seger   'closure', n
    e.   sograyim   'parentheses', n
    f.   misgeret   'frame', n

Marvin (2002) and Di Sciullo (2004, 2005) argue on additional independent grounds that the Phase Impenetrability Condition holds for these "morphological phases" created by *a*, *n*, and *v*.

It is interesting at this juncture to compare this inventory of phase heads to Chomsky and Halle's (1968: 366) rule of phonological phrase-building. In *SPE*, a # boundary is automatically inserted "at the beginning and end of every string dominated by . . . one of the lexical categories 'noun,' 'verb,' 'adjective,' or by a category such as 'sentence,' 'noun phrase,' 'verb phrase.'" PDbP provides a new and principled way of understanding why precisely *these* objects should constitute phonological domains.

---

[12] Note however that Borer (2009) points out a problem with another one of Arad's examples, based on the root $\sqrt{xsb}$. Arad takes the meaning of the denominal verb *hitxašben* 'to settle accounts' based on the noun *xešbon* 'arithmetic, account, calculus' as an example of the predictable meaning of denominal verbs as opposed to the variable, idiosyncratic meanings available to root derivatives. However, Borer notes that *hitxašben* actually has an idiosyncratic meaning 'to retaliate' which *xešbon* does not have with any light verb. This reading may be literally translated from the English idiom 'to settle an account' (as Borer admits), however, in which case it is unclear to me whether this constitutes a true counterexample to Arad's generalization.

The strongest claim made by the PDbP approach (call it the 'strong PDbP thesis'), and the one to which I will adhere, is that spell-out domains are the *only* domains that phonology and operations at the syntax–phonology interface need. In other words, this is PDbP's answer to Cole's (1995) desideratum (1), quoted in the previous section: both the levels of Lexical Phonology and domains of phrasal phonology come for free when we assume Distributed Morphology and a phasal syntax. Phonological domains are directly imposed by morphosyntactic structure, and phonology need not erect any boundaries. It has been recognized for at least forty years (i.e. at least back to *SPE*) that phonological domains correspond—in some fashion—to morphosyntactic ones. If the correspondence is not one of exact congruence, then phonology must construct (or adjust) boundaries. But if the correspondence *is* exact, then phonology can simply "read" the structures it is given. Theories that assume exact correspondence and describe phonological domains in terms of syntactic primes are sometimes called "direct reference" theories; see Kaisse (1985); Odden (1990); Cinque (1993). In recent literature, it is common to read that direct reference cannot be correct because there are mismatches between syntactic and phonological domains. This is the position held by proponents of "indirect reference" theories such as Selkirk (1984), Nespor and Vogel (1986), Truckenbrodt (1995), Seidl (2001), and many others. If PDbP is correct, there is no need for the extensive restructuring of domains proposed by most indirect reference theories. In fact, the situation is even better: phonology doesn't have to "read" syntactic boundaries, it just applies to each chunk as it is received.

4.3.2 *How Derivations Proceed*

Now that I have described the basic skeleton of PDbP, let me put some flesh onto its bones. The story of PDbP properly begins at the syntax-to-phonology transfer: in other words, at the top of the chart in (17). For the sake of simplicity, I will gloss over immobilization and morphosyntax here, and skip straight to spell-out, the point at which phonological content enters the derivation (recall the Distributed Morphology hypothesis of Late Insertion), and the output of which is a directed graph. Remember that transfer does not occur until two phase heads are present in the syntactic derivation: upon the introduction of the *second* phase head, the complement domain of the *first* phase head is transferred. This first phase head (*v, n,* or *a*) then licenses vocabulary insertion for the material in its complement (again, subsequent to immobilization, which we are ignoring here). For empirical reasons that we shall see shortly, it is understood that vocabulary insertion proceeds bottom-up within each cycle.

Another property which I take to be characteristic of spell-out is that it can produce objects which are ill-formed (or more accurately, not yet fully formed) for phonological purposes: for instance, the phonological material which is inserted may be phontactically illicit or combine with previously inserted material to create a non-asymmetrical structure. Serialization can therefore be seen as "interface-driven repair" in the sense of Calabrese (1995, 2005). In the next chapter we will specify the range of available repairs more clearly, but for now, we will stick to simple examples of phonology-internal repairs (such as, for example, schwa insertion to break up phonotactically illicit clusters) and focus on *when* these repairs occur rather than the mechanics of the repairs themselves. The simple answer to the question of when repairs occur is that they happen immediately, and because of the Phase Impenetrability Condition, never later.[13] We are forced to adopt this view if "looking ahead" in the derivation is not permitted (a standard assumption given that the impossibility of looking ahead is an inherent property of stepwise derivations in general). For instance, the phonological system cannot know that the phonotactically illicit structure in the current cycle will be rendered licit by a suffix which has not yet been transferred. Its only choice is to make the necessary repairs immediately, just in case.[14]

A point which may at first be difficult to understand is that this first complement to be transferred—a root transferred by virtue of being the complement of a categorizing phase head—does not undergo phonological operations on its own. Instead, the root and *everything accessible to it under the PIC*—which in the absence of specifiers or adjuncts in the sub-word-level architecture means only the first categorizing head—undergo phonology together.[15] It may be helpful to think about this issue from a different angle in order to understand that this is not a purely phonological issue. One of the most important ideas in Distributed Morphology is the idea that a root and its sister form a special domain for semantic interpretation, allomorphy, and phonology as well. Here is one classic argument, which comes from Marantz (2001). Marantz was concerned with countering the argument against strict

---

[13] I should clarify that by "immediately" I mean "within that cycle." I maintain that phonological rules must be extrinsically ordered within a cycle: in other words, that their ordering must be learned (see Bromberger and Halle 1989 and Vaux 2008 for arguments to this effect).

[14] To enforce this, Piggott and Newell (2006: 16) propose a "codicil" to the Phase Impenetrability Condition which they call Phase Integrity: "Conditions on the well-formedness of prosodic categories are imposed on all elements that emerge within a phase *a*, if the elements are solely within phase *a*." This formalizes the prohibition against look-ahead, but I feel it is superfluous to do so when the very nature of stepwise derivations is such that they do not permit look-ahead.

[15] See Newell 2008 on the possibility of morphological adjuncts; their existence is commensurable with my approach, although I will not discuss this issue further.

lexicalism articulated by Dubinsky and Simango (1996). The evidence presented by Dubinsky and Simango comes from the behavior of stative and passive morphemes in Chichewa. These two morphemes differ in several respects, in fact exactly parallel to the way adjectival (stative) passives differ from eventive passives in English, as summarized below (modified slightly from Marantz 2001: 5). (The % symbol denotes a sentence which is unacceptable under a particular interpretation which is noted in parentheses.)

(37) Stative affix

    a. can create idioms
       cf. *the die is cast*

    b. won't attach to applicative morpheme
       cf. %*The men are baked a cake.* (stative interpretation impossible)

    c. won't attach to causative morpheme
       cf. %*These tomatoes are grown.* ("cultivated" interpretation impossible)

    d. meaning is connected to aspectual class of root
       cf. *These children are grown/bathed/stunned.*

    e. can trigger stem allomorphy

(38) Passive affix

    a. can't create idioms

    b. may attach to applicative morpheme
       cf. *The men were baked a cake.*

    c. may attach to causative morpheme
       cf. *These flowers were grown by farmers.*

    d. meaning is independent of root
       cf. *The flowers are being grown/bathed/stunned.*

    e. doesn't trigger stem allomorphy

While Dubinsky and Simango (1996) take the differences between the stative and the passive to argue that the former is constructed in the lexicon while the latter is constructed in the syntax, Marantz (2001) claims instead that these formations are created in two different places, but both *in the syntax*. Specifically, Marantz argues that a head which is the sister of a root, and which categorizes that root, enjoys special privileges because of its syntactic position. This, he claims, follows from the phase system: the categorizing head defines the edge of the associated root's phase domain, so the two undergo semantic and phonological interpretation together. The interpretation of the root in the context of the categorizing head is negotiated using information from the Encyclopedia (the component which lists the relations between vocabulary items and their various meanings) at this stage. Given the restrictions imposed by the Phase Impenetrability Condition, any subsequent material attached outside this core head+root structure cannot see the properties of the root, only of those of the head. The meaning of the root cannot then be "re-negotiated" at this stage (as the Georgian and Hebrew examples presented earlier in this chapter are also meant to show). This is taken to follow from the Phase Impenetrability Condition. The contrast between the stative (37) and passive (38) thus reduces to a syntactic difference: the stative is a *v* head merged directly to the root (39a), while the passive is merged outside *v* (39b).

This distinction between "inner" and "outer" affixes is particularly attractive from a phonological perspective because it can be correlated with the Class 1 (stem-level) versus Class 2 (word-level) distinction familiar from Lexical Phonology. Take, for example, formations involving the root √*meter*. Let us assume (following Chomsky and Halle's 1968) that the underlying phonological form of the root is /mitr/, which contains an illicit consonant cluster. If this cluster appears word-finally, a rule of schwa epenthesis breaks it up, as occurs in the noun [mirəɹ] (with epenthesis feeding tapping) and similarly in the verb [hɪndəɹ] from /hɪndr/. It has also long been noted that vowel-initial suffixes can obviate the need for epenthesis, since the offending root-final consonant can be syllabified with the suffix: thus, /mitr/ plus the adjectival suffix *-ic* yields [mɛtɹɪk] (a different rule adjusts the quality of the stem vowel). However, not all vowel-initial suffixes allow a root to escape epenthesis in this way. Though there is no prima facie phonological or phonetic reason why /mitr/ plus *-ing* ought to be syllabified any differently from /mitr/ plus *-ic*, still we see epenthesis in [mirəɹɪŋ]. As it happens, all stem-level (Class 1) suffixes behave like *-ic* with respect to epenthesis, and all word-level (Class 2) suffixes behave like *-ing*; indeed, for this reason, the possibility of resyllabification was used by Kiparsky (1982) as a diagnostic for affix class membership.

Marvin (2002) suggests that this pattern of epenthesis can be described in the spirit of Marantz (2001) if we adopt these structures, equating Class 1 with merger to the root and Class 2 with merger outside the initial categorial head:

(40)   a.   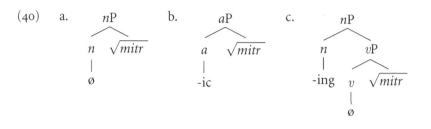   b.   c.

In (40a), √*mitr* undergoes phonological operations upon construction of *n*P, and since the illicit cluster finds no affixal support, epenthesis applies. In (40b), phonological operations apply when *a*P is constructed, and because the root and the *a* head undergo interpretation together, epenthesis fails to apply: the phonology receives the string /mitr+ɪk/, which does not have a cluster in need of repair, and the result is [mɛtɹɪk]. But in (40c), in contrast, the root is subject to phonological operations at *v*P, before *-ing* enters the derivation. It must therefore undergo epenthesis, which explains why the resulting form is [mirəɹɪŋ], not *[mitɹɪŋ].

Again, the root and innermost head form a special domain for semantics as well as phonology. Marvin (2002) provides several examples of minimal pairs in which one member is semantically compositional and phonologically behaves as though it has undergone Class 1 affixation, while the other member is semantically opaque and phonologically looks as though it has undergone Class 2 affixation. These include *twink[əl]ing* (gleaming) vs. *twin[kl]ing* (an instant) and *short[ən]ing* (making shorter) vs. *shor[tn]ing* (fat used in cooking). Marvin (2002: 31) explains this phenomenon thus, in keeping with the proposal by Marantz (1997, 2001):

[T]he attachment site of category-forming affixes is relevant for both meaning and pronunciation. If an affix is attached directly to the root, the meaning of the whole can be idiosyncratic (unpredictable). This follows from the fact that the root meaning itself is unpredictable and encyclopedic knowledge has to be evoked in order to negotiate the meaning of the root in the context of the category-forming head. If an affix is attached on top of the root that already has a category-forming affix attached, the meaning of the whole is predictable from the meaning of the upper affix and the unit it attaches to, because the meaning of this unit, comprising the root and lower category-forming affix, has already been negotiated at this point.

Thus, the regular forms in the minimal pairs mentioned above are made by *-ing* attaching to a previously-constructed *v*P, which entails that the root is repaired (by schwa-insertion) prior to the introduction of *-ing*. The opaque forms, by contrast, involve (in Marvin's view) direct affixation of *-ing* to the a-categorial root, or (in my view) may be stored directly in the lexicon as a simplex form.[16]

I illustrate this graphically in (41) below with the case of *twin[kl]ing* ∼ *twink[əl]ing*, adopting the structures posited by Marvin.

(41)

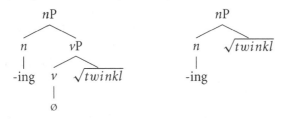

This example also illustrates another important difference between Lexical Phonology and phase-based phonology. In Lexical Phonology, one would say that *-ing* exhibits "double membership": *-ing* acts as a Class 2 (word-level) suffix in the transparent cases and as a Class 1 (stem-level) affix in the opaque cases. The ubiquity of double membership was seen by some as problematic (Aronoff 1976). In a phase-based framework, affix classes can be abolished. Instead, affixes subcategorize for different types of complements (*a*, *n*, *v*, final stress, animate, etc.). Double membership merely reflects the fact that a given affix can appear in different structural positions relative to a root; that is, it can subcategorize for more than one type of complement. (It would in fact require an additional stipulation, and run counter to much empirical evidence, to rule out this possibility.) If a root has already been rendered opaque by the Phase Impenetrability Condition prior to the introduction of a given affix, the affix will not be able to change that root, and it will thereby act (in that particular instance) as though it belongs to Class 2. Otherwise, if the affix attaches directly to the root without any intervening phase head, it can effect changes on the root.

Another advantage of phonological derivation by phase is that the phase-head status of derivational affixes, the Phase Impenetrability Condition, and binary branching conspire to produce exactly Lexical Phonology's Affix Ordering Generalization (Selkirk 1982): only one affix in a given derivation—the innermost—may (potentially) belong to Class 1, because a root can only have one sister. All other affixes will find the root inaccessible and must there-fore act as though they belong to Class 2. In the case where the root merges

---

[16] Which of these options is ultimately correct does not affect the outcome of the derivation. If the opaque forms are stored as simplex forms, one might argue that the derivationally produced forms of *lightning* and *shortening* consist of √*light*/√*short* plus a verbal head *-n* and then a nominal head *-ing*. Either way, the first phonological cycle will operate over the root and its sister: *lightn-* and *shortn-* in the predictable cases but *lightning* and *shortening* in the opaque cases. Thus, the desired contrast is still achieved.

first with a null categorial head, any affixes which may attach subsequently will all still act as though they are in Class 2. Another morphological consequence of derivational affixes being phase heads is that, assuming all morphological operations occur phase-by-phase, they undergo vocabulary insertion on different cycles and thus cannot undergo fusion. This explains an observation attributed to David Perlmutter to the effect that there are no portmanteaux derivational affixes; see Embick (2010) for discussion.

All this evidence runs in the same direction as a long-recognized generalization, namely that all cyclic phonological processes are dependent on there being two cycles' worth of strings in the workspace. This is the general force of the Strict Cycle Condition, which can now be replaced with the Phase Impenetrability Condition.

(42)   STRICT CYCLE CONDITION (SCC; here from Kenstowicz 1994: 208)[17]
    A cyclic rule may apply to a string x just in case either of the following holds:

    a. (SCC_1) The rule makes crucial reference to information in the representation that spans the boundary between the current cycle and the preceding one.

    b. (SCC_2) The rule applies solely within the domain of the previous cycle but crucially refers to information supplied by a rule operating on the current cycle.

To sum up this discussion, the first phonological cycle for any word applies to the root and its sister (the innermost categorizing phase head). At this stage, the phase head and complement are visible to each other, so phonological rules can affect these two objects. Even if the categorizing head is phonologically null, its complement nevertheless becomes completely opaque on subsequent cycles.

This process is iterated. Every time another string is sent to the phonology, some set of phonological rules gets the chance to apply: when the structural description of a phonological rule is newly satisfied by the material entering in that phase, the rule can modify anything which is accessible under the Phase Impenetrability Condition. Moreover, since $\{n, v, a\}$ are all phase heads, every derivational affix triggers a phonological cycle.[18] This system predicts

---

[17] The biclausal, disjunctive version here forms the basis for most phonological discussions of strict cyclicity and "derived environment" effects. However, it is worth noting that syntacticians may have in mind a different version of the Strict Cycle Condition, which was first proposed for syntax by Chomsky (1973: 243): "No rule can apply to a domain dominated by a cyclic node A in such a way as to affect solely a proper subdomain of A dominated by a node B which is also a cyclic node."

[18] It is interesting to note that this entails the possibility of a language that has "no phonology" (or more accurately, no lexical rules) because it has no derivational affixes. This is precisely what Sandler

exactly the type of strictly local opacity effects that are visible in allomorph selection, phonological rule application, and compositional interpretation. Having one cycle per morpheme also yields as a theorem the relationship between phonological cyclicity and semantic compositionality known as the Natural Bracketing Hypothesis:

(43)   NATURAL BRACKETING HYPOTHESIS (Brame 1972)
       A substring ψ of a string ϕ is a domain of cyclic rule application in phonology only if it shows up elsewhere as an independent word sequence which enters compositionally into the determination of the meaning of ϕ.

There are counterexamples to this generalization on the surface: ψ is sometimes not a word, as in many *-ation* nouns that are not paired with corresponding *-ate* verbs. However, it is the exception that proves the rule, and the ease which with words are backformed to fill such gaps (*conversate, orientate, constellate*) gives weight to the hypothesis. A different type of counterexample is provided by words which are well-behaved phonologically—that is to say, they have exactly the number of cycles one would expect given the number of morphemes involved—but are semantically idiosyncratic. Harley (2009*a*, *b*) notes several cases in which words have idiosyncratic meanings that appear to be computed over chunks larger than the initial root + first categorizing head. Some examples include *editorial, naturalized, sanitarium, auditorium, nationalize, institutionalize,* and *hospitality* (compare the specialized meanings of these words with *edit, nature/natural, sane/sanitary, audit/auditor/auditory, nation/national, institute/institution/institutional*). The existence of such idiosyncratic meanings leads Harley to conclude, following Marantz (1997) but contra Arad (2003) and more recent writings by Marantz, that the domain of semantic idiosyncrasy is in fact larger than just the root + first sister; for Harley, meaning is fixed by a flavor of *v* which introduces an Agent, called Voice by Kratzer (1996). Marantz (2010) counters that that such putative counterexamples fall into a particular class which he does not view as problematic. The hypothesis which Marantz advances is that once a particular alloseme of a root is selected (upon merging with the first categorial head), it is impossible to reverse this selection. For instance, for $\sqrt{globe}$ there are three allosemes, corresponding to three meanings of *global*: one meaning "spherical," one meaning "pertaining to the Earth," and one meaning "considering all aspects of a situation." All further derivatives must stick with the particular alloseme

---

(2008*b*) has claimed for Al-Sayyid Bedouin Sign Language, in which the only morphological process is compounding, and only in compounds is a "kernel of proto-phonology" in the form of assimilation beginning to emerge.

that was chosen at this first-categorizing-head level. So *globalization* may have a rather special meaning, but it still *cannot* mean "the act of turning something into a sphere" since the allosome for "pertaining to the Earth" was selected on a previous cycle. I will have nothing more to say about this debate, which is semantic at its core, but let me reiterate that none of these forms are remarkable phonologically; if Marantz is correct, they are not remarkable semantically, either, and the phase-mediated parallel cyclicity across linguistic modules (Chomsky's "best-case scenario") remains.

The Phase Impenetrability Condition also constrains allomorph selection and the phonological readjustment of allomorphs which have already been inserted. First, let us consider a case in which a particular tense triggers phonological readjustment of the verb stem (we will ignore the base position of the external argument, which does not seem to have any effect here):

(44)

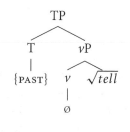

$$\sqrt{tell} + \{\text{PAST}\} \rightarrow told$$

This tense-root interaction is licit under the Phase Impenetrability Condition: the root in the complement of *v* is accessible to material in the *v*P phase edge, including T. A phonological readjustment rule triggered by {PAST} can therefore affect the root, changing the vowel in the context of the past tense.

There are also effects that run in the opposite direction: not only can the presence of a particular tense affect the exponence of the root, the presence of a particular root can affect the exponence of T, selecting *-t* rather than the usual *-ed*, as shown here:

(45)

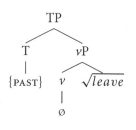

$$\sqrt{leave} + \{\text{PAST}\} \rightarrow left$$

Again, since the root and the *v*P phase edge are accessible to one another, the root can have a hand in determining which exponent of T is inserted. Embick (2010: 31) notes that the following generalization seems to hold about interactions like these, between a root (or non-cyclic head) and another non-cyclic node:

A non-cyclic (i.e. non-category-defining) head *X* can see a Root in spite of intervening cyclic node *x*, but this seems to happen only when *x* is non-overt. This is the situation in the English past tense, where the phonologically null *v* head does not prevent the T[past] head from having its allomorphy conditioned by the identity of the Root.

Embick hypothesizes that the cyclic node involved (here, *v*) must be null to license this type of allomorphy because this allows it to be "pruned" during linearization, creating linear adjacency between the root and the non-cyclic node T; vocabulary insertion then takes place at the stage where this local relationship has been established. This is consonant with the order of operations at the syntax–phonology interface for which I have argued earlier (and see Lohndal and Samuels 2010). The adjacency requirement here is the phonological counterpoint to the restriction on allosemy proposed by Marantz (2010) and introduced above.

One question which remains open concerns a potential asymmetry between cases like *told* in (44) and *left* in (45). We have already seen that it is possible for the properties of one node to affect allomorph choice of a morpheme which is higher up in the structure: one such case is $\sqrt{leave}$ conditioning insertion of -*t* rather than -*ed* in the past tense. This is called inwards sensitivity. Inwards-sensitive allomorphy can depend on phonological properties of the lower element: for example, an affix may be sensitive to the stress properties or number of syllables in a root. This is taken as evidence that vocabulary insertion proceeds from bottom up within a phase. Outwards-sensitive allomorphy such as (44), in which the exponence of an inner node depends on the content of an outer node, is also possible in a phase-based system provided the necessary participants are accessible to one another under the Phase Impenetrability Condition. In contrast to the inwards-sensitive case, if vocabulary insertion within a given domain occurs strictly from bottom to top, then we predict— seemingly correctly, see Bobaljik (2000)—that outwards-sensitive allomorphy cannot be conditioned by the phonological content of the outer morpheme, only its morphosyntactic features.

We also correctly predict under the phase system that interactions between two cyclic heads are extremely local. "Category-changing" heads cannot see the root at the core of their structure; only the first, category-establishing head can do so. This follows directly from the Phase Impenetrability Condition if *v, n*, and *a* are all phase heads. Embick (2010) illustrates this with the case of the nominal suffix *-ity*. This suffix can only attach to a certain set of roots, including $\sqrt{atroc}$ and $\sqrt{curious}$. However, *-ity* is fully productive in its ability to nominalize adjectives in *-able*. This "potentiation" of *-ity* is understandable given the Phase Impenetrability Condition: the *n* head (i.e. *-ity*) is prevented from seeing a root which has already been categorized by *-able* (or any other head, even if it is not phonologically overt). We need only describe the conditions for insertion of *-ity* as something like what is shown below, following Embick (2010: 32).

(46) $n \leftrightarrow$ -ity / X_
          X = Roots ($\sqrt{atroc}$, $\sqrt{curious}$ ...); [a, -able]

In short, combining Distributed Morphology with the phase architecture allows the Phase Impenetrability Condition to account for restrictions on contextual allomorphy and allosemy in addition to regulating the cyclic application of phonological rules.

4.3.3 *Cyclicity and Lexical Rule Application*

Stress assignment provides a good example of how a phase-based analysis, which provides one phonological cycle for each derivational affix, makes the correct predictions. Along the same lines as the earlier discussion of *meter ∼ metric ∼ metering*, formations built off the root $\sqrt{parent}$ illustrate the role of the Phase Impenetrability Condition in stress assignment. It is useful in this regard to compare the stress contour of *párent* to *paréntal* and *párenthood*, following Marvin (2002). Notice that *paréntal* shows stress retraction when compared to *párent*, while *párenthood* does not. This difference is in fact the primary diagnostic of English affix class membership in Lexical Phonology: Class 1 affixes affect stress, while Class 2 affixes do not. In PDbP, this finds an explanation in terms of locality, namely that the Class 2 affix is too far from the root to affect its stress. A Class 1 affix will be merged directly with the root, while a Class 2 affix will attach outside a previous categorizing head:

(47)   a.   b.   c.

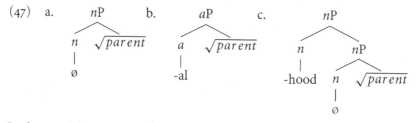

In the case of *parent*, stress assignment rules will first to the $n + \sqrt{}$ structure, constructing a unary foot and yielding stress on the first syllable. In the case of *parental*, involving a root-attached suffix, the input to the stress rules will be the $a + \sqrt{}$ structure, and the result will be regular penultimate stress. *Párenthood* contrasts with *paréntal* because it undergoes two cycles. The first cycle applies to $n + \sqrt{}$, with the same result as in the noun/verb *párent*. Next, -*hood* is added, but by this time the root is inaccessible because of the Phase Impenetrability Condition. For this reason, the accent assigned to the initial syllable is maintained, and the result is antepenultimate stress. It is interesting to note, along with Marvin (2002), that the Phase Impenetrability Condition forces us to adopt a view of stress assignment more like that of Chomsky and Halle's (1968) than Halle and Vergnaud (1987): whereas stress is built up cyclically in *SPE*, in Halle and Vergnaud (1987) previously assigned stresses are wiped clean and built up anew upon each instance of affixation. This wholesale erasure of stresses from earlier derivational stages is impermissible if the Phase Impenetrability Condition opacifies previous cycles as the derivation unfolds.

There are also structural minimal pairs in terms of stress, such as *compárable* ("able to be compared") and *cómparable* ("roughly the same"). The latter, which is semantically idiosyncratic, also exhibits the stress pattern of a Class 1 formation. In contrast, *compárable* exhibits semantic transparency and exhibits the stress pattern of a Class 2 formation: that is, it has the same stress as the verb *compáre* from which it is derived. This case is exactly parallel to *twin[kl]ing* ~ *twink[əl]ing*, with the semantically transparent form undergoing one more phonological cycle than the semantically idiosyncratic form.

Let me now explain more about the nature of phonological rules in PDbP and how they come to apply. While Minimalists pursue the idea that syntax is universal, and one of the main goals of the present work is to describe a universal core of phonological operations and representations, there is one part of language which undoubtedly must be learned and cannot be universal: the lexicon. It makes sense, then, to reduce as much cross-linguistic variation as possible to this very component; this is often expressed as the idea that "all parameters are lexical," dating back to Borer (1984) and sometimes called the Borer–Chomsky Conjecture (see Boeckx (2010*b*) for lucid discussion). I take an approach to phonology which reduces variation in large part to properties of lexical items as well. We will return to the issue of variation across individuals' phonological systems in much more detail in Chapter 6, but for now, I want to focus on how lexical items can vary in their phonological behavior.

Often when phonological rules are discussed, the situation seems very black and white: a rule applies if its structural description is met; if not, the rule fails to apply. But at least certain kinds of rules can have exceptions, and particular morphemes may simply be exempt from them. For instance, in Irish, there are three homophonous possessive pronouns: the third person singular masculine, third person singular feminine, and third person plural are all pronounced as [ə]. However, each has a different effect on the initial consonant of the following noun (possessee), as shown in (48) with the noun *cat* /kat/ meaning the same as English "cat":

(48)   a. [ək]at 'her cat' (no mutation)

      b. [əx]at 'his cat' (lenition)

      c. [əg]at 'their cat' (eclipsis)

It is hard to imagine how this effect could be captured, if not by rules specific to the individual possessive pronouns. (Establishing three separate allomorphs of every noun in the language—one unmutated, one lenited, and one eclipsed— seems a far less parsimonious option.)

On the other hand, there are some rules that seem to be completely exceptionless given the correct phonological and syntactic environment, and these rules also share a number of other commonalities. In Lexical Phonology, these are called "post-lexical" rules, since another salient property of rules in this class is that they apply across word boundaries (again, in the appropriate syntactic context). It has long been noted that such "late" rules have different properties from the earlier, cyclic lexical rules (see Coetzee and Pater (forthcoming) for a recent overview).[19] While lexical rules are subject to exceptions on a morpheme-by-morpheme basis in precisely the manner illustrated by (48), post-lexical rules are exceptionless from a morphological point of view. However, they can be sensitive to syntax, as has been recognized since Chomsky, Halle, and Lukoff (1956). This, of course, is exactly what PDbP is meant to capture. Post-lexical rules also tend to be gradient, and to be sensitive to performance factors such as speech rate/style/register and lexical frequency (which I will not discuss in depth here), whereas lexical rules are not.

I maintain the distinction between these two rule types by arguing that all phonological rules obey the Phase Impenetrability Condition, but in one of two different ways. Lexical rules must obey the Phase Impenetrability Condition at both the morpheme level (phase heads *n*, *a*, etc.) and the clausal level (phase heads *v*, C, etc.). Post-lexical rules obey the Phase Impenetrability Condition only at the clausal level. The way I use the terms

---

[19] These differences run parallel to the observation made by Di Sciullo (2004, 2005): morphological selection is similar to but more restricted than syntactic selection. Lexical rules are similar to (in fact, often the same as) post-lexical rules but more restricted.

"lexical" and "post-lexical" here roughly corresponds to the distinction between "concatenation" and "chaining" rules in Pak (2008). There is also another, more subtle point of difference between lexical and post-lexical rule domains: a lexical rule applies to everything which is *accessible* under the Phase Impenetrability Condition, whereas a post-lexical rule applies to a single transfer domain. In other words, the domain of a post-lexical rule is a phase head's complement, whereas the domain of a lexical rule is a phase head's complement *and edge*. This will become clearer as I introduce additional examples throughout the rest of this chapter.

Upon observing a particular alternation, how can a phonologist determine whether it results from a lexical or a post-lexical rule? As I have already noted, descriptively they differ in a number of ways. For instance, lexical rules are subject to lexical exceptions. Taking this to its logical conclusion, and in keeping with the Minimalist desire to place all idiosyncrasies in the lexicon, I adopt the *SPE* position that individual lexical entries can be specified as [-rule X]. One might think of there being an ordered list of rules which are automatically triggered by individual lexical items unless otherwise specified. Post-lexical rules, in contrast, are germane only to functional categories: they are triggered only by the clause-level phase heads *v*, C, etc., and apply to the whole complement domain of the head on which they are carried, down to the next phase head. (It is possible, as Samuels 2010*b* argues for Basque, for clause-level phase heads to trigger lexical rules also.) Recall that, unlike lexical rules, post-lexical rules apply to only *one* (clause-level) spell-out domain. As I will show in the next section (primarily §4.4.3), this creates a situation in which a lexical rule can span a boundary between two clause-level domains while a post-lexical rule cannot.[20]

4.4 Prosody without Hierarchy

In the previous sections, I focused on how PDbP captures some of the fundamental insights of Lexical Phonology while improving on it in several respects. However, this is but one way in which PDbP changes the picture of phonology and its interfaces. The model developed in the previous sections can also lead to a new understanding of phrase-level phonology, one that has the potential to eliminate the construction of a distinct set of phonological domains (i.e. the prosodic hierarchy). To paraphrase p. 9 of *SPE*, whether the output of the

[20] This is another way in which the theory presented here differs from that of Pak (2008). For Pak, concatenation rules are not only limited to two morpheme-level domains which are within a single clause-level spell-out domain; we will see examples later in which it is important that lexical rules can apply across *any* two adjacent morphemes even if they span a clause-level phase boundary.

syntactic component and the input of the phonological component are the same in this respect is an empirical issue. And as Scheer (2008*b*) notes, the relationship between Lexical Phonology and Prosodic Phonology has always been unclear, leading to claims that Lexical Phonology is redundant and should be eliminated (e.g. Selkirk 1984; Inkelas 1990). In this section I hope to show that PDbP can cover all the territory that was uneasily divided between Lexical Phonology and Prosodic Phonology.

Evidence for phonological constituents falls into three major classes: (*a*) phonological rules for which they serve as domains of application, (*b*) phonological processes which occur at their edges (primarily supraseg-mental, e.g. boundary tones), and (*c*) restrictions on syntactic elements relative to their edges (e.g. second position clitics). It has been recognized since the beginning of the generative enterprise that the phonological domains identified on the basis of these criteria correspond—in some fashion—to morphosyntactic domains. If the correspondence is not one of exact congruence, then phonology must construct (or adjust) boundaries. But if the correspondence *is* exact, then phonology can simply "read" the structures it is given. Theories that assume exact correspondence and describe phonological domains in terms of syntactic primes are sometimes called "direct reference" theories; see Kaisse (1985), Odden (1990), and Cinque (1993). In recent literature, it is common to read that direct reference cannot be correct because there are apparent mismatches between syntactic and phonological domains. This is the position held by proponents of "indirect reference" theories such as Selkirk (1984), Nespor and Vogel (1986), Truckenbrodt (1995), and many others. One famous mismatch, already noted by Chomsky and Halle's (1968), is shown in (49). Brackets represent clause boundaries and parentheses represent intonational phrase boundaries.

(49)   a. Syntax: This is [the cat that caught [the rat that stole [the cheese]]]

b. Phonology: (This is the cat) (that caught the rat) (that stole the cheese)

Note however that the purported isomorphism only exists if one considers NPs/DPs in the syntax. The prosodic constituents in fact line up perfectly with the left edges of the CPs, an observation made by Phillips (1999), Scheer (2004), Samuels (2009*b*), Shiobara (2009), and Wagner (2010), among others.

A number of phase-based approaches to phonological phrasing now exist, occupying a spectrum from those such as Seidl (2001), who maintain that indirect reference is still necessary, to those such as Samuels (2009*b*) and the present work, in which I pursue the idea that phases provide a means for reinterpreting purported non-isomorphisms as structures which in fact show exact correspondence of syntactic and phonological domains.

4.4.1 *Prosodic Hierarchy Theory*

I will not seek to give a comprehensive primer in Prosodic Phonology/prosodic hierarchy theory here; I direct the reader to Inkelas and Zec (1995), on which I base the brief introductory discussion below, for an overview. Since Selkirk (1978), and in classic works on prosodic hierarchy theory such as Selkirk (1984) and Nespor and Vogel (1986), a hierarchy of phonological constituents has been identified. The most standard of these are (from smallest to largest, or weakest to strongest) the phonological word (ω), the phonological phrase (ϕ), the intonational phrase (I-phrase), and the utterance (U).

It is commonly (though not exceptionlessly) thought that this hierarchy of constituents obeys the conditions in (50)–(51) (Selkirk 1984; Nespor and Vogel 1986):

(50)   STRICT LAYERING HYPOTHESIS
A given nonterminal unit of the prosodic hierarchy, X^P, is composed of one or more units of the immediately lower category, X^{P-1}.

(51)   PROPER CONTAINMENT
A boundary at a particular level of the prosodic hierarchy implies all weaker boundaries.

That is, the prosodic hierarchy is non-recursive and no levels can be "skipped."[21]

The fundamental hypothesis of prosodic hierarchy theory is that the constituents suggested by phonological processes (again, diagnosed by the domains of post-lexical rules and phenomena which occur at domain edges) are similar but not isomorphic to syntactic constituents. For this reason, proponents of the prosodic hierarchy claim it is necessary to erect and adjust boundaries in the phonology on the basis of syntactic information.

Paraphrasing Seidl (2000), both sides acknowledge that there are phonologically relevant domains at the phrasal level. The difference is that direct reference theories state these domains in terms of syntactic primes, while indirect theories state them in terms of phonological primes. For indirect reference theories, prosodic constituents are constructed from a syntactic

---

[21] Though see Dobashi (2003), Truckenbrodt (1995 et seq.), and Itô and Mester (2007) for arguments against non-recursivity and Schiering, Bickel, and Hildebrandt (2010) for arguments against strict layering.

representation, as should be obvious from (52)–(53), which illustrate the two general schools of thought on how this is construction is undertaken. The relation-based mapping approach in (52) is represented by Nespor and Vogel (1986), and the edge- or end-based mapping approach is (53) represented by Selkirk (1986) and, in Optimality-Theoretic terms, Truckenbrodt (1995, 1999).[22]

(52)   Relation-based ϕ-construction (Nespor and Vogel 1986: 168 ff.)

    a. *ϕ domain*
       The domain of ϕ consists of a C [clitic group] which contains a lexical head (X) and all Cs on its nonrecursive side up to the C that contains another head outside of the maximal projection of X.

    b. *ϕ construction*
       Join into an n-ary branching ϕ all Cs included in a string delimited by the definition of the domain of ϕ.

    c. *ϕ restructuring (optional)*
       A nonbranching ϕ which is the first complement of X on its recursive side is joined into the ϕ that contains X.

(53)   End-based ϕ-construction (Truckenbrodt 1995: 223)
    A language ranks the two following universal constraints:

    a. ALIGN-XP, R: ALIGN (XP, R; ϕ, R)
       For each XP there is a ϕ such that the right edge of XP coincides with the right edge of ϕ.

    b. ALIGN-XP, L: ALIGN (XP, L; ϕ, L)
       For each XP there is a ϕ such that the left edge of XP coincides with the left edge of ϕ.

Many arguments against the prosodic hierarchy exist, particularly in light of Bare Phrase Structure (Chomsky 1995a), in which it is impossible to refer to syntactic projections (i.e. XP), as both relation- and edge-based approaches must (see Dobashi 2003: 10 ff.). I will not attempt to recap these arguments here. The analyses presented in Seidl (2000, 2001) and the conceptual arguments in Scheer (2008b) are to my mind particularly devastating for prosodic hierarchy theory, and I encourage the reader to consult these works.

---

[22] An OT implementation of end-based ϕ construction, the Strict Layer Hypothesis, and Proper Containment requires many more constraints than just the ALIGN family, such as WRAP-XP, NONRECURSIVITY, EXHAUSTIVITY, LAYEREDNESS, and HEADEDNESS. See Truckenbrodt (2007) for an overview.

4.4.2 *Phonological Phrases as Phases*

A quote from the final chapter of Dobashi (2003) points to the potential of the phase framework for simplifying the syntax–phonology mapping:

> [I]f the mapping to Φ occurs as the syntactic derivation goes on, and if phonological rules apply as the mapping takes place, it would be unnecessary to create a p-phrase [= ϕ] in Φ. That is, the phonological rules apply when a phonological string is mapped to Φ, and such a phonological string becomes inaccessible when another phonological string is mapped to Φ later in the derivation. If so, the p-phrase is unnecessary. That is, the apparent p-phrase phenomena are reduced to the derivational properties of syntax and the cyclic mapping to Φ.   (Dobashi 2003: 223)

This should be the null hypothesis (as opposed to any other mechanism of ϕ-construction) since it does not require any additional interface machinery beyond the spell-out mechanism and phase domains which are already independently motivated and required. Let us now pursue this null hypothesis and consider what prediction a phase-based system makes about ϕ-construction, compared to prosodic hierarchy theory. I will limit the discussion further to the simplest possible case, namely that the spell-out domains prescribed by the phase system are imported to phonology directly, without any readjustment. Also aligned with this goal are Sato (2008, 2009b) and Pak (2008), though my theory differs from theirs in several respects, as I discuss in Samuels (2009b).

Let us first consider what prediction a phase-based system makes about ϕ-construction, compared to prosodic hierarchy theory. Dobashi (2003) shows how the theories in (52) and (53) make different predictions with regards to the syntactic structure in (54):

(54) $[_{IP} \text{ NP}_{Subj} \text{ Infl } [_{VP} \text{ V NP}_{Obj}]]$

The relation-based model in (52) will construct (55a), and if the optional restructuring rule applies, (55b). The end-based model in (53), if ALIGN-XP, R outranks ALIGN-XP, L, will construct only (55b).

(55) ϕ boundaries for (54):

      a. $(\text{NP}_{Subj})_\phi \ (\text{Infl V})_\phi \ (\text{NP}_{Obj})_\phi$

      b. $(\text{NP}_{Subj})_\phi \ (\text{Infl V NP}_{Obj})_\phi$

The two models agree that the subject must always be phrased separately, but they differ as to whether it is possible to phrase the object alone as well. Now let us see how this matches with a known slice of the cross-linguistic typology. Narita and Samuels (2009), building on the survey of Romance and Bantu varieties presented by Dobashi (2003), demonstrate that the following phrasing possibilities are attested for transitive sentences like (54):

(56)   Typology of ϕ-domains

    a. $(S)_\phi \ (V)_\phi \ (O)_\phi$
         $(S)_\phi \ (V \ O)_\phi/(O \ V)_\phi$ if O is non-branching

    b. $(S \ V)_\phi \ (O)_\phi$ if S is non-branching
         $(S)_\phi \ (V \ O)_\phi/(O \ V)_\phi$ if O is non-branching
         $(S \ O \ V)_\phi$ if S and O are non-branching

In short, it appears, looking at these languages, that branching arguments are phrased separately from the verb in structures like (54), but when it comes to non-branching arguments there are two options: some languages permit any non-branching argument to be phrased with the verb, while others allow a non-branching subject, but not a non-branching object, to be phrased with the verb. Languages in which the subject is always phrased separately include Italian (Ghini 1993; Nespor and Vogel 1986), Kimatuumbi (Odden 1987, 1996), and Aŋlɔ Ewe (Clements 1978). I give illustrative examples below from Ewe and Kinyambo, with phonological phrasing shown as brackets. First, Ewe:

(57) a.   *[mí] [ā-dzó]*
         we   FUT-leave
         'We will leave'

    b.   *[kpɔ́] [ānyí]*
         see   bee
         'saw a bee'

    c.   *[mē] [kpě flě-gé]*
         I   stone buy-PRT
         'I'm going to buy a stone'

The mid tones on the tense marker in (57a) and the initial syllable of the object in (57b) would raise to extra-high tones if contained within the same phonological phrase as the surrounding high tones. Thus the fact that none of them raise is diagnostic of phrase boundaries after the subject and before the object. However, in (57c), the mid tone on the first syllable of the verb (under-lying form *flēgé*) does in fact raise, indicating a lack of boundary in the case where the object is non-branching; the SOV order seen in this sentence is only permissible in such cases as well. Languages of the other type, in which any non-branching argument(s) may be phrased with the verb, include Kinyambo, as diagnosed by deletion of non-phrase-final high tones. The absence of a high tone on *abakozi* (underlying form *abakózi*) in (58a) shows that there is no boundary after the non-branching subject. Yet in (58b), the high tone retained on *bakúru* shows that there is a boundary between a branching subject and following verb. With a non-branching object (58c), there is no boundary between the verb and the object, as evidenced by the deletion of the high tone on *okubon* (underlying form *okubón*).

(58)   a.   *[abakozi bákajúna]*
            workers   help.PST.3PL
            'The workers helped'

       b.   *[abakozi bakúru]* *[bákajúna]*
            workers   mature   help.PST.3PL
            'The mature workers helped'

       c.   *[okubon ómuntu]*
            see   person
            'To see the person'

There is still much typological work to be done in documenting phonological phrasing (see Samuels 2010*a*), so at this stage it is certainly premature to make universal statements, but the data pattern at present poses a snippet of typology which finds a ready explanation using phase theory.

The proposal begins with a basic assumption introduced earlier, namely that a phase head's complement domain (minus what has already been spelled out) corresponds to a phonological (ϕ) phrase. The inventory of phase heads which are relevant for this purpose includes C (or at least one head in an expanded Left Periphery), v, and D—but crucially not n and a (or v within a deverbal word; see Samuels 2009*b*, §5.3.2 for discussion); i.e. only the "clause-level" phase heads, not the derivational affixes. Say the verb raises to v or to T. We are then concerned with the structure:

(59) $[_{CP}$ C $[_{TP}$ *Subj* T $[_{vP}$ v *Obj* $]]]$

It so happens that in all the languages discussed in this section there is evidence for V-to-T raising, but even if the verb only raises to v, an *in situ* object will be in the complement domain of v, and thereby phrased separately from the verb.

We also have to account somehow for the typological fact that branching arguments behave differently from non-branching ones. Narita and Samuels (2009) provide an account under which movement of a branching object will still result in its being phrased separately, if movement of a branching phrase requires prior spell-out of the phase head's complement. A simplex object which raises out of VP may be phrased with the verb, for instance if it instantiates D (e.g. a pronoun) or undergoes N-to-D raising (e.g. a proper name; see Longobardi 1994); there is also the possibility that some languages which do not exhibit overt determiners may not even have D, as argued by

Bošković (2005), in which case the prediction is that in such a language a raised NP object could phrase with a verb in T or *v* regardless of branchingness.

Italian, Ewe, and Kimatuumbi are all alike in having the subject undergo A′-movement to TopicP (on the connection with *pro*-drop in Italian, see Alexiadou and Anagnostopoulou 1998 and Frascarelli 2007). For example, a subject can be followed by a complementizer in Kimatuumbi (Odden 1990), which shows that subjects can be quite high in this language. The fact that subjects and preposed elements all behave alike with regard to phonological rules diagnostic of the ϕ domain in this language also suggests that this may be correct. It has also been independently argued for Bantu that subjects typically appear in Topic (see Demuth and Mmusi 1997 and references therein on Sesotho and Bantu more generally; also Pak 2008 on Luganda). Simplex objects (at least; recall the previous paragraph) may raise in all three languages.

The difference between French and Kinyambo on the one hand and Italian, Ewe, and Kimatuumbi on the other hand is the height of the subject: in the former, the subject has only moved as far as Spec,TP, so a non-branching subject can be phrased with a verb in T. Thus, there is a contrast in phrasing between the two types of languages with respect to non-branching subjects.

In sum, the phonological phrasing exhibited in these languages depends on the interaction of three things, holding constant the position of the verb in T/*v*: whether the subject is in an A′ position, whether the object has raised out of VP, and whether the arguments branch. There is no need for any readjustment of domains on the way from syntax to phonology, or for any purely phonological conditions tying prosodic phrasing to branchingness.

If this purely phase-based account of phonological phrases is correct, it makes explaining rules which apply within the domain ϕ simple: they are simply post-lexical rules that clause-level phase heads trigger on their complement domains. The same approach would apply to rules which refer to the edges of ϕ-domains, such as the placement of boundary tones. By tying phase domains directly to prosodic phrasing, we also derive the Maximal ϕ Condition of M. Richards (2004):

(60)   MAXIMAL ϕ CONDITION
         A prosodic phrase ϕ (... ω, etc.) can be no larger than a phase.

This provides an interesting counterpoint to the conclusions of Compton and Pittman (2007), who argue that the phase defines a single prosodic word in Inuktitut; Piggott and Newell (2006) argue the same for Ojibwa. This suggests that at the opposite end of the spectrum are isolating languages such as Chinese: for them, it is almost as if every terminal defines a prosodic word.

This could perhaps be thought of as the prosodic word being defined as a morpheme-level phase rather than a clause-level one. There are two ways, then, that the edges of these domains can be marked. A post-lexical rule triggered by the phase head could do the job: this way it is possible to mark either edge, since a post-lexical rule sees the entire domain as a single string without any internal boundaries. The other alternative is to appeal to a lexical rule triggered by the phase head. Because lexical rules are responsible to the Phase Impenetrability Condition at the morpheme level, this will only work for rules that mark the left (least-embedded) edge of the complement; the right edge of what is accessible to a lexical rule (i.e. the morpheme-level domain) will typically not extend all the way to the right edge of the clause-level domain. We would also expect that these two types of domain limit rules could be distinguished on the basis of whether or not they exhibit the properties characteristic of post-lexical rules: exceptionlessness with respect to lexical items, optionality, and so on (recall §4.3.3).

It would be a massive undertaking to show that phase domains suffice for every rule with a claimed domain of ϕ, but already there are many successful empirical studies in phase-based phonology on a wide variety of languages, including Seidl (2001) primarily on Bantu and Korean; Marvin (2002) on English and Slovenian; Kahnemuyipour (2009) on Persian, English, and German; Piggott and Newell (2006) and Newell (2008) primarily on Ojibwa; Sato (2009b) on Taiwanese, French, Gilyak, Kinyambo, and Welsh; Ishihara (2007) on Japanese; Bachrach and Wagner (2007) on Portuguese; Michaels (2007) on Malayalam; Kamali and Samuels (2008a, b) on Turkish; Samuels (2010b) on Basque; and more programmatically, Embick (2010), Samuels (2009b), N. Richards (2010), and Scheer (2008a, b, forthcoming). I attempt to lend further support to PDbP later in this chapter by using obstruent voicing in Korean as a case study. I demonstrate that the Phase Impenetrability Condition predicts the application and blocking contexts of this process, both above and below the word level, in exactly the way I have just described.

4.4.3 *Overlapping Rule Domains*

In the previous sections I discussed how phenomena that have typically been described as ϕ-level can be accounted for within a phase-based framework, and without the construction of any boundaries in phonology, via a combination of procedural and representational approaches. In this section, I answer the objection raised by Seidl (2001), who argues that, while phase domains are indeed very important to phonological computations, they do not suffice to cover all the attested phenomena. Seidl argues for a "minimally indirect" interface theory, in which phonology has access to two sets of syntactically determined domains: first, the "early parse" or "morphosyntactic parse" consisting of spell-out domains, and second, the "late parse" or "phonological parse" which may include rebracketing of clitics with their hosts, and the projection of boundaries at the edges of θ-marking domains. Rules which refer to this late parse would seem to preclude the possibility of getting by without a mechanism for creating purely phonological domains. For reasons of space I cannot describe and reanalyze all the data covered by Seidl here, but I will try to give evidence that the PDbP system of allowing lexical rules to span a phase edge and its complement but confining post-lexical rules to one clause-level domain can accommodate both "early-parse" and "late-parse" rules.

One example Seidl gives of the early-/late-parse dichotomy comes from Oyo Yoruba, and specifically the overlapping domains of high-tone deletion and ATR harmony in this language. The data presented in (61) is reported in Akinlabi and Liberman (2000) and (62) is from Akinbiyi Akinlabi (p.c.); both are reported by Seidl (2000). I give a few simple cases of the tone deletion process below: underlying high tone on an object clitic deletes when it follows a verb that also carries a high tone. Thus, the high tone appears on the clitics *mí* 'me' and *wá* 'us' in (61a, b) since they follow a verb with low tone (*kò* 'divorced'), but the high tone deletes on the clitics in (61c, d), following a verb with high tone (*kó* 'taught').

(61)   a. *ó   kò   mí   → ó kò mí*
           he divorced me

        b. *ó   kò   wá   → ó kò wá*
           he divorced us

        c. *ó   kó   mí   → ó kó mi*
           he taught me

        d. *ó   kó   wá   → ó kó wa*
           he taught us

Note that the adjacent high tones on the subject and verb in the preceding examples are not repaired. However, when ATR harmony is added to the picture, the opposite is true: the subject clitic harmonizes with the verb, but the object clitic is unaffected.

(62)   a. *ó   kó   wá   → ɔ́ kó wa*
           he taught us

        b. *ó   lé   wá   → ó lé wa*
           he chased us

Because of this domain overlap, Seidl argues that the tone deletion rule applies on the early phase-based parse within the spell-out domain of VP, while harmony applies to the late parse, after the subject has cliticized to the verb, and the object is parsed in its own domain.

I agree with Seidl that high-tone deletion takes place within the spell-out domain to which the verb and object both belong; in my account it is a post-lexical rule. However, there is no reason that harmony needs to be computed over a different parse. I propose instead that subject clitics are harmonic (i.e. they are underspecified for [ATR], as I will discuss in §5.4), while object clitics are not. A simple lexical rule will take care of the harmony. The fact that high-tone deletion is exceptionless but harmony has lexical exceptions—for instance, only singular subject clitics participate—lends support to my view. Seidl instead takes the position that late-parse rules tend to have exceptions, in contrast to early rules, but this does not follow from any independent principle of her theory. Seidl claims that whether or not θ-marking domain boundaries are projected is dependent on speech rate/register, which can account for optionality in the application of late rules. However, this cannot account for the type of systematic pattern that Oyo Yoruba vowel harmony exhibits, with the plural subject pronouns never participating. Furthermore, as we saw earlier in this chapter, *post-lexical* rules—corresponding to Seidl's *early* rules—are the ones known to exhibit sensitivity to extragrammatical variables.

Many of the rules that Seidl argues are sensitive to θ-marking domain boundaries come from Bantu languages. She details the syntactic differences between "symmetric" Bantu languages such as Kinande and "asymmetric" ones such as Chicheŵa, then argues that the differences in the boundaries projected at the edges of the θ-marking domains in these two types of languages yield different domains for rules such as tone sandhi. Symmetric languages exhibit a single domain with the indirect object (IO) and direct object (DO) phrased together, while asymmetric ones show two domains, (IO)(DO). Seidl says this results from the DO raising to the specifier of ApplP in symmetric languages but remaining *in situ* in asymmetric ones; in either case, the edge of the θ-marking domain, VP, projects a phonological phrase boundary, but if the DO has raised, there is nothing left in that domain so everything gets phrased together. McGinnis (2001) shows that reference to θ-marking domains is unnecessary; the phrasing facts immediately follow from spell-out domains when we appreciate that the difference between symmetric languages and asymmetric ones, following Pylkkänen (2002), is that the former have a high applicative (ApplHP) between vP and VP, while the latter have a low applicative (ApplLP) within VP. (The high applicative head is a phase head, while the low applicative head is not, though this is not crucial here.) For McGinnis, then, one object raises in both types of language: the DO raises to the edge of the ApplHP phase in a symmetric language while the IO remains *in situ*, and the IO moves to the edge of the *v*P phase in an asymmetric language while the DO remains *in situ*. This is shown below in (63)–(64), modified slightly from McGinnis (2001: 27).

(63)   High applicative (symmetric)

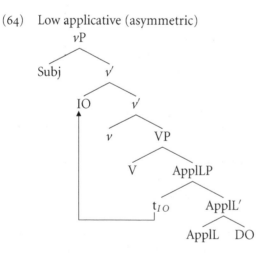

(64)   Low applicative (asymmetric)

The symmetric case in (63) will have both objects in a single spell-out domain: nothing remains in ApplH's complement domain, but both objects sit in ApplHP's edge and will be spelled out together as the complement of *v*. In the asymmetric case, (64), the DO is in *v*'s complement but the IO is in its edge, so they will be spelled out separately.

Seidl makes a further assumption that the subject and verb move out of *v*P in both types of language, with the subject landing in Spec, TP and the verb also moving into the TP domain. This makes a good prediction for asymmetric languages—the subject, verb, and IO will all be spelled out together with the DO separate, and it generates the correct S V IO DO word order. For symmetric languages, though, neither leaving the subject and verb in *v*P or raising them predicts the single (S V IO DO) domain which Seidl claims is necessary. Whether or not the subject and verb remain in *v*P, the result is still (S V)(IO DO). I will illustrate with Seidl's example from Kinande that, by adding one additional parameter to the way post-lexical rules apply in PDbP, it is possible to reconcile a two-domain analysis with this type of data.

Kinande shows lengthening of the penultimate vowel in a domain. Lengthening does not affect the verb if it has an object after it, nor does it affect the first object in a ditransitive. The high tone found on the penult is also absent when an object follows.[23]

(65)   Kinande penultimate vowel lengthening (Hyman and Valinande 1985)

   a. *er-rí-túːm-a*   (→ **er-rí-túm-a*)
      IV-INF-send-FV

   b. *er-rí-tum-a*   *valináːnde* (→ **er-rí-túːm-a valináːnde*)
      IV-INF-send-FV   Valinande
      'to send Valinande'

   c. *tu-ká-βi-túm-ir-a*   *omúkali valináːnde* (→ **omúkaːli*
      we-PST-T-send-BENE-FV   woman   Valinande
      valináːnde)

      'We have just sent Valinande to the woman'

In short, a couple of post-lexical rules are needed in order to capture the distribution of these two processes.[24] These rules will apply to the last element in the complement of *v*, or if the complement is empty (i.e. all material to be pronounced has evacuated the domain), to the last element in the edge of *v*P. To account for this behavior, I propose a modification to the application of post-lexical rules which I call the Empty Complement Condition:

---

[23] In the following Kinande examples, IV and FV stand for Initial Vowel (augment) and Final Vowel, respectively.
[24] See Hyman and Valinande (1985); Hyman (1990); Mutaka (1994) on the independence, and post-lexical nature, of these processes.

(66)   EMPTY COMPLEMENT CONDITION
        If the complement of a phase head α is empty, a post-lexical rule on α
        may apply to the edge of αP.

Kahnemuyipour (2004: 125 ff.) proposes a similar condition to account for
unexpected stress on sentence-final prepositional phrases (both adjunct and
argument) in English.

(67)   a. John saw Mary in the <u>park</u>.

        b. John put the milk in the <u>fridge</u>.

        c. John gave the ball to <u>Bill</u>.

He suggests that the base order for such sentences is as follows:

(68) $[_{TP}$ Subj $[_{\nu P}$ V DO $[_{VP}$ t$_V$ $[_{PP}$ IO $]]]]$

The PP evacuates the νP, and then what remains of the νP moves around
the indirect object. Thus nothing is left in the lowest spell-out domain (the
complement domain of ν). In such a case, stress is assigned to the closest
element in the next higher domain.

  The Empty Complement Condition accounts for the phenomenon noticed
by Kahnemuyipour, but as the discussion of Kinande here shows, it is not
limited to stress assignment. If the phrasal high tone and penultimate vowel
lengthening rules in Kinande are both subject to this condition, then there
is nothing to contradict the (S V)(IO DO) phrasing predicted by PDbP as
applied to McGinnis's analysis of symmetric languages. The effects of the
Empty Complement Condition are most apparent for ν, because of ellipsis,
intransitives, and object raising; however, we nevertheless predict that if the
circumstances are right, the Empty Complement Condition will manifest itself
in other domains. For instance, the complement of C is empty when there
is clausal pied-piping of the type which Basque exhibits (Samuels 2010*b*).
However, some rules do not appear to be subject to the Empty Complement
Condition and apply *only* if there is an overt complement (and never to the
edge). I leave open the question of whether the applicability of the Empty
Complement Condition may be predictable with regard to whether it always
applies to some types of rules but not others.

4.5 A Case Study: Korean Obstruent Voicing

Throughout the previous sections, we have seen several examples of how
lexical phonological rules, allomorphy, and allosemy are constrained by
the Phase Impenetrability Condition, and we have also seen how post-
lexical tonal/intonational processes apply to larger phonological phrases, again

restricted by the phase system. To close this chapter, I will provide an analysis of a post-lexical segmental rule, namely obstruent voicing in Korean.

In Korean, three processes—obstruent voicing, stop nasalization, and homorganic nasal assimilation—apply within the same domain, which has been called the (minor) phonological phrase (see Cho 1990; Jun 1993). I will discuss only the first of these because its effects are the most easily visible, though we will be able see the others in a few cases. The data presented here comes from Cho (1990: 48 ff.), but I have in some cases corrected glosses and terminology. The obstruent voicing rule, as stated by Cho, is given below.

(69)   Obstruent Voicing
     [−CONT, −ASP, −TENSE] → [+VOICE] / [+VOICE] _ [+VOICE]

It is immediately apparent upon inspecting its pattern of application that obstruent voicing in Korean applies in a a wide variety of environments both within and across words. I will first show some examples from the nominal domain. In the present analysis I represent Case marking on the head of K(ase)P, with the noun moving to Spec,KP and no DP being projected. Nothing critical rides on this assumption; it could also be that there is a DP layer, but the noun moves into its edge.[25]

In this configuration, the root and case morphemes are in the same spell-out domain, so obstruent voicing can apply.

(70)   *kæ-ka*   →   *kæga*
     dog-NOM   'dog'

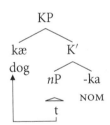

A demonstrative/adjective and a noun can interact such that one can provide the environment to voice an obstruent in the other. Again, this is because no clause-level phase head intervenes. Here I show *a*P as adjoined to KP, loosely following Bošković's (2005) adoption of Abney's (1987) "NP-over-AP" hypothesis for languages without DP, but a number of variations are possible; all that matters is that these elements are ultimately spelled out together, which will be the case if there is no D in between them.

---

[25] For simplicity's sake, I do not show structure internal to the *n*P.

(71) a. *kɨ   cip*   → *kɨ jip*
          that house   'that house'

      b. *motɨn kilim*   → *modɨn girim*
          every picture   'every picture'

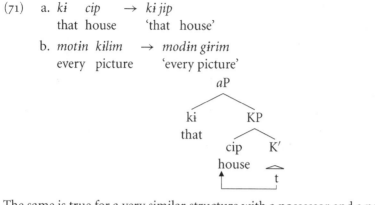

The same is true for a very similar structure with a possessor and a possessee:

(72) *Suni-ɨy   cip*   → *Suniɨy jip*
       Suni-GEN house   'Suni's house'

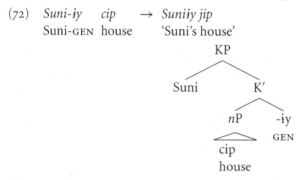

With nominals being so accessible, it is possible to see obstruent voicing between an object and a verb. In order for the object and verb to be spelled out together in the matrix clause, it is important that the verb does not move too high: if it is in *v* or higher, the verb and object would be in separate clause-level domains (unless the object also raises). Evidence for or against verb raising in Korean is very hard to come by (see Han, Lidz, and Musolino 2007[26]). For the rest of this section I will leave both the object and verb in their base-generated positions. As we will see, this makes the correct predictions about where obstruent voicing can apply: between the verb and the (direct) object, but not between the indirect object and the verb in a ditransitive, or between the subject and the verb in an intransitive. I show the VP without movement (except, of course, the root moving into Spec,KP) below:

(73) *kilim-ɨl   pota* → *kirimɨl boda*
       picture-ACC see   'look at the picture'

---

[26] In fact, Han *et al.* suggest that learners may choose a grammar with or without verb raising at random. A study of the correlations between the variation they found in scope judgments and possible variation in phonological domains could be enlightening.

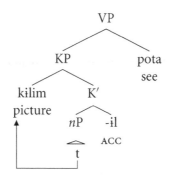

But only the *direct* object is within the same domain as the verb. This is apparent in a ditransitive sentence:

(74)   *ai-eke   kwaca-lɨl   cunta → aiege kwajarɨl junda*
       child-DAT candy-ACC give   'he gives a candy to the child'

The reason for this is that, as I alluded to earlier in this chapter, ApplH is a phase head. The applied argument in its specifier is therefore spelled out by *v*, separately from the direct object and the verb, which are spelled out by ApplH.

(75)

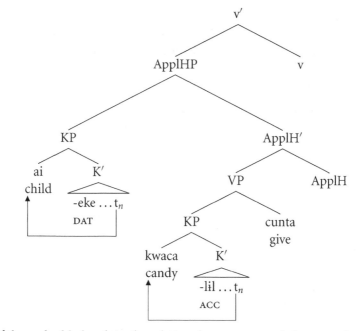

Similarly, if the embedded verb in the relative clause structure below remains in VP, then *v* will spell it out along with the head noun *pap* 'rice.' Note that it is crucial here that the verb does not move to *v* or higher. If it did, then *pap*

would be spelled out by *v* and the verb would not be spelled out until the next phase.

(76) [[*ki-ka   mǝk-nin*]_{CP} *pap*]_{NP} → *kiga mǝŋ nin bap*
      he-NOM eat-ASP   rice   'the rice he is eating'

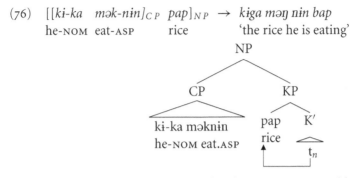

A lack of verb raising also explains why obstruent voicing is blocked between a subject and a verb, even in the absence of D: one is spelled out in the complement of *v*, and the other by C.

(77) *kæ-ka   canta* → *kæga canda*
      dog-NOM sleep   'the dog is sleeping'

Further support for the PDbP analysis comes from the fact that no obstruent voicing applies between a subject and an object in a transitive sentence. This again suggests that the verb and object remain in VP; whether the subject stays in its base-generated position of Spec,*v*P or moves to Spec,TP is immaterial. Either way, (S)(OV) domains result.

(78) *kæ-ka   pap-il   mǝk-ninta* → *kiga pabil mǝŋninda*
      dog-NOM rice-ACC eat-ASP   'the dog is eating rice'

Given that a subject in its usual position is too far from the verb to trigger in obstruent voicing, it should come as no surprise that a topicalized argument is also blocked from participating:

(79) *sakwa-nin pǝl-inta* → *sagwanin pǝrinda*
      apple-TOP throw-ASP 'apples, they throw away'

The final blocking context we will discuss involves conjunction: the second conjunct cannot undergo obstruent voicing that could ostensibly be triggered by the vowel-final conjunction *wa*.

(80) *horaɲi-wa koyaɲi* → *horaɲiwa koyaɲi*
      tiger-CONJ cat   'the tiger and the cat'

This effect could be explained in keeping with the proposal by Schein (1997) that conjoined elements are always CPs. A blocking effect would result because the first conjunct and the conjunction itself would be spelled out by the C associated with that first clause, and the second conjunct would be spelled out separately by its own C. Alternately, one could suppose that the conjunction itself is a phase head. A similar proposal is made by Narita (2009a), and it is suggestive that cross-linguistically, a conjunction forms a prosodic unit with the second conjunct in head-initial languages and with the first conjunct in head-final languages (Zoerner 1995: 11). This is demonstrated by the contrast between English (81)–(82) on the one hand, and Japanese (83)–(84), which patterns with Korean (and apparently also Sanskrit; Mark Hale (p.c.)), on the other:

(81)   a. Robin, and Kim, like apples.

       b. *Robin and, Kim, like apples.

(82)   a. Robin slept, and Kim slept.

       b. *Robin slept and, Kim slept.

(83)   a. *Hanako-to,   Naoko-wa   kawai-i.*
          Hanako-and Naoko-TOP pretty-PRES
          'Hanako and Naoko are pretty.'

       b. *Hanako, to Naoko-wa kawaii.

(84)   a. *Ame-ga   hur-u   si,   kaze-ga   huk-u.*
          rain-NOM fall-PRES and wind-NOM blow-PRES
          'Rain falls and wind blows.'

       b. *Ame-ga hur-u, si kaze-ga huk-u.

The data from both word-internal obstruent voicing and voicing across word boundaries are quite amenable to analysis in terms of a post-lexical rule applying uniformly within a clause-level spell-out domain, both within and across words, but blocked from applying across two separate domains.

4.6 Conclusions

In this chapter I hope to have given 'proof of concept' for PDbP: looking closely at syntax allows us to identify language-specific phonological domains, without the need to build up hierarchy in the phonology. At this point, I believe this is the most one can offer given that the syntax upon which a theory of the syntax–phonology interface must depend remains in flux. For this reason, the details of how to implement PDbP may well have to be renegotiated later. The ultimate message of this chapter is that, if we want to understand cross-linguistic variation in phonology, we need to understand cross-linguistic variation in morphosyntax better. This calls for collaboration between phonologists, morphologists, and syntacticians, all working together towards the common goal of describing the range of linguistic structures that are available.

Nevertheless, as I noted earlier, already there is a quickly growing list of empirical successes which have been achieved by tying phonological rule application directly to spell-out domains. While some of these varied approaches differ substantially from the way I have implemented PDbP here, I hope that the theoretical framework and case studies given here will provide a guide for the limited reanalysis that would make these earlier studies compatible with my claims; the literature on phonology and prosody is rife with obvious candidates for PDbP analyses.

Now that we have some understanding of the timing of all the operations which turn syntactic representations into phonological ones, we can dig a bit deeper into the question of how those operations work. Of course, this necessitates further discussion of the representations which are manipulated by these operations, and it is this matter to which we next turn.

5

Representations and Primitive Operations

5.1 Introduction

In this chapter, I first undertake the task of defining phonological representations which provide a workspace for the operations to be explicated in the second portion of the chapter. I will concentrate here on sub-word-level representations; this thread runs parallel to the issues we discussed in Chapter 4 concerning the domains of cyclic rule application both within and across words, and how these domains are derived from syntactic structure. In other words: Chapter 4 dealt with *when* rules apply, and Chapter 5 is concerned with *how* rules apply. Starting with the smallest units of phonological representation, I begin with discussion of phonological features and how they are structured. I argue for a theory of "archiphonemic" underspecification along the lines of Inkelas (1995), as opposed to "radical" or "contrastive" underspecification. This allows me to maintain a distinction between a perseverant form of underspecification that persists at all stages of the phonological and phonetic representations (see Keating 1988; Hale, Kissock, and Reiss 2007) and a resolvable type that is potentially repaired. Later in the chapter, I will discuss the organization of features, arguing for the algebraic approach of Reiss (2003*a*, *b*) as opposed to the feature-geometric approach (e.g. Clements 1985).

Zooming out, I next discuss the organization of segmental and suprasegmental material into strings. I focus on the idea that phonological representations are "flat" or equivalently, "linearly hierarchical" (Neeleman and van de Koot 2006). I compare phonological syllables and syntactic phrases, which have been equated by Levin (1985) and many others, with some even claiming that phrase structure was exapted from syllable structure (Carstairs-McCarthy 1999), despite strong evolutionary arguments against this view (see Fitch 2010: §10.5). I provide evidence, following Tallerman (2006), that these analogies are false, and that many of the properties commonly attributed to syllabic structure can be explained as well or better without positing innate structure supporting discrete syllables in the grammar. Once I have laid out the details of what phonological representations look like, I will present a theory of rule application which relies upon primitive operations SEARCH, COPY, and DELETE. I show that these operations combine to produce the necessary typology of phonological processes, and furthermore the same SEARCH and COPY operations do work at the syntax–phonology interface, specifically concatenation of morphemes upon spell-out. Finally, I attempt to show that these operations are plausible from an evolutionary perspective, continuing the discussion begun in Chapter 3.

5.2 Phonological Features

One of the most important advances in twentieth-century phonological theory was Roman Jakobson's proposal that segments can be decomposed into distinctive features to which phonological processes refer.[1] Over the past fifty years, a huge number of phonological feature systems have been proposed, and debates in many areas of feature theory continue to the present day. Are features privative (present/absent), binary $(+/-)$, or equipollent $(+/-/\emptyset)$? Are they articulatory or acoustic? Are they organized hierarchically (and if so, how)? Another set of questions concerns whether lexical entries can have featural representations which are less than fully specified, and if so, what principles govern this underspecification. Finally, there is a constellation of questions surrounding what one might call "applied feature theory," or how features can be manipulated in the phonology.

As a means of approaching some of the issues just mentioned, I will address the following question: what are features meant to explain? The basic answer is that they are meant to capture the fact that various groups of sounds behave alike (i.e. they are all affected by or trigger a particular rule, or they are all subject to a particular distributional restriction). When one examines such groups of sounds, one finds that they typically—though not always—have in common a property which is acoustic (for instance, all the sounds' first formants fall within a given frequency range) or articulatory (all the sounds are produced with vibration of the vocal folds).

Phonologists call these groups of similar sounds "natural classes." The standard view, as expressed by Kenstowicz (1994: 19), is that "the natural

---

[1] The idea of decomposing speech sounds into features really dates back to Alexander Melville Bell's *Visible Speech*, published in 1867, but this discovery gained little ground prior to the reintroduction of features into phonology by Jakobson in 1928. See Halle (2005) for an overview of the history of feature theory.

phonological classes must arise from and be explained by the particular way in which UG organizes the information that determines how human language is articulated and perceived." This is typically taken to mean that natural classes are defined by features which reflect phonetic properties, and those features are part of UG. By hypothesis, the phonological grammar operates over features; the sounds in question pattern together because there is a phonological process which refers to the feature they share. Thus, an equation is made between *phonetically natural* classes, *featurally natural* classes, and *phonologically active* classes, definitions of which I provide below, from Mielke (2008: 12–13).

(85) a. PHONETICALLY NATURAL CLASS

A group of sounds in an inventory which share one or more phonetic properties, to the exclusion of all other sounds in the inventory.

b. FEATURALLY NATURAL CLASS

A group of sounds in an inventory which share one or more distinctive features, to the exclusion of all other sounds in the inventory.

c. PHONOLOGICALLY ACTIVE CLASS

A group of sounds in an inventory which do at least one of the following, to the exclusion of all other sounds in the inventory:

- undergo a phonological process
- trigger a phonological process, or
- exemplify a static distributional restriction.

The main task of feature theory, then, is to find the phonetic features which accurately describe the attested phonologically active classes in the world's languages. This goal has been met with varying degrees of success. A large-scale survey of 6,077 phonologically active classes from 648 language varieties representing fifty-one language families, undertaken by Mielke (2008), sought to quantify the accuracy of the major feature theories in this regard. The results of this survey show that about three-quarters of these active classes comprise a natural class (i.e. they can be characterized by a conjunction of features) within each of the three theories he tested: the *Preliminaries to Speech Analysis* (Jakobson, Fant, and Halle 1952) system, based on acoustics; the *SPE* (Chomsky and Halle's 1968) system, based on articulation; and the Unified Feature Theory (Clements and Hume 1995), also articulatory.

This raises an interesting question: why do acoustic and articulatory feature theories perform so similarly? One possible answer is provided by models such as that of Coen (2006), which I already mentioned in §3.2. A major advantage of using data from multiple modalities to construct phonological categories, as Coen does, is that it allows for categories to be constructed from a mix of acoustic and articulatory properties; that is, features can be of either type. This provides a ready account for the observations made by Brunelle (2008); S. Anderson (1981) provides several similar examples. Brunelle obtained very interesting results from his acoustic and electrographic studies of register in Cham: different speakers appear to realize register contrasts in different ways. They utilize the various phonetic cues which distinguish registers (pitch, breathiness, etc.) to varying degrees, and moreover, some appear to use different articulatory targets for each register, rather than acoustic ones. On the basis of these data, Brunelle concluded that register contrasts cannot be the result of a universal pitch feature, but instead that learners of Cham induce different hypotheses about the phonetic correlates of the distinction made in their language. In short, the phenomenon makes sense only if learners have a much wider range of possibilities for how to realize a particular contrast than is available if features are tied to articulation or acoustic properties only.

The idea that a particular feature/contrast can have multiple different articulatory or acoustic targets is not new. To take but one example, the feature commonly known as [ATR] has the following correlates in various languages:

(86)   Articulatory correlates of [ATR] contrast (Lindau and Ladefoged 1986)

- Tongue root advancement/retraction and larynx lowering/raising (Akan, Igbo, Ijọ)
- Tongue height (Ateso)
- Phonation difference and tongue root advancement/retraction (Shilluk, Dinka)
- Tongue height or root movement and sometimes larynx height (Luo)

Additional examples from both articulatory and acoustic properties can be found in Lindau and Ladefoged (1986) and Pulleyblank (2006). The picture that emerges from all these studies is that the dichotomy between acoustic and articulatory features is a false opposition. In keeping with the position that phonology is a system of abstract symbol manipulation (the basis for substance-free phonology), I regard features as where phonology "bottoms out." Just as the semantic content of roots is inaccessible to morphosyntax, the phonetic content of features is inaccessible to phonology. Following Hall (2007: 17), whether features refer to acoustic or articulatory properties is immaterial to both phonology and phonetics:

The phonological component does not need to know whether the features it is manipulating refer to gestures or to sounds, just as the syntactic component does not need to know whether the words it is manipulating refer to dogs or to cats; it only needs to know that the features define segments and classes of segments. The phonetic component does not need to be told whether the features refer to gestures or to sounds, because it is itself the mechanism by which the features are converted into both gestures and sounds. So it does not matter whether a feature at the interface is called [peripheral], [grave], or [low F2], because the phonological component cannot differentiate among these alternatives, and the phonetic component will realize any one of them as all three. In light of this, phonological features might not need names at all; for the purposes of describing the phonology of any given language, it would be possible to use arbitrarily numbered features $[\pm 1]$, $[\pm 2]$, $[\pm 3]$, and so on.

Of course, that would be highly inconvenient for the reader, so throughout this work, I use the names for articulatory and acoustic features that appear in the various literature from which I have obtained my examples. The reader should feel free to substitute his or her own favorite labels when extensionally equivalent.

5.2.1 *Underspecification*

The next matter which needs to be discussed is whether to allow feature or feature-value underspecification, and if so, to what degree. I will then connect the conclusions from this section to the phonological operations for which I will argue later in this chapter.

From a certain perspective, phonology exists to reconcile two conflicting sets of needs brought by the lexicon and the externalization system: it serves to unpack the minimal representations required by our limited memory capacity into full representations which contain all the appropriate instructions for the articulators.[2] For example, since the aspiration of stops in English is predictable on the basis of their distribution, it is not necessary to specify aspiration in the lexicon; it can be supplied by rule in the phonology. Steriade (1995: 114) succinctly defines these two *SPE*-era assumptions about phonological representations:

(87) a. LEXICAL MINIMALITY: underlying representations must reduce to some minimum the phonological information used to distinguish lexical items.

  b. FULL SPECIFICATION: the output of the phonological component must contain fully (or at least maximally) specified feature matrices.

---

[2] See e.g. Bromberger and Halle (1989: 58): "phonology is concerned with the relationship between representations that encode the same type of information—phonetic information—but do so in ways that serve distinct functions: articulation and audition, on the one hand, memory, on the other."

However, both Lexical Minimality and Full Specification have been rejected in some subsequent literature, and I think rightly so. In Ch. 3 of Samuels (2009*b*), I review the history of thought concerning underspecification in phonology and argue for a variant of "archiphonemic underspecification" (Inkelas 1995; Reiss 2008*a*), as opposed to the "radical" (Kiparsky 1982; Archangeli and Pulleyblank 1994, etc.) or "contrastive" (Clements 1987; Steriade 1987; Calabrese 1988; Dresher 2003, etc.) types. I am convinced—particularly given the failure of both Lexical Minimality and Full Specification as guiding principles—that there is ample reason to reject both radical and contrastive underspecification, but that some degree of underspecification can and indeed must be admitted. In what follows, I will outline my proposal. As has been widely noted, there are two kinds of underspecification (see e.g. Steriade 1995). One type, with which we will not concern ourselves here, is the "trivial" or "intrinsic" underspecification which arises automatically from the use of privative features.[3] Any phonologist who uses privative features or anything like feature geometry has to accept this. The more interesting type of underspecification is (potentially) resolvable. I follow Inkelas (1995) and Reiss (2008*a*) in arguing that lexical representations are underspecified when there is evidence of alternating forms which contrast with non-alternating ones, and the alternation is predictable. Inkelas calls this "Archiphonemic Underspecification." The case typically used to illustrate Archiphonemic Underspecification is feature-filling harmony; we will see several examples throughout this chapter. This very restricted type of underspecification is reminiscent of the Alternation Condition (Kiparsky 1968) and (part 1 of) the Strong Naturalness Condition, here from Goyvaerts (1978: 125): "lexical representations of non-alternating parts of morphemes are identical to their phonetic representations."

---

[3] In early theories (e.g. Jakobson *et al.* 1952; Chomsky and Halle's 1968, etc.), phonological features were represented as binary oppositions. For example, Jakobson *et al.* (1952) introduce pairs of opposing monovalent features in their analysis of English: vocalic/consonantal, compact/diffuse, grave/acute, nasal/oral, tense/lax, and optimal constrictive/optimal stop. They then note that the number of features can be halved if each of these pairs is "compressed" by allowing each feature to take two opposing values. Thus, they arrive at a binary system containing [±vocalic], [±compact], [±grave], and so forth.

More recently, many phonologists (see e.g. Steriade 1995) have moved towards systems in which features are monovalent or 'privative,' positing features such as [VOICE]. Others utilize a mixture of both privative and binary features; e.g. Sagey (1990), Halle (1992), Clements and Hume (1995), and Clements (2003) use the following mixed set:

(1)   a. [LABIAL], [CORONAL], [DORSAL], [RADICAL], [SPREAD GLOTTIS], [CONSTRICTED GLOTTIS]

      b. [±SONORANT], [±CONSONANTAL], [±DISTRIBUTED], [±ANTERIOR],
        [±STRIDENT], [±LATERAL], [±VOICE], [±NASAL], [± CONTINUANT]

See Kim (2002) and Samuels (2009*b*: §3.2.2) for in-depth arguments against a solely privative system.

In short, this type of underspecification arises when a morpheme's exact featural content is unlearnable because it exhibits alternation of a contrastive feature value. Underspecification is potentially resolvable only in polymorphemic words because a morpheme already present in the derivation may provide featural specifications that subsequently added morphemes can utilize. When the underspecified morpheme is concatenated with its host, only then does the needed feature value information become available. One typical such process is vowel harmony of the type manifested by Tangale, which I will discuss in more detail later in this chapter. For present purposes, it suffices to note that the suffix vowels shown in capital letters in the left column take on the ATR value of a vowel in the root; thus, there is alternation in suffixes between [u] and [ʊ], as shown in the (a) and (b) forms:

(88)   Tangale [ATR] harmony (modified from Mailhot and Reiss 2007: 36)
      a. seb-U   [sebu]   'look' (imper.)
      b. kɛn-U   [kɛnʊ]   'enter' (imper.)
      c. dob-Um-gU [dobumgu] 'called us'

Given Archiphonemic Underspecification, we could (as I will indeed argue shortly) think of there being a single suffix underspecified for [ATR] which receives a value for that feature upon concatenation with a root. Phonological rules then get the chance to apply, resolving the underspecification with the host morpheme's feature values. In the absence of derivational look-ahead, underspecification can be resolved only by looking *back* into the derivation: an underspecified morpheme cannot simply wait and hope that a potential valuator will enter the derivation, preventing it from crashing.

Note that I have claimed only that underspecification *can* be resolved in polymorphemic words, not that it *must*. I do not claim that all underspecification must be resolved, or that only polymorphemic words can be underspecified. There are two other logical possibilities: (*a*) underspecification in monomorphemic words, which will not be resolvable, and (*b*) underspecification in polymorphemic words, which is nevertheless unresolved. Both of these phenomena are attested. They provide incontrovertible evidence against the principle of Full Specification, which demands that the output of a phonological computation is fully/maximally specified.

There are several well-known examples of "perseverant" or "phonetic" underspecification which persist from the underlying representation straight through to the phonetic component. Keating (1988) discusses examples such as English [h] and Slavic [x]. This type of underspecification is often characterized by gradient transitions from the specifications one flanking segment to the other, passing straight through the underspecified segment. It can also be characterized by a wide range of phonetic variation. Vaux and Samuels (2005) discuss this point with regards to laryngeal features: stops which are unspecified for the laryngeal gestures that produce aspiration (or lack thereof) exhibit a wide range of voice onset time values, and are often utilized by languages which do not have an aspiration contrast.

One particularly striking example of perseverant underspecification comes from Marshallese and has been described by Bender (1968), Choi's (1992), Hale (2000), and Hale *et al.* (2007). Bender (1968) analyzes the underlying vowel inventory of this language as being specified along only two dimensions: ATR and height. Choi's (1992) phonetic study shows that the vocalic formants show a smooth transition between the points of articulation of the flanking consonants, which may be plain (C), palatalized (Cʲ), or labialized (Cʷ). Thus, the surface vowel inventory is quite large, varying along the front/back, round/unround, high/low, and $+/-$ATR axes:

(89)   Marshallese surface vowel inventory (Hale *et al.* 2007)

	Cʲ_Cʲ	C_C	Cʷ_Cʷ	Cʲ_C	Cʲ_Cʷ	C_Cʲ	C_Cʷ	Cʷ_Cʲ	Cʷ_C
[+HI, +ATR]	i	ɯ	u	iɯ	iu	ɯi	ɯu	ui	uɯ
[+HI, +ATR]	ɪ	ɣ	ʊ	ɪɣ	ɪʊ	ɣɪ	ɣʊ	ʊɪ	ʊɣ
[−HI, +ATR]	e	ʌ	o	eʌ	eo	ʌe	ʌo	oe	oʌ
[−HI, −ATR]	ɛ	ɐ	ɔ	ɛɐ	ɛɔ	ɐɛ	ɐɔ	ɔɛ	ɔɐ

This is true for all vowels in Marshallese: affixes, too, remain underspecified. Since no vowels are ever specified for backness or rounding, morpheme concatenation cannot rectify this situation. There is no donor from which a vowel could ever obtain a value for these features. With this example, I conclude our discussion of underspecification, and of phonological features. I will make heavy use of the conclusions drawn here about underspecified representations later in this chapter, as we focus on phonological operations. The role of Archiphonemic Underspecification in particular will be explored more fully at that point, as will feature geometry. For the time being, I will move on to a discussion of how the feature bundles we call segments are themselves arranged and grouped.

5.3 Towards a Flat Phonology

5.3.1 *Syllables Are Not Like Phrases*

One conclusion I would like the reader to take away from the present work is that, while phonology and syntax may look similar on the surface—and this is not likely to be a coincidence—upon digging deeper, crucial differences between the two modules begin to emerge. I focus here on one area where surface similarities hide striking differences: the comparison between phonological syllables and syntactic phrases. The idea of the syllable as a phonological constituent arose shortly after World War II with Pike and Kuryłowicz, when constituency in syntax was a new and hot topic, thanks to Bloomfield (Goldsmith forthcoming). In more recent decades, syllables and phrases have been equated by Levin (1985) and many others, with some going so far as to claim that phrase structure was exapted from syllable structure (Carstairs-McCarthy 1999). I argue that these analogies are false, and that many of the properties commonly attributed to syllabic structure can be explained as well or better without positing innate structure supporting discrete syllables in the grammar. Before I address the myriad questions about syllables that have arisen in the past half-century, it is instructive to highlight the critical differences between the traditional views of syllables and syntactic phrases, even though the two have been explicitly equated. Compare the structures in (90):

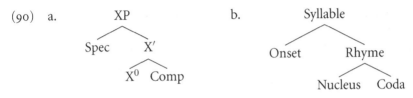

(90) a. XP b. Syllable
Spec X′ Onset Rhyme
X⁰ Comp Nucleus Coda

On the left in (90a) is a generic X′ template of the type used in syntax (since Chomsky 1970), and on the right in (90b) is a typical characterization of syllabic structure (since Fudge 1969). Both are right-branching, and both observe binarity of branching. However, one important property immediately differentiates the two structures. The syntactic structure is recursive in a way that the phonological structure is not: the complement of X can be YP—itself the maximal projection off Y, which can have its own specifier and complement and so on ad infinitum. Syllables, in contrast, are like beads on a string; no syllabic or subsyllabic node can dominate another node of the same type. Scheer (2004), who also denies the validity of (90b), attributes the lack of recursion to the phonological component's inability to create arboreal structure. He further claims that the absence of hierarchical notions such as binding, locality, and relativized minimality in phonology provide evidence for a lack of the dominance dimension in this domain; in his view, such concepts "make sense only when certain chunks of the linear string, hierarchically speaking, do not stand on a par with others" (Scheer 2004: 238 ff.). I believe Scheer's conclusion here is correct, but the evidence could be better chosen. Locality is certainly a valid notion in an object with any number of dimensions, though of course, it must be defined appropriately to the specific geometry. No one would deny that there are local phenomena in phonology: assimilation may occur only between two adjacent segments, and a great many processes in any given language are limited to applying locally within a larger domain (for instance, a prosodic phrase). Similarly, minimality has been captured in phonology by the No [Line-]Crossing Constraint (Goldsmith 1976) holding over autosegmental representations. This constraint is intended to rule out spreading of one feature value (here, [−HIGH]) across an instance of the opposite feature value (here, [+HIGH]):

(91)   X   X   X

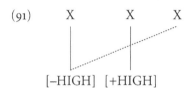

[−HIGH]   [+HIGH]

Rizzi (2002), following Halle, has also argued that the concept of minimality is relevant in this domain. (I will adopt a similar position.) It is not, then, that these notions are absent in phonology, but simply that in phonology, unlike in syntax, they must be defined in linear terms. That is to say, there is no evidence for a hierarchically defined relation like c-command in this module (Carr 2006).

There are also properties of syllables which syntactic phrases lack. Syntactic elements belong strictly to one phrase or another,[4] but phonological elements can act as though they are members of two adjacent syllables at once ("ambisyllabic"). Some words which have been taken by various theories to involve ambisyllabicity are listed here; these and more examples can be found in Kahn (1976: 34 ff.).

(92)   Hammer, being, booing, bidding, money, lemon, pony, happy, attic, collie

Another point of contrast between syntax and phonology involves the status of segments that violate the Sonority Sequencing Principle (e.g. the /s/ in the

---

[4] Excluding the potential case of parallel merge (Citko 2005). But note that even in the claimed parallel merge cases (such as Right-Node Raising; see e.g. Bachrach and Katzir 2007), the situation is different from phonology. The configuration we find in phonology is one element behaving as both coda and onset of two adjacent ("sister") syllables, which would be equivalent to one syntactic element behaving as both complement and specifier. As far as I am aware, the parallel merge cases are either one element behaving as a complement or specifier to two sister phrases (but always the same position in both, as in right node raising), or as the complement to one head and the specifier of a higher one (as in *wh*-movement).

word *string*), which have been called "appendices," "stray segments," "extrasyllabic material," or "demisyllables" (see Vaux 2009*b* for a review of the literature on this topic). Various approaches exist for dealing with these segments: some consider the stray to be its own degenerate syllable, while others treat it as unsyllabified material that attaches to a higher node (usually the prosodic word) in the phonological structure. In either case, there is no analogue in syntax. The closest parallel would be with adjuncts, but adjuncts have a place within X' structure; they are not exempt from it, and they are not degenerate phrases.

Finally, a couple of ostensive syntax-phonology similarities are points of contention. These controversial notions are headedness and endocentricity. On one side of the debate are those who, like Scheer (2004), Hornstein (2005, 2009), Tallerman (2006), and Carr (2006),[5] do not see these concepts as being applicable to syllables. The opposite view is taken by Carstairs-McCarthy (1999), who claims that syllables are endocentric, with peaks/nuclei (i.e. vowels) as their heads.[6] Clearly, if the syllable has a head, the only good candidate is the nucleus. The nucleus is always the most prominent segment in terms of sonority, and no syllable can exist without a nucleus. However, the first of these observations is a circular definition, and the second disappears when we consider that the method used to count "syllables" is actually just counting peaks—when we ask subjects to identify syllable edges, their judgments break down (see, *inter alia*, Kahn 1976 and Steriade 1999). One type of task used to obtain such judgments indirectly involves asking subjects to perform infixation. Assuming that the infix is inserted at a syllable boundary (though see §5.7), variability in performance on such tasks indicates uncertainty about syllabification. Such a study on expletive infixation in English was undertaken by Pritchett (1984). Pritchett found that in many cases of infixation into $V_1 sTV_2$ sequences (where T stands for a voiceless stop), subjects tend to "split" the [s], producing forms like *des-fucking-spotic* or *des-fucking-structable*. Steriade (1999: 29), I believe correctly, "interpret[s] segment splitting as the strategy followed when speakers are uncertain how to parse the string." This follows from the fact that the subjects split [s] most commonly when V_1 was lax and V_2 was stressed (i.e. in words such as *despótic*). On the view that syllable divisions follow from phonotactics (to be explicated shortly), the prohibition on lax vowels word-finally argues against

---

[5] Carr also argues against other notions of "headedness" in phonology, such as the Government Phonology conception of segments as consisting of head and subsidiary features.

[6] Carstairs-McCarthy further equates nouns with consonants (syllable margins) and verbs with vowels (syllable heads). I will not discuss the issue here, but I refer the reader to Tallerman (2006) for extensive criticism of this position.

a syllable boundary after V_1; the unaspirated stop after [s] argues against a syllable boundary after [s]; a stressed vowel word-initially is also disallowed (it should in that case be preceded by a glottal stop). This means that *de-fucking-spotic*, *des-fucking-potic*, and *desp-fucking-otic* should all be malformed; speakers therefore experience uncertainty when parsing the string. We will see the consequences of this more fully in §5.3.4.

Returning to the question of endocentricity, it is true, as J. C. Brown and Golston (2004) note, that onsets and codas are more like each other than they are like nuclei. The same is true of specifiers and complements to the exclusion of heads, but onsets and codas cannot be interchanged (Tallerman 2006), whereas complements frequently become specifiers via syntactic movement. Furthermore, the head of an onset is considered to be its least sonorous element, while the head of the rhyme is taken to be its most sonorous element (van der Hulst and Ritter 2003; van der Hulst 2007). This is illustrated below with the syllable *tram*, from van der Hulst and Ritter (2003: 164); the heads of each constituent are in boldface.

(93)   syllable

        onset   **rhyme**

         t r   a m

In syntax, this would be as if the possible heads of specifiers were a different set from the possible heads of complements. We may also note another curiosity related to headedness, namely that within a syllabic onset, sonority typically rises (i.e. it is left-headed; van der Hulst and Ritter (2003)), but within a rhyme/coda, it usually falls. If the least sonorous element is taken to be the head of the coda, then this means the coda is right-headed. Again, this is very different from what we see in syntax (see Tallerman 2006); it would be as if the head parameter were always reversed in specifiers.

I hope to have shown in this preliminary discussion that the equation between syllables and phrases is not tenable, and based on this conclusion, that syllables ought to be rethought on their own terms. That is the task to be undertaken in the remainder of this section.

5.3.2 *Mysteries of the Syllable*

Apart from failing to explain the differences between syllables and syntactic phrases detailed in §5.3.1, mainstream theories of syllable structure also lack explanatory adequacy where many phonological phenomena are concerned. In the current section I will describe these problems, and in §5.3.4

we will return to see how they are accounted for by the theory proposed here.

It has long been the conventional view that the primary problem with syllables is not how to count them, but how to divide them. However, Duanmu (2008: 1) shows that even this is not so clear in certain cases, such as when what might be deemed syllabic resonants appear. He lists several different works and their differing views (some inferred) on the number of syllables in the words *hour, flour, flower,* and *shower*:

(94)

	hour	flour	flower	shower
Jones (1950)	1	1	1	1
Hanks (1979)	1	1	2	2
Baayen *et al.* (1993)	2	2	2	2
Kenyon and Knott (1944)	1	1	1 or 2	1 or 2
Kreidler (2004)	1	1	1	1
Merriam-Webster (2004)	1 or 2	2 or 2	1 or 2	1 or 2
Gussmann (2002)	2	2	2	2

This highlights the fact that how to count syllables and how to divide them are intrinsically related problems, with the latter already a subject of controversy in the 1970s (see e.g. Kahn 1976. See also Duanmu 2008 and references therein on more recent experimental studies). Moreover, it is not clear that tests which purport to probe judgments on syllable boundaries actually do so. Duanmu (2008) discusses one such test, proposed by Giegerich (1992): ask speakers to pronounce each syllable of a word twice, beginning with unambiguous words and then moving on to more difficult cases such as *apple* or *city*. But what can we conclude when (as Giegerich reports) the result of testing subjects on *apple* is *ap-ap-ple-ple*? Duanmu (2008: 53) comments:

[D]oes it mean that the syllables are *ap-ple*, or does it mean that *le-le* [l̩-l̩] is an unusual sequence of syllables which the speaker would avoid? Second, consider the word *text*. If the result is *tek-tek-st-st*, one might conclude that the syllable is [tɛk] and [st] is outside the syllable. However, if the result is *text-text*, does it mean that the syllable is [tɛkst], or does it mean that the speaker is trying to avoid repeating a non-syllable cluster [st]? Finally, Giegerich does not discuss whether speaker judgment is always clear. My own test with some native speakers shows that the judgment can vary. For example, the output for *city* can be *cit-cit-ty-ty* or *ci-ci-ty-ty*. Therefore, the test does not seem to provide conclusive answers.

Harris (2004) makes similar arguments against tests intended to probe syllabification, pointing out that in such tasks, the fact that certain syllables (e.g. ones which end with short vowels, such as [sɪ] in *city*) are too small to be phonological words interferes with speakers' judgments. The notorious variability of native-speaker judgments on syllable boundaries in languages such as English that allow a range of syllable shapes is all the more striking when contrasted with judgments on phonotactics, which are clear and robust (Steriade 1999). Since phonotactic restrictions are traditionally defined over subsyllabic constituents, one wonders why this sharp dichotomy exists. Discussions of syllabification also lead to questions about universality. Does all phonological content have to be syllabified (Vennemann 1988), and if not, could there be a language that does not have syllables, as argued by Hyman (1985)? One might also wonder about variation: why is syllabification never contrastive within a language, while across languages identical sequences can be syllabified in different ways (Hayes 1989; Blevins 1995)? Steriade (1999) mentions the difference between Spanish and Cairene Arabic in this respect. When presented with (C)VTRV sequences, Spanish speakers give $(V)_\sigma(TRV)_\sigma$ syllabifications but Arabic speakers instead judge such sequences to be split up as $(VT)_\sigma(RV)_\sigma$. Yet there is no language in which, for instance, *at.ra* means something different from *a.tra*. At the very least, then, syllabification is not invariant across languages, and the apparent impossibility of sustaining two different syllabifications of the same string within a language suggests that the syllabic parse is not lexically stored.

Other questions concern syllables as they are put to use describing other phonological processes. At least since Kuryłowicz (1948) it has been acknowledged that codas and word-final consonants behave alike in many respects (i.e. they often form a single environment for phonological rules, their phonetic realizations are often alike, they both tend to be lost over time, etc.), and that onsets and word-initial consonants also behave alike. Scheer (2004), calling these positions the "coda" and "coda-mirror" respectively, wonders why this should be. Moravcsik (1978) and McCarthy and Prince (1986) have noted that references to the syllable are notably absent from the domain of reduplication: a reduplicant can be of CV or CVC shape, but there are no processes that copy the first syllable of a stem regardless of its shape. For example, in Tohono O'odham, a CV chunk is repeated to indicate plurality or plural agreement (Raimy 2000a: 112).

(95) a. ?um   ?u-?um   'thigh(s)'
      b. hon   ho-hon   'body/bodies'
      c. gimai   gi-gimai   'braggart(s)'
      d. pualt   pu-pualt   'door(s)'

In contrast, Ilokano uses CVC reduplication to mark plurality on nouns and the progressive aspect on verbs (Raimy 2000a: 128):

(96) a. kaldíŋ   kal-kaldíŋ   'goat(s)'
      b. púsa   pus-púsa   'cat(s)'
      c. sáŋit   ʔag-saŋ-sáŋit   '(is) cry(ing)'

Both these processes are more complicated than presented here, but the generalization still holds—a syllable-based analysis does not make the correct
predictions, whereas a string-based one does. I argue later in this chapter
that affixation, too, operates independently of syllable boundaries (see also
Raimy 2008, 2009). These morphophonological processes readily make use of
morpheme boundaries, so why can they not use syllable boundaries also, if
they have the same status in phonology?

The third and final set of questions that I will attempt to address concerns
subsyllabic constituents. Over the past half-century, a great many parts of the
syllable have been posited: onset, nucleus, body, margin, pre-margin, margin
core, head, coda, rhyme/rime, and mora, to name some of the more popular
ones. Some of these divisions are mutually exclusive; for instance, the onset-
rhyme model is opposed to the view that the onset and nucleus form a constituent to the exclusion of the coda. It is natural, then, to ask (as Blevins 1995
does) which of these competing models should be adopted. In the Government Phonology tradition, a popular position is that a proper conception of
subsyllabic constituency and/or lateral relations can eliminate the need for a
syllable node entirely (see e.g. Harris 1994; Scheer 2004; Aoun 1979 provides
an early example of such reasoning). This makes the need to identify the
"real" nodes all the more pressing. Ultimately, a theory of syllable structure
should also explain the numerous onset-rhyme (or onset-coda) asymmetries
that we find. Why does only the rhyme figure into the computation of metrical
weight—or alternatively, if the few putative cases of onset-dependent stress
are real (Everett and Everett 1984), why are they so rare? The answer to this
is typically something like "because only rime segments are moraic" (Hayes
1989), which simply begs the question. Additionally, why, as Scheer (2004)
asks, are the coda and the coda-mirror virtually opposite in their tendencies?
A related query has been posed in Optimality Theoretic terms: why should the
constraints ONSET (penalizing onsetless syllables) and NoCODA (penalizing
syllables with codas) exist instead of their opposites, NoONSET and CODA (see
e.g. Haspelmath 1999; Scheer 2004)?

In sum, current theories of syllable structure are at a loss to explain
many important generalizations in phonology. The entire genre of approaches
based on syntactic phrase structure has left many questions unanswered, and
I have already suggested one major reason why: syllables are just not like

phrases. Let us keep this, and the questions posed in this discussion, in our minds as we endeavor now to approach syllables from an entirely different angle.

5.3.3 *A String Theory of Syllables*

I have already noted that syllables range widely in shape across languages. In (97) I give examples from opposite ends of the spectrum: a series of three CV syllables in (97), and a syllable in (98) that has a branching onset as well as a branching coda, and additionally an appendix. The relative heights of the segments in (97)–(98) represent an abstract scale of sonority (I do not intend to be making a claim about the units of this scale).

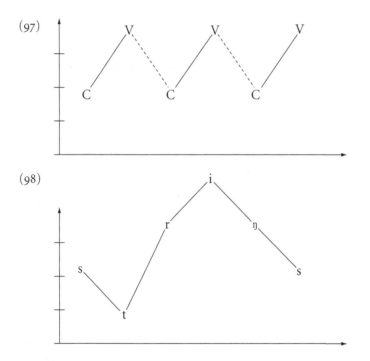

(97)

(98)

Much ink has been spilled in an attempt to accommodate patterns as different as (97) and (98) in a single framework, as alluded to in the previous section. When we move away from viewing one syllable in isolation and consider a continuous stream of speech, however, a different picture emerges. Multiple syllables of any of the attested shapes concatenate roughly as shown in (99).

(99)

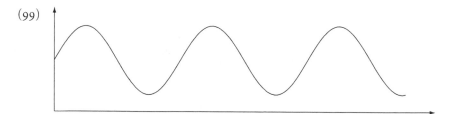

The peaks and troughs may not be so evenly dispersed, and they may not all be of the same amplitude, but the general shape is the same no matter whether the sonority values being plotted come from syllables that are CV, CVC, sCRV:CRs, and so forth, or any combination of these. This is hardly a new observation; it dates back to Lepsius and Whitney (1865) and de Saussure (1916). Ohala and Kawasaki-Fukumori (1997: 356) point out that it is inevitable:

> Just by virtue of seeking detectable changes in the acoustic signal one would create as an epiphenomenon, i.e. automatically, a sequence showing local maxima and minima in vocal tract opening or loudness. In a similar way one could find 'peaks' (local maxima) in a string of random numbers as long as each succeeding number in the sequence was different from the preceding one.

I take the wavelike sonority profile, therefore, to be a fundamental property of speech. It is an inevitable consequence of differentiation in the acoustic signal, which is necessary if there is to be more than one possible phonological output.[7]

Like any wave, the plot of sonority over time can be broken up into periods—one period of the sonority wave is essentially the definition of a syllable proposed by Pike (1947), minus the "chest pulses" debunked by Ladefoged (1967); see also Goldsmith and Larson (1990). I suggest that the ability to break the wave up into periods aids with one of the primary tasks of language acquisition and perception, namely the identification of morpheme/word boundaries (for the moment, I will conflate these two notions).[8] If one morpheme is equivalent to one period of the sonority wave, then the task of parsing the speech stream into morphemes/words reduces to finding local minima/maxima in the wave and making the "cut" when one

---

[7] As a reviewer has pointed out to me, differentiation in sonority is not *quite* inevitable: one could imagine high-frequency alternations such as *ssssssffffffssssss*. However, once one grants the existence of both consonants and vowels (or simply multiple manners of consonants or heights of vowels; even having both voiced and voiceless types of a single manner of consonant will suffice), then the signal begins to look like (99).

[8] See also Kaye (1989) and Scheer (forthcoming) on phonology's role as a facilitator of morphological parsing and Clements (2009) on sharp sonority drops facilitating parsing.

is reached. We already know that very young children—and tamarins—are sensitive to local maxima and minima (of probability distributions) in speech (see Gambell and Yang 2005 for references), so it is not implausible to suggest that the task may be accomplished in this way.

How might this parsing process be facilitated? Intuitively, the best strategy is to make the edges to be identified as different from the middles of morphemes as possible, either in terms of sonority or in some other fashion. There are numerous ways in which this might be accomplished. In (100) I give a partial list of possibilities, all of which appear to be used in natural languages.

(100)   Strategies for word-edge identification

   a. Tag every word-end with a special marker.
      Parsing strategy: place a word boundary after the end marker has been identified. Allowing only CV words would be a special case of this, in which vowels serve as the word-end markers.[9]

   b. Allow only C_1VC_2 words, where C_1 and C_2 are selected from disjoint sets.
      Parsing strategy: place a word boundary after C_2 has been identified.

   c. Make word beginnings and ends mirror images of each other.
      Parsing strategy: place a word boundary at the axis of symmetry. The Sonority Sequencing Principle/Generalization (word beginnings rise in sonority; word ends fall in sonority) is a frequent manifestation of this strategy.

These strategies never fail to produce unambiguous boundaries when every word in the language subsumes at most one period of the sonority wave. When words are longer, however, the situation becomes more complicated. Now, the parsing strategies that used to pick out word boundaries will sometimes be in error: they will sometimes identify a boundary that is actually word-internal. By simply increasing word length while holding everything else constant, words are suddenly "overparsed" into sublexical chunks that we call syllables. We have empirical confirmation that strategies which, like those in (100), yield unambiguous boundaries lead to successful word identification.

---

[9] Having a closed set of word-end markers with cardinality >1 is more economical than having only one because the markers can bear a phonemic opposition and therefore support words that differ only in their markers but still contrast lexically. Put in a different way, imagine two languages with the same phonemic inventory. Language A contains only words of the shape CV! (where ! is an edge marker), and Language B contains words only of the shape CV (vowels = edge markers). The number of possible unique lexical items in both languages is the same, yet Language B is more economical on the basis of having shorter words.

Simulations of acquisition scenarios show that "the success of the conditional probability analysis in identifying words (and excluding nonwords) depends upon the clarity of syllable boundaries in the input" (Swingley 2005: 112). On this view, it is no accident that word edges and syllable edges look the same (an intuition that dates back 2,000 years and is supported by experimental data; see Haugen 1956; Vihman *et al.* 1985; Blevins 2003, and Flack 2009 for variations on this point): they *are* the same. The resemblance between word beginnings and onsets on the one hand and word endings and codas on the other hand has been formalized as the Law of Initials/Finals.

(101)   LAW OF INITIALS (Vennemann 1988: 32)
         Word-medial syllable heads [= onsets—B.D.S] are the more preferred, the less they differ from possible word-initial syllable onsets of the language system.

(102)   LAW OF FINALS (ibid. 33)
         Word-medial syllable codas are the more preferred, the less they differ from possible word-final syllable codas of the language system.

Duanmu (2008: 54–5) weakens these laws to state simply that word-initial onsets/rhymes should resemble word-final onsets/rhymes. His rationale for doing so is essentially that some word-final rhymes, such as the [-kst] in *text*, do not occur word-medially (really, morpheme-medially; consider compounds like *textsetting*). Moreover, it is true, as Duanmu notes, that affixation can create word edges which include more consonants than are typically found in monomorphemic contexts; examples include *texts, helped,* and *sixths*. This could actually help with parsing morphemes: if parsing proceeds as usual and a "normal-sized" syllable is separated from the extra material, the result will be detection of the morpheme boundary. (And if the affix is larger, containing a vowel as well as a consonant, then parsing will also give a fair approximation of morpheme boundaries.) This idea of syllables as being epiphenomena of edge-detection also explains why there are no hard restrictions on what onsets can go with which rhymes/codas, though there are surely some extragrammatical factors, such as difficulty of production (Kessler and Treiman 1997), which make onset-coda pairs containing certain gestures less prevalent than others; this results from the mere proximity of the two gestures, and should not be seen as a function of them being parsed into the same unit. (This is consistent with my view that identity-avoidance effects in phonology typically attributed to constraints such as the Obligatory Contour Principle emerge from perception and production difficulties, not a constraint in the grammar; see Walter 2007.)

I suspect many phonologists would accept the story I have just told, since up to this point we have been in the realm of virtual conceptual necessity. However, I depart from standard theory in saying that, not only are syllables not like syntactic phrases, as I argued in §5.3.1; apart from the existence of "overparses," there is nothing more to syllables. This eliminativist approach is in keeping with the guiding question of Chomsky (2007: 4) and the Minimalist emphasis on 'Third Factor' principles, which we discussed in the previous chapter: "how little can be attributed to UG while still accounting for the variety of I-languages attained?" My proposal is also in the spirit of *SPE*, treating the syllable as epiphenomenal. The phonological portion of a lexical representation, in my view, is (as I already hinted in the last chapter) just a linear string of segments marked by a start marker # and an end marker %, *à la* Raimy (2000*a*), and with no internal structure.

(103) $\# \rightarrow X_1 \rightarrow X_2 \rightarrow X_3 \rightarrow X_4 \rightarrow \%$

The remainder of this chapter will be devoted to discussing the implications of representing phonological objects in this way.

From this perspective, it is unsurprising that syllable structures vary so much; the more interesting question is what, if not syllable structure, constrains the variety of shapes that words take? Here, several factors are at play. One class of factors clearly involves articulation: some sounds are difficult to make in sequence because the movement needed to transition between them is too large to accomplish rapidly, or because of articulator fatigue induced by repeating the same gestures (an "articulatory OCP;" see Walter 2007); also, there is a general tendency for speech sounds to arrange themselves in a way such that the jaw opens and closes in a smooth cycle, which yields rough correspondence to the Sonority Sequencing Generalization/Principle (Redford 1999). The jaw cycle also explains, at least partially, a preference for single consonants interspersed with vowels, rather than consonant clusters:

All consonant segments are articulated during the closed portion of the jaw cycle and all vowels are articulated during the open portion (Redford 1999). Thus, in a cycle that contains multiple consonants and vowels, multiple articulations must be achieved quickly as the jaw moves continuously to or from a closed position. In contrast, a cycle with a single consonant and vowel, a single consonantal gesture, begun at the point of maximal closure, is continued through the opening phase and a single vocalic gesture, begun just before the point of maximal aperture, is continued through the closing gesture. Maximizing differences in jaw openness between adjacent segments therefore reduces the number of segments within a cycle and increases articulatory ease.   (Redford, Chen, and Miikkulainen 2001: 35)

This may not be the *sole* explanation for the Sonority Sequencing Generalization, but I concur with Cairns (2009: 158) that this violable principle is not part of UG, but rather "belongs to one or more of the phonetic sciences." Another class of factors involves perception. Certain types of sounds are more perceptible in certain contexts than in others, and phonological changes such as metathesis frequently reorder sounds so as to enhance perceptibility (Blevins and Garrett 2004); less perceptible sounds are often simply lost, as famously happens to word-final consonants.

Memory constraints may also contribute to limiting the length of words or the distances between word-internal boundaries. Perhaps it is not an accident that the maximum number of elements in a traditional syllable (branching onset, nucleus, branching coda, plus two appendices) is seven, as in Miller's (1956) Magical Number 7 ± 2. It may also be relevant that the more usual number of elements between boundaries is less than four (i.e. a CV or CVC syllable), a cardinality that is within the grasp of humans' (and animals') parallel tracking abilities (Kaufman *et al.* 1949; recall also discussion in Ch. 3). Interestingly, Golston (2007) argues on the basis of such working memory limitations that feet, not syllables, may be the chunks of phonological material stored in working memory. His evidence for this comes from long words such as *Apalachicola*: at twelve segments, the word is too long to be stored segment-by-segment, and storing each of its six syllables is not much better. But breaking it into three or four feet (depending on one's position on degenerate footing in English) is achievable. This theory makes the prediction that no morpheme can have more than five feet, under Golston's experimentally supported assumption that 4 ± 1 is the limit of working memory. I am not aware of any evidence to the contrary.

Computational research also suggests that syllable shapes can emerge from functional constraints, lending support to the view that no innate structure constrains syllables. Redford, Chen, and Miikkulainen (2001) ran computer simulations with a set of constraints very similar to the ones discussed above—penalties for articulatory and perceptual difficulty, word length, and vocabulary size—and produced artificial languages whose syllable shapes and frequencies corresponded very closely to those found cross-linguistically.

5.3.4 *Parsing and Underparsing*

In the previous section I proposed that syllables are the result of overparsing the speech stream when words subsume more than one period of the sonority wave. In the section to follow, we will discuss underparsing, other factors that interact with the strategies in (100), and how words ultimately come to be identified even if they are at first incorrectly parsed.

Though the task of identifying words becomes more difficult as words get longer, stress-based clues to correct parsing also become available. Though not all languages utilize stress, in those which do, primary stress occurs precisely once per word.[10] As a result, whenever a listener hears two primary stresses, he can safely assume that there is one word boundary between them (Gambell and Yang 2005); this "culminative function" of stress had been noticed already by Trubetzkoy. For example, consider the string:

(104) $C_1 V_1 C_2 \acute{V}_2 C_3 V_3 C_4 \acute{V}_4 C_5 V_5 C_6 \acute{V}_6$

This string must comprise precisely three phonological words: no more, and no less. The boundaries of those words must be somewhere between V_2 and V_4, and between V_4 and V_6.

Moreover, many languages restrict stress to the same relative location in every word, and infants are sensitive to such prosodic information by 6–9 months of age (Jusczyk, Houston, and Newsome 1999). If the stress is placed relative to the tail end of the word, there is a simple strategy: place a word boundary at a certain location after the stress. (This, too, was noticed by Trubetzkoy: the "delimitative function" of fixed stress.) For example, recalling the string above, if the stressed vowel is always final, then the word boundaries must occur at C_3 and C_5 (on one side or the other). With stress placed relative to the beginning of the word, the same procedure can be applied retroactively; a word boundary will be located at a certain location before that stress. This is a less efficient strategy because it requires backtracking in the signal, and the amount of backtracking is increased the further back in the word the stress is. I suggest that this may explain the relative scarcity of initial versus final stress, the especially strong asymmetry between penultimate stress (frequent) and post-initial stress (rare), and the fact that antepenultimate stress is attested while post-post-initial stress is not (Heinz 2007). Combining fixed stress placement with one of the strategies in (100) narrows down the possible parses, as we will soon see.

Each language differs phonotactically; that is, different word-ends are found in different languages, and parsing strategies vary accordingly. These strategies are probably the result of statistical generalizations that infants are able to make over the lexicon based on transitional probabilities, prosody, allophonic variation, and other cues. I depart from most theories of word-identification by rejecting the assumption that syllabification must be accomplished before word boundaries can be parsed, and I go one step farther than Steriade (1999: 32), who argues that "syllabic parsing is an inference process based largely

---

[10] In languages which have tone but not stress, the predictability of particular tonal patterns may serve a similar function.

on word-edge properties." Instead, I argue that a uniform parsing procedure applies only once to the incoming speech stream, with the purpose of finding word boundaries and the side-effect of (potentially incomplete) syllabification. This is supported by the results of simulations undertaken by Cairns *et al.* (1997), who demonstrate that simply locating syllable boundaries is sufficient for the location of lexical boundaries. In the sense described in the previous paragraph, the parser is looking for word boundaries, but at the same time it will also return some overparses ("false positives"), which are what linguists have called syllable boundaries. The segmented speech stream then interfaces with the lexicon via analysis-by-synthesis, along the lines of Poeppel, Idsardi, and van Wassenhove (2007).

At this stage we may revisit two related questions mentioned in the previous section and now cast in a new light; why are syllabification judgments so tricky, and why is there something like ambisyllabicity? It has long been noted that for sonority in particular, finding local minima or troughs is much more difficult than finding the highly salient local maxima or peaks (Smalley 1968; Kahn 1976). Peaks are intrinsically acoustically prominent; they are selected from a class of segments determined by a language-specific cut-off on the sonority scale (sonority of n or higher is eligible to be a peak; see Dell and Elmedlaoui 2002), which, following Jespersen (1904) is roughly thus.[11]

(105) Sonority scale
       Voiceless stops < voiced stops/voiceless fricatives < voiced fricatives < nasals < liquids < high vowels < non-high vowels

Additionally, languages are not required to be organized in a way that allows for the failsafe disambiguation strategies in (100) to apply—following the logic laid out in Chapter 2, such properties are favored over evolutionary time, but they are not necessitated. For this reason, unambiguous trough location, which is already inherently difficult, may not even be possible in principle in a given language.

I argue that when no unambiguous parse is available given the particular parsing algorithm that is in use, no parsing on the basis of phonotactics actually occurs. When the parser doesn't return a word boundary that it should, this will become apparent before too long; it will come across another primary stress, for example. Context and comparisons with the lexicon will in most cases resolve the issue. If not, the result could be a metanalytic change, such

---

[11] I remain agnostic about the exact nature of sonority, although I am sympathetic to the claim that it is a derived notion. For discussion see, among others, Ohala (1992), Ohala and Kawasaki-Fukumori (1997), Ségéral and Scheer (2008), Cairns (2009), Clements (2009), and references therein.

as *a napron* becoming *an apron*. If there is no word boundary at stake, the "underparse" is allowed to remain; this is when we find variable judgments, as in *lemon* (as if lem.mon), *atra* (a.tra, at.ra, or at.tra) and the similar cases discussed earlier in this chapter. Note that this latter example demonstrates why syllabification cannot be contrastive, a phonological universal we pondered earlier: it is precisely in the case where two different syllabifications are available in a single language (because multiple parses create possible word beginnings and endings) that an underparse occurs and no boundary is posited at all. The possibility of underparsing provides an answer to another question raised in §5.3.2, namely why morphophonological processes such as reduplication and infixation do not make use of syllable boundaries (see the extensive empirical investigation in Samuels 2010*d*); it also explains why there are virtually no true syllabaries (Poser 2004; Samuels 2005), contra Ladefoged (2001) and Gnanadesikan (2008), and why speech errors fail to provide evidence for the existence of syllables (Shattuck-Hufnagel 2008). This follows naturally from the theory presented here, namely that there are fewer word-internal boundaries than typically assumed. This does not mean we have to give up all the benefits of syllables—we can still distinguish monosyllables from polysyllabic words, for example—but rather, we must understand that we are really just talking about the peaks on a continuous curve, not clearly demarcated, discrete units. I follow Kahn (1976: 33 ff.) on this point:

There need not correspond to every pair of adjacent syllables [read: peaks—B.D.S.] a well-defined syllable boundary. It would seem reasonable to maintain, then, that while hammer is bisyllabic, there is no internal syllable boundary associated with the word. As an analogy to this view of syllabic structure, one might consider mountain ranges; the claim that a given range consists of, say, five mountains loses none of its validity on the basis of one's inability to say where one mountain ends and the next begins.

In many cases, syllable boundaries are simply not present; this is why they cannot be anchors for reduplication and infixation. Interestingly, when they are present—as in a language that disallows consonant clusters, vowel hiatus, and codas (e.g. is rigidly CVCVCV)—they may be anchors, but this fact is obscured by the fact that there are other possible analyses of the process in question that do not make reference to syllables, as will be discussed in §5.7 (see also Yu 2007: 133). For instance, an infix in the hypothetical language just outlined might be described as occurring after the first syllable or after the first vowel, and there would be no means of disambiguating between these two possibilities.

5.3.5 *Explanation without Syllabification*

Naturally, if anyone is to take this proposal seriously, it will have to be shown that the processes traditionally described with reference to syllable boundaries can be analyzed in different ways. The phenomena used to motivate the syllable, and to which we must therefore respond, fall into three basic types (here from Redford 1999: 7, based on Kenstowicz 1994; see also Goldsmith forthcoming):

(106)   Phenomena used to motivate the syllable

    a. The existence of segment sequencing constraints in language

    b. Phonological rules, such as those for linguistic stress assignment, are simplified by the concept of syllable

    c. Certain phonological operations, such as the insertion of an epenthetic vowel, are best understood with reference to syllable structure

I will treat each of these in turn, while keeping in mind the goal of providing more satisfying answers to some of the nagging questions in §5.3.2. Some of these have already been mentioned in the two previous sections, and the remainder will be addressed in the discussion to follow.

Let me first discuss segment sequencing constraints (phonotactics), which have typically been considered to operate on the syllabic level: the onset and rhyme are taken to be two distinct domains, both subject to well-formedness conditions (e.g. Kahn 1976), though not to co-occurrence restrictions, as I mentioned earlier. Kahn (1976) and Larson (1993) have argued that some phonotactic restrictions are best understood in a linear framework, and the possibility of characterizing phonotactic restrictions in a purely string-based manner has recently garnered increasing attention. This is the approach taken by Steriade (1999) (and see also Blevins 2003), who argues for the independence of phonotactics from syllabification ("Segmental Autonomy"), thus resolving the paradox of why judgments on phonotactics are clear while on syllabification they are anything but. The keystone of her theory is Licensing by Cue (as opposed to the syllable-dependent Licensing by Prosody), the notion that the presence of a particular featural contrast is correlated with its degree of perceptibility in given context. Although I may disagree with the Optimality Theory implementation of Licensing by Cue, there are nevertheless many important insights to be gained from it.

One crucial observation is that perceptibility is asymmetric; for instance, consonantal place cues are more perceptible before a vowel than after one (see Ohala 1990 for a summary of the literature), which may partially explain the preference for CV over VC sequences (i.e. the Onset Principle). Complementing the string-based theory of co-occurrence restrictions, Heinz (2007) proposes a simple procedure for learning local phonotactics and then implements representation of local phonotactic constraints using finite-state machines (sitting alongside other finite-state machines which represent long-distance phonotactics, such as harmony, and stress patterns). He obtains very good results with a learner that considers two consecutive segments and nearly perfect ones with a learner that considers three segments in a row.

The second and third arguments for the syllable, those based on phonological rules and operations, are similarly weak. A representative statement comes from Côté (2000: 14): "phonological processes that are expressed with reference to the syllable can always be reformulated in sequential terms." She discusses two large categories of processes, epenthesis and deletion, which are often viewed as phonological repairs of ill-formed syllable structures (for instance, syllables which would violate the Sonority Sequencing Principle) and argues extensively that, while syllabically based approaches to some of these phenomena may be empirically adequate, some are not, and in general such analyses suffer from a number of weaknesses:

(107)   Weaknesses of the syllabic approach (Côté 2000: 22)

   a. *The syllabic approach is insufficient:*

      - Epenthesis and deletion often fail to apply in contexts where syllable well-formedness predicts them to be applicable.
      - Epenthesis and deletion often apply in contexts where syllable well-formedness does not predict them to be applicable.

   b. *The syllabic approach is inadequate:*
      Upon closer examination, the syllabic account cannot be maintained for several of the cases of epenthesis and deletion for which it has been proposed.

   c. *The syllabic approach is unnecessary:*
      For the patterns that are naturally compatible with a syllabic analysis, an equally simple sequential account that makes no use of syllable well-formedness conditions is easily available.

To illustrate these points, Côté (2000: 32–3) offers a list of consonant deletion processes which have been claimed to result from stray erasure (i.e. the deletion of unsyllabifiable material). The languages in question include

Attic Greek, Diola Fogny, Icelandic, Hungarian, Korean, Turkish, Menomini, Kamaiurá, Basque, Lardil, Québec French, and English. Côté claims that "[t]hese languages can be divided into two main groups. The [Attic Greek, Diola Fogny, Icelandic, and Hungarian cases] appear to be incompatible—or at least clearly problematic—for the Stray Erasure account. For the rest, the syllabic analysis could be maintained, but I argue that an equally simple sequential analysis is available." Specifically, the constraints banning certain configurations in syllabic terms can be restated sequentially without any loss of generalization:

(108) Correspondences between syllabic and sequential constraints (Côté 2000: 35)

a.	Korean/Menomini:	*Syllabic:*	*COMPLEX (CVC template)
		Sequential:	Consonants are adjacent to vowels
b.	Kamaiurá:	*Syllabic:*	*CODA (CV template)
		Sequential:	Consonants are followed by a vowel
c.	Lardil/Basque	*Syllabic:*	*F/CODA (coda condition) (F a feature or combination of features)
		Sequential:	F is followed by a vowel
d.	Québec French	*Syllabic:*	Sonority does not increase from the nucleus to the edges of the syllable
		Sequential:	Sonority maxima correspond to possible sonority peaks

All these sequential conditions are implementable as conditions on the DELETE operation to be formalized later in this chapter, as we will see: it is possible in the framework developed here to delete a segment provided its neighbors have particular properties. That is, we can state a rule of Kamaiurá: "delete a consonant if it is followed by another consonant." Similarly for Québec French, we can have a rule which deletes a consonant word-finally provided its sonority is greater than that of the segment preceding it. This obtains the correct results for final sonorant deletion:

(109) Final sonorant deletion in Québec French (Côté 2000: 22)
   a. /putr/   [pʊt]   'beam'
   b. /kateʃism/ [kateʃɪs]   'catechism'

A parallel approach, using an insertion/COPY procedure also formalized later in this chapter, would produce patterns of epenthesis rather than deletion. Take, for example, epenthesis in Chaha. Unless a final consonant cluster has falling sonority (i.e. (110a–b)), an epenthetic vowel appears. That is to say, the same configuration which triggers deletion in French—a word-final consonant which is more sonorous than its neighbor to the left—triggers epenthesis in Chaha. Again, no reference to syllables is necessary.

(110)   Vowel epenthesis in Chaha (Rose 1997; Côté 2000: 22)
     a. /srt/   [sɨrt]   'cauterize!'
     b. /kft/   [kɨft]   'open!'
     c. /dβr/   [diβir]   'add!'
     d. /rkʼm/   [nikʼim]   'pick!'

Even early proponents of the syllable conceded this point, saying that "all phonological processes which can be stated in a general way with the use of syllable boundaries can also be stated without them" (Vennemann 1972: 2). Put a different way, syllable affiliation can be determined entirely on the basis of looking at the relative sonority of two adjacent consonants (Scheer 2004: 240); we can simply add this information to the structural descriptions of phonological rules. The issue is not that some processes *necessitate* syllable boundaries, but rather that Vennemann, Hooper (1972), Kahn (1976), and others felt that, in the absence of the syllable, certain analyses served to obscure rather than enlighten (see Lowenstamm 1981 on this point and the uncompelling nature of the arguments involved).

I see two problems with the line of argumentation begun by Vennemann, Hooper, and Kahn. First, the tremendous difficulties that linguists have had over the past century with formulating a coherent and usable structural (or physiological, or phonetic) definition of the syllable militate against the idea that the appeals to syllable structure in phonological rules are somehow explanatorily deep. A truly deep explanation brings into service the principles of perception, production, cognitive organization, and whatever else may be relevant. It is fine, though not explanatory, to say informally (for example) that consonants delete in coda position, so long as we are clear that this is a shortcut which allows us to express concisely the underlying reasons for the behavior in question, such as the fact that an adjacent consonant masks some of the cues that lead to accurate perception (see references in Ohala 1990). Such factors influence the shape of languages over evolutionary time (recall the discussion of Blevins 2004 in Ch. 2), creating patterns that can turn into synchronic phonological rules—still expressible in syllable-free terms. Secondly, as others have already argued, "conceptual economy, that seeks to minimize the set of primitive notions ... [argues] against the syllable as a basic unit in phonology" given the fact that the syllable is never strictly necessary (Côté 2000: 14). The illusory "simplification" of phonological rules brought about by positing innate syllable structure comes at a high theoretical cost. It entails radically enriching lexical representations, and/or a phonological module that will syllabify and resyllabify strings as warranted. This seems too high a price to pay for a construct that can be eliminated without sacrificing empirical coverage. In fact, segment-based analyses are sometimes better than syllable-based ones, as Steriade's (1999) work on phonotactics demonstrates. And as I discussed above, Côté (2000) has done the same for two other processes that traditionally depend on syllabification; she argues that for deletion and epenthesis patterns, syllabic analyses are not only unnecessary but also insufficient and inadequate. The recent trend of linear analyses continues: Steriade (2008), taking seriously the "interlude theory of weight" advocated by Sturtevant in the early twentieth century, moves away from an entirely syllable-based approach to metrical weight and emphasizes the rhythmic importance of the consonantal interlude, or the distance between two vowels, independent of syllabification. If the string-based theory proposed here is correct, this work certainly represents a step in the right direction. Still, much work remains to be done in this area, particularly with the relationship between syllable peaks, feet, and metrics. It should be stressed at this juncture that the notion of the metrical foot is completely independent from the syllable; one can exist without the other. If we accept that there is a metrical tier (the bracketed grid of ×-marks familiar from Halle and Vergnaud 1987 and many others subsequently), then "[t]he metrical foot ... is a group of marks defined by brackets on lines of the metrical tier. There is no sense in which metrical feet gather up or dominate syllables or segments, directly or indirectly" (Cairns 2009: 147).

As a final note before I shift gears, I would like to mention that the conclusions reached here about syllables are in some ways separable from the remainder of the present work. That is to say, if the reader finds the idea of doing phonology without structural syllables to be distressing, he or she need not be discouraged from reading on. Nevertheless, the arguments presented in Chapter 4 for doing without hierarchical structure-building in phrasal phonology (i.e. the prosodic hierarchy) make more sense if there is no hierarchy in phonology below the word level, either. With this caveat stated, let us now turn to the procedural side of phonology.

5.4 Harmony: Introducing SEARCH and COPY

Armed with a basic understanding of the structure of phonological representations, we can now begin to consider the repertoire of phonological computations which operate over these objects. Three operations will be formalized
here: SEARCH, COPY, and DELETE. I introduce the first two using the example of
vowel harmony, then show how the SEARCH mechanism can be extended to a
theory of "generalized" SEARCH in conjunction with COPY and DELETE. In the
course of this discussion, I will pick up a loose thread from our discussion of
features in the previous chapter, namely whether feature geometry is necessary
and/or sufficient for explaining the range of attested phonological phenomena. I then connect the SEARCH and COPY operations with the concepts of
precedence relations and looping representations proposed by Raimy (2000*a*,
et seq.) to capture a wide range of morphophonological processes including
reduplication, affixation, and subtractive morphology; this also harkens back
to the discussion of spell-out and serialization in Chapter 4. In this section
I motivate the phonological operations while focusing on one phenomenon,
vowel harmony. In Samuels (2009*a*) and (2009*b*: §4.2) I argue against models
of harmony which require hierarchical or tiered structure, concluding that
vowel harmony can be accommodated using linear representations combined
with simple search and copy operations which find parallels elsewhere in
linguistics, and which may not even be specific to language, as we will see
in §5.8. Here I will skip directly to the search-based proposal which I adopt,
but first, let me discuss the typology of vowel harmony in terms that are as
theory-neutral as possible. Vowel harmony takes the general shape in (111),
taken from Turkish. A morpheme, typically a suffix, takes on a feature value—
here, [αBACK]—from a vowel in the root. Thus, we see alternation in the plural
suffix between [e] and [a], and in the genitive between [i] and [ɨ] depending
on whether the root contains a front or back vowel.

(111)   Turkish [BACK] vowel harmony (Mailhot and Reiss 2007: 33)

	NOM.PL	GEN.SG	
a.	ip-ler	ip-in	'rope'
b.	kɨz-lar	kɨz-ɨn	'girl'
c.	sap-lar	sap-ɨn	'stalk'

Not every case of vowel harmony is this straightforward (and in fact, as we will
see, the Turkish case is itself more complicated than shown above). In some
languages, there are "opaque" vowels which do not participate in harmonic
alternations, and which appear to block suffixal vowels from obtaining their
features from harmonic vowels in the root. Illustrated in (112) is one such

case, [ATR] harmony in Tangale. Tangale has a nine-vowel system comprised of the [+ATR] series /i u e o/ and the [–ATR] series /ɪ ʊ ɛ ɔ a/. In the more abstract left column below, the high back vowel is represented as capital /U/ to indicate its surface alternation between [u] and [ʊ], shown in the middle column.

(112)   Tangale [ATR] harmony (modified from Mailhot and Reiss 2007: 36)
      a. seb-U   [sebu]   'look' (imper.)
      b. kɛn-U   [kɛnʊ]   'enter' (imper.)
      c. dob-Um-gU [dobumgu] 'called us'
      d. peer-na   [peerna]   'compelled'
      e. pɛd-na   [pɛdna]   'untied'
      f. dib-na-m-gU [dibnamgʊ] 'called you (pl.)'

The forms in (112a) and (112b) act in a fashion parallel to the forms in (111): The suffixal vowel represented as /U/ takes on a value for [ATR] that matches the value of the root vowel to its left. In (112c) we see that when /U/ appears more than once in a word, each token winds up with the same valuation. Examples (112d) and (112e) show that [a] does not undergo any phonetic alternation itself, regardless of the [ATR] values of the other vowels in the word. Finally, (112f) speaks to the opaque nature of [a]. When [a] comes between a [+ATR] root vowel and /U/, the suffixal vowel unexpectedly appears in its [–ATR] variant.

In (113) I present another case of [ATR] harmony, from Wolof, which provides an interesting contrast with the Tangale case. In this language, there are seven long vowels (/iː uː eː oː ɛː ɔː aː/) and eight short ones (/i u e ə o ɛ ɔ a/). The high vowels [i] and [u] do not alternate themselves, but they are "transparent" to harmony processes. As above, capital letters in the left column represent vowels with surface alternations; long vowels are transcribed as double (e.g. < ee > = [eː]).

(113)   Wolof [ATR] harmony (Mailhot and Reiss 2007: 38)
      a. toxi-lEEn   [toxileen]   'go and smoke' (imper.)
      b. tɛkki-lEEn [tɛkkilɛɛn] 'untie' (imper.)
      c. seen-uw-OOn [seenuwoon] 'tried to spot'
      d. tɛɛr-uw-OOn [tɛɛruwɔɔn] 'welcomed'

In Wolof, unlike in Tangale, the non-alternating vowels act as if they simply do not exist for the purposes of computing harmony. The alternating vowels /E/ and /O/ can undergo harmony with the other mid vowels in the root, skipping over [i] and [u].

Consonants may participate in this type of alternation process as well. Here again in (114) Turkish provides an example.

(114)   Turkish [BACK] harmony with laterals (Nevins 2004: 40)

	NOM.SG	ACC.SG	
a.	usul^y	usul^y-ü	'system'
b.	sual^y	sual^y-i	'question'
c.	okul	okul-u	'school'
d.	meʃgul^y	meʃgul^{y}düm	'busy' (past)

This is the same [BACK] harmony as in (111), illustrated now with different stems and a different case form, and with the added complication of rounding harmony (which only certain affixes participate in), creating the possibility of having four different vowels appear in the accusative suffix. Turkish /l/ comes in a [+BACK] version, [l], and a [−BACK] palatalized version, [l^y]. If a root ends in one of these laterals, a suffixal vowel will take on the backness value of the lateral, regardless of the values of the vowels in the root.

Mailhot and Reiss (2007; henceforth M&R) propose a new method of computing harmony via a search.[12] They begin with the theory of precedence proposed by Raimy (2000a) for phonological representations as directed graphs (introduced in Ch. 4) and formally define SEARCH and COPY operations over such strings. Here in (115) and (116) is the formalism, where ς and γ when unindexed are feature specifications, and when indexed are tokens of segments with those features:

(115)   SEARCH algorithm (M&R 30)
        Search(Σ, ς, γ, δ)

    1. Find all x in Σ subsumed by ς and index them:
       $\varsigma_0, \varsigma_1, \ldots, \varsigma_n$
    2. For each $i \in \{0, \ldots, n\}$:
       (a) Proceed from ς_i through Σ in the direction δ until an element subsumed by γ is found
       (b) Label this element γ_i
    3. Return all pairs of coindexed standards and goals, (ς_i, γ_i)

(116)   COPY algorithm (M&R 32)
        Identify αF on γ_i and assign αF to ς_i if the set of conditions C on γ_i are satisfied.

---

[12] Harmony via search had previously been explored by Nevins (2004). See Samuels (2009a) and Samuels (2009b: §4.2) for a comparison of the two approaches.

Assuming Archiphonemic Underspecification (recall discussion in §5.2.1), only a segment that does not already have a specification for the harmonic feature(s) can have a feature value copied onto it (in the absence of some mechanism for overwriting/deleting existing feature values), i.e. ʂ can only be an alternating vowel. Less complicated cases such as the Turkish [BACK] harmony in (111) thus follow straightforwardly: SEARCH in Σ to the left (δ) for a segment specified for [BACK] (γ), then COPY the value of [BACK] from the target (γ) onto the standard (ʂ). As yet I have made no provisions for feature-changing harmony, but as we will see, the addition of DELETE to the repertoire of operations makes this formally possible.

Note further that viewing harmony in this way turns the traditional "donor–recipient" conception of harmony (and other feature-spreading processes) on its head. Rather than a donor vowel looking for recipients for a particular feature, instead segments which *lack* a feature search for a valuator. As M&R discuss, this yields a "non-symmetric" notion of locality. Take a string such as:

(117)   C V$_1$ C V$_2$ C V$_3$

Assume only V$_1$ is specified [+ROUND]; V$_2$ and V$_3$ have no specification for [ROUND]. The autosegmental spreading approach would have V$_1$ spreading [+ROUND] to the right, and in order to do so, it would have to proceed iteratively to V$_2$ and from there to V$_3$. But if instead, as in the SEARCH/COPY model, V$_2$ and V$_3$ both search for valuators, there is no need for iterative steps. The searches will converge on V$_1$, which is the closest potential valuator to both segments. The non-symmetric or non-reversible property of this locality relation is that, while V$_1$ is the closest valuator to V$_3$, it is not the case that V$_3$ is the closest valuee to V$_1$.

Another way in which search-based models of harmony represent an improvement over autosegmental ones is that they can capture dependencies that run afoul of the No Line-Crossing Constraint on autosegmental representations. This constraint makes it difficult to capture transparency of the type in (113) and rules out empirically attested cases like the one in (118), which would in autosegmental terms involve spreading of the type shown in (119), where "uvularization" is spreading of [−HIGH]:

(118)   Height/dorsalization harmony in Sibe (Nevins 2004: 85, 168 ff.)
         Descriptively: a [−HIGH] vowel anywhere in the root triggers uvularization of a suffix-initial dorsal consonant.

    a. ildi(n)-kin   'bright'
    b. muxuli(n)-kin   'round'
    c. sula-qin   'loose'
    d. ulu-kun   'soft'
    e. tɔndɔ-qun   'honest'
    f. χɔdu(n)-qun   'quick'

(119)   [−CONS, DORSAL]   [−CONS, DORSAL]   [+CONS, DORSAL]

                [−HIGH]   [+HIGH]

The + variant of [HIGH] is invisible to the search for a value of [HIGH] for the suffixal consonant. If line-crossing were strictly prohibited, there would be no way to account for this skipping in the association process given that all instances of [HIGH] are on the same tier; a search, on the other hand, can circumvent the issue by referring directly to [−HIGH], ignoring [+HIGH] entirely.

Another area in which M&R's theory diverges notably from previous accounts is that opacity and transparency, rather than being taken as properties of vowels (or vowel systems), are properties of the rules of SEARCH. Opaque and transparent vowels have something in common, namely they are already specified for the harmonic feature. Thus, they are unaffected by the SEARCH and COPY procedure. This allows for a simple account of the Tangale data in (112) and repeated below, in which [a] is opaque: SEARCH to the left for [αATR], then COPY [αATR] to the initiator.

(120)   Tangale [ATR] harmony (M&R 36)
         a. seb-U   [sebu]   'look' (imper.)
         b. kɛn-U   [kɛnʊ]   'enter' (imper.)
         c. dob-Um-gU   [dobumgu]   'called us'
         d. peer-na   [peerna]   'compelled'
         e. pɛd-na   [pɛdna]   'untied'
         f. dib-na-m-gU   [dibnamgʊ]   'called you (pl.)'

Crucially, this search does not fail or require an atypical method of valuation: [a] donates its own [−ATR] feature for copying. That value is not the default in any sense; it results from successful application of SEARCH and COPY.

Transparency illustrates the independence of SEARCH and COPY. For Wolof, as in (113) and repeated below, there is a SEARCH left for γ specified [−HIGH, αATR], but only [αATR] is targeted by COPY to value ʂ.[13]

(121)   Wolof [ATR] harmony (M&R 38)
    a. toxi-lEEn   [toxileen]   'go and smoke' (imper.)
    b. tɛkki-lEEn   [tɛkkilɛɛn]   'untie' (imper.)
    c. seen-uw-OOn   [seenuwoon]   'tried to spot'
    d. tɛɛr-uw-OOn   [tɛɛruwɔɔn]   'welcomed'

Rounding out the typology, there are cases like Kirghiz, as shown in (122). The Kirghiz vowel system includes the unrounded /i e ɨ a/ and the rounded /ü ö u o/.

(122)   Kirghiz vowel harmony (M&R 42)

	ACC.SG	DAT.SG	
a.	taš-tɨ	taš-ka	'stone'
b.	iš-ti	iš-ke	'job'
c.	uč-tu	uč-ka	'tip'
d.	konok-tu	konok-ko	'guest'
e.	köz-tü	köz-gö	'eye'
f.	üy-tü	üy-gö	'house'

The dative suffix, which is specified as [−HIGH], picks up [+ROUND] from a [+HIGH, +BACK] vowel, but not from a [+HIGH, −BACK] one.[14] This is captured by a condition on COPY: SEARCH left for [αROUND], then COPY [αROUND] if γ is [−BACK]. The difference between Kirghiz and Wolof has been described with the following analogy:

Suppose you are told to go out into the world, find a man with a hat, and take his hat. On the assumption that there are such things as men with hats and that they are findable, you will always return with a hat. But the outcome is potentially different if you are told to go out, find a *person* with a hat, and take the hat *only if that person is a man*. You may in this case return hatless, if the first behatted person you met was a woman. The first task involved a condition on the search termination—take the hat of the first person you meet who is both a man *and* a hat-wearer; the second involved

---

[13] More complicated data require a combination of this approach plus rule ordering—multiple instances of harmony within a language, like [BACK] and [ROUND] harmony in Turkish, are treated as separate processes (in accordance with Chomsky's 1967 Principle 6, the force of which we will discuss shortly) so it is possible for them to be ordered with respect to one another, and for unrelated rules to apply between them. See M&R on Hungarian for an example of such an analysis.

[14] [BACK] is also independently harmonic and can be described through an independent SEARCH and COPY process. See the previous footnote.

a condition on the hat-taking (COPY) operation—take the hat of the first hat-wearer, only if that person is a man.   (M&R 43)

Kirghiz, with the condition on COPY, corresponds to the "find a person with a hat ..." case; Wolof, with its more restrictive SEARCH criteria, corresponds to the "find a man with a hat ..." case.

The M&R approach is particularly well-suited to the theory I have developed throughout the present work since it can operate over a flat phonology (i.e. it does not need tiers or trees to establish the relations between the donor and recipient segments). Moreover, the model is inherently substance-free and as such, makes no recourse to phonetics or to any particular qualities of the vowel systems of harmonic languages.[15] It achieves appropriate empirical coverage with minimal apparatus, and the SEARCH and COPY procedures that it does require are independently motivated elsewhere in linguistics (and in other domains): they seem to be used widely in syntax, for instance. We will see in the remainder of this chapter that SEARCH in particular has very broad applications in phonology and at the syntax–phonology interface. Indeed, all phonological processes and even the concatenation of morphemes which happens during spell-out can be captured through a combination of SEARCH paired with two other operations: COPY and DELETE.

5.5 Generalized SEARCH and COPY

Now that I have explained how SEARCH and COPY work for vowel harmony, I will extend them to all phonological rules (I call this the generalized theory of SEARCH and COPY) and introduce the third and final primitive operation, DELETE.

As early as *SPE*, it was recognized that rule application could be seen as a search plus modification procedure:

To apply a rule, the entire string is first scanned for segments that satisfy the environmental constraints of the rule. After all such segments have been identified in the string, the changes required by the rule are applied simultaneously.

(Chomsky and Halle's 1968: 344)

I want to emphasize the fact that describing phonological processes with a search-plus-modification procedure is completely compatible with the major results of rule-based phonological theory of the generative era; for example,

---

[15] This is unlike earlier proposals, such as Nevins 2004, which refer to markedness and sonority in describing opaque/transparent segments. Note that it is still possible to highlight contrastive/marked specifications (along the lines of Nevins 2004 and Calabrese 2005, 2009) in this framework without a theory of markedness or without abandoning underspecification.

the notion that rules apply serially and are extrinsically ordered. In fact, using SEARCH simplifies rules, allowing them to be expressed as parameters of a simple and invariant schema, and preserves important insights from autosegmental phonology while streamlining representations. The ability of SEARCH to simplify rule application can be seen clearly in the case of the "subscript zero convention," in which the symbol C_0 is used as an abbreviation for a string of zero or more consonants.[16] The following hypothetical rule, which will add a feature F to the final vowel in a word, makes use of this convention:

(123) $V \rightarrow [+F] / \_ C_0 \#$

By convention, this rule is an abbreviation for an infinite set of simultaneously applying rules:[17]

(124)   a. $V \rightarrow [+F] / \_\#$
        b. $V \rightarrow [+F] / \_ C\#$
        c. $V \rightarrow [+F] / \_ CC\#$
        d. $V \rightarrow [+F] / \_ CCC\#$
        e. $V \rightarrow [+F] / \_ CCCC\#$
             $\vdots$

I agree with the argument which has been made more or less explicitly by Odden (1994) and others since the 1970s that the subscript zero convention should be eliminated, and that the notion of infinity relevant to this example should be reinterpreted in terms of *locality* (of the type I discussed in the previous section, following M&R). That is to say, when two segments appear to interact at a distance, they are actually adjacent to one another on some abstract level. In recent years, this has been achieved representationally, by separating features onto separate planes (i.e. feature geometry combined with autosegmental tiers) and enforcing some type of constraint against crossing association lines; we saw this approach already while discussing harmony.

[16] See Reiss (2008*b*), which goes some distance towards developing a generalized SEARCH and COPY mechanism, for additional discussion of this issue. Reiss also proposes SEARCH-based accounts for several "Path-type rules" (see §5.5.1 of the present work), including the Sundanese nasalization case which I will soon discuss.

[17] Following Howard (1972: 18), "The claim that these phenomena should be handled by *infinite* schema rather than by an abbreviation . . . is justified by the fact that the upper limit on the number of consonants is an arbitrary one contingent only upon the maximal number to be found in the strings of that language. If a word with four final consonants should be added to the language we would fully expect it to behave as predicted by [(124e)]. The fundamental fact here is that the number of consonants is *entirely irrelevant* to the operation of the rule."

Adopting a SEARCH-based view of rule application allows us to maintain this basic result, but without appealing to autosegmental tiers, feature geometry, or constraints. In other words, the approach taken here is procedural rather than representational. More concretely, (123) can be replaced by the following SEARCH and COPY procedure, which is quite similar to what we just saw for harmony; the only difference is that there's no underspecified segment which can be seen as the initiator of the SEARCH. Instead, I take [+F] to be the initiator (ς) of SEARCH. In other words, I treat [+F] as something like a "floating feature" (a notion familiar from autosegmental phonology) to be concatenated with the string in the phonological workspace.[18] The formal change I am forced to make in order to do this is to divorce the beginning point of SEARCH from the target of COPY. This is necessary when one considers that the feature to be added (i.e. ς) is not yet integrated into the string in the phonological workspace when SEARCH takes place (that integration, of course, being the result of SEARCH and COPY); if ς is not in the string which will be scanned, then it is impossible for SEARCH to begin from there. I therefore introduce a new variable, β, which represents the starting point of SEARCH in the string Σ to which ς (here, [+F]) will be added. Although SEARCH is starting from β, I still consider ς to be the "initiator" and assign it that variable. So the parameters for the SEARCH and COPY operations to place [+F] on the last vowel of a word would be:

(125)   a. ς (initiator of SEARCH): [+F]

      b. γ (target of SEARCH): First V

      c. δ (direction of SEARCH): L

      d. β (beginning point of SEARCH): %

      e. COPY ς to γ

No matter how many consonants come between % and the last vowel in the word, SEARCH will converge on the correct target.

Another thing to note about the procedure in (125) is that, rather than COPY adding a feature *from* the target (γ) *to* the initiator (ς) as we have seen for harmony, in this case COPY applies the other way around. This will require some modification to the COPY algorithm, as shown below.

---

[18] One might take exception with my use of "copy" in this loose sense; the operation here is more akin to insertion than copying. But as Hornstein (2001) points out, "insertion" is merely copying from the lexicon. I prefer to use the term "copy" to emphasize parallelism with the other types of processes discussed throughout this chapter.

(126) Copy algorithm (bidirectional version)
       Identify αF on γ_i and assign αF to ς_i if the set of conditions C on γ_i are
       satisfied <u>or</u>
       Identify αF on ς_i and assign αF to γ_i if the set of conditions C on γ_i are
       satisfied.

Adding the ς-to-γ copy operation alongside the γ-to-ς type could be seen as
increasing the symmetry of the theory, a potentially welcome consequence.
Any conditions on copy are still restricted to the γ variable.

   I argue that there is a principled distinction to be made here between
harmony or spreading-type processes and insertion-type processes such as the
one characterized by (125). Indeed, this is a distinction which Archangeli and
Pulleyblank (1994) made in their theory of parametric rules. These authors
proposed that all phonological rules can be described using combinations of
four parameters: Function, Type, Direction, and Iteration. The parameters
and their possible values are:

(127) a. Parameter: **Function**
           Values: {Insert, Delete}

       b. Parameter: **Type**
           Values: {Path, F-element}

       c. Parameter: **Direction**
           Values: {Left-to-right, Right-to-left}

       d. Parameter: **Iteration**
           Values: {Iterative, Non-iterative}

Direction corresponds directly to the δ parameter on search. The Function
parameter corresponds roughly to my distinction between copy and delete
operations (with a caveat to be added later concerning the possibility of
mimicking deletion using only search and copy). I will suggest shortly that
delete is a primitive operation which can be ordered with respect to search
and copy. I will discuss iterativity at various points throughout the rest of this
chapter.

   The Type parameter is what distinguishes rules which have the effect of
spreading features which are already present in the string (Type: Path) from
those which introduce new features into the derivation (Type: F-element).
For example, a rule like the one in (123) would have the Type parameter set
to F-element because [F] was not present in the derivation prior to the rule's
application. A harmony or assimilation rule, on the other hand, would have
Type set to Path because the rule creates copies of a feature which is already

present.[19] I would like to maintain the distinction between these two kinds of processes, which I will call Path-type and FE-type for convenience, using SEARCH.

5.5.1 *Path-type Rules*

One of the fundamental insights of M&R is that, as I alluded to in §5.4, by turning the "donor–recipient" conception of harmony on its head, a number of phenomena fall out of the theory for free. Such phenomena include the behavior of "opaque" and "transparent" vowels and blocking effects previously attributed to the No Line-Crossing Constraint. These results are achieved by making the *target/recipient* the initiator (in their terms, the "standard" ς) of SEARCH. As M&R note (and again recall the discussion of non-symmetric locality in the previous section), multiple standards may converge on the same goal (γ); in other words, a single segment may donate a feature value to multiple recipients. This is to be preferred over the converse, which would be the case if the donor initiated the search. Multiple donors with conflicting feature values could converge on the same recipient, and there would have to be some mechanism for resolving this conflict.

As an example, let us look at nasal spread in Sundanese. This language has a process which nasalizes all vowels to the right of a nasal consonant; the spreading is blocked by all oral consonants except /h/ and /ʔ/. Following Padgett (1995) and acoustic analyses by Cohn, these two transparent consonants actually undergo nasalization themselves when in the appropriate environment (this is not shown in the transcription below).

(128)   Sundanese nasal spread (Robins 1957; Cohn 1990)
    a. ŋãĩãn   'to wet'
    b. kumãhã   'how'
    c. mĩʔãsih   'to love'
    d. ŋãtur   'to arrange'
    e. mãwur   'to spread'

Even though this may at first seem counterintuitive, I will posit a SEARCH with the following parameters to account for this process:

---

[19] Strictly speaking, the difference between PATH and F-ELEMENT does not depend on whether the feature in question is already in the derivation; it is instead whether there exists a token of that feature *upon which the rule depends*. In other words, there could be a F-ELEMENT rule which inserts a feature already present on some segment in the string, so long as there is no relationship between the pre-existing and newly added occurrences of that feature.

(129)   a. ς (initiator of SEARCH): $\forall X$ (i.e. all segments)

       b. γ (target of SEARCH): $[\alpha\text{NASAL}]$

       c. δ (direction of SEARCH): L

       d. β (beginning point of SEARCH): ς

       e.   COPY $[\alpha\text{NASAL}]$ from γ_n to ς_n

This will make every segment look to its left for the closest segment specified for [NASAL], then copy that segment's value for [NASAL] onto the initiator of the search. This will obtain the correct results since COPY is incapable of overwriting feature values. In other words, COPY only succeeds if the standard is not specified for [NASAL]. Otherwise, it fails. Thus, this will be a typical "feature-filling" rule.[20]

Another interesting property of performing nasal spread in this way is that each segment can perform its SEARCH simultaneously, with the result being what has traditionally been termed "iterative" application. To illustrate this, take the derivation of *kumāhā* 'how'. I assume that the underlying representation is /kumaha/. Then according to the SEARCH and COPY procedure outlined above, every segment will simultaneously initiate its own search, returning an ordered pair of the form (ς_i, γ_i) where γ_i is a segment which is specified for [NASAL]. I list these ordered pairs below (with the goal of the failed SEARCH from the leftmost segment represented as ø). Recall that at this stage we assume that only /k/ and /m/ are specified for [NASAL], so these are the only possible goals for SEARCH.

(130)   (k, ø), (u, k), (m, k), (a, m), (h, m), (a, m)

Next, COPY applies. Since /k/ and /m/ are already specified for [NASAL], they cannot be affected. However, {u, a, h, a} are all unspecified for [NASAL] and will receive a value for that feature from the goals of their respective searches. The result of this will be /u/ receiving /k/'s [-NASAL] and {a, h, a} receiving /m/'s [+NASAL].

In (129), the target of SEARCH was narrowly specified, leading to termination only on consonants specified for [NASAL]; COPY had no restrictions on it. Now we will see what happens in the converse situation: when the target of SEARCH is quite broadly specified and there are conditions on COPY. Consider what pattern would be produced by the following:

---

[20] Also note that, while M&R did not use universal quantification in their original formulation of SEARCH and COPY for harmony phenomena, feature-filling harmony can be expressed with $\forall V$ or $\forall X$ as initiating SEARCH. Since there is no possibility of "overwriting" feature values in the absence of combining COPY with DELETE, only underspecified segments will be valued by the COPY procedure associated with such a SEARCH.

(131)   a.   ʂ (initiator of SEARCH): ∀C

      b.   γ (target of SEARCH): X

      c.   δ (direction of SEARCH): R

      d.   β (beginning point of SEARCH): ʂ

      e.   Copy [αVOICE] from $γ_n$ to $ʂ_n$ if $γ_n$ is [+CONS].

This would initiate a SEARCH from each consonant to the nearest segment to its right. If that segment is a consonant, the initiator will receive the voicing specification of the target. In other words, this combination of SEARCH and COPY will produce regressive voicing assimilation in clusters. Because every consonant's search terminates at the segment immediately adjacent to it, the assimilation is inherently local or "non-iterative." If the segment to the right of the initiator is a vowel, COPY fails so nothing happens; the initiator cannot be affected by a consonant which is non-adjacent to it, unlike in the nasalization case, where there was no limit on the distance over which the SEARCH algorithm could travel, and therefore over which [NASAL] could spread.

It is also possible to describe a nasal assimilation process like this one (or, of course, any other process one might have in mind) as feature-changing, not feature-filling. If there is some reason to suspect that the consonants involved should be underlyingly specified for [VOICE], then regressive assimilation should be able to "overwrite" those values. On the other hand, I would also like to capture the noted generalization that the feature-filling case is the more frequent state of affairs (see Kiparsky 1985, Archangeli and Pulleyblank 1994). I argue that this is because feature-changing processes are inherently more complicated, involving the application of the operation DELETE between SEARCH and COPY; DELETE has the ability to remove feature values. For example, if all consonants were underlyingly specified for [VOICE], the procedure in (131) could be modified as follows:

(132)   a.   ʂ (initiator of SEARCH): ∀C

      b.   γ (target of SEARCH): X

      c.   δ (direction of SEARCH): R

      d.   β (beginning point of SEARCH): ʂ

      e.   DELETE [αVOICE] from $ʂ_n$ if $γ_n$ is [+CONS].

      f.   Copy [αVOICE] from $γ_n$ to $ʂ_n$.

The conditions placed on COPY in (131) have been instead been stated on DELETE, but the procedure remains the same otherwise. This rule will ensure that two adjacent consonants agree in voicing regardless of whether the leftmost of the pair is specified for [VOICE] or not.

Another use of DELETE is to remove a feature from the target of SEARCH after COPY has applied; this is the equivalent of the "spread-and-delink" paradigm familiar from autosegmental theory. Take, for example, the case of high tone spread in Tonga. In this language, a lexical H-tone spreads to all vowels to its left, then deletes from the original location. (Another rule then inserts a low tone on the toneless syllables; I will return to this later.)

(133) Tonga H-spread and deletion (Archangeli and Pulleyblank 1994: 292)
       Underlying   Surface
       a. imakáni   ímákànì   'news, affairs'
       b. imusimbí   ímúsímbì   'girl'

The SEARCH, COPY, and DELETE processes which generate H-tone spread and deletion are shown here:

(134)   a. ς (initiator of SEARCH): $\forall$V

        b. γ (target of SEARCH): H (i.e. V with H tone)

        c. δ (direction of SEARCH): R

        d. β (beginning point of SEARCH): ς

        e. Copy H from γ_n to ς_n.

        f. DELETE H from γ_n.

In short, DELETE can apply either before COPY (to ς) or after COPY (to γ). A feature-changing spread-and-delink rule would therefore contain two applications of DELETE.

5.5.2 *FE-type Rules*

I now turn to FE-type rules, the ones which involve the addition of new features into the derivation rather than "donation" of a feature present on the goal to the standard. As I have already argued, FE-type rules should be see as akin to affixation; the initiator of SEARCH in such a rule is essentially a very small affix—a feature bundle smaller than a segment—looking for a host. As such, this affix is the initiator of SEARCH (starting from within the string in the workspace: $\beta = \{\%, \#\}$), and COPY applies to affix's feature value(s) to the goal(s) of this SEARCH, subject to any conditions which may be on COPY. The reason why FE-type rules differ from Path-type rules in this respect is simple: the segments ultimately affected by the rule cannot initiate SEARCH because there is nothing in the string to search *for*. But in all other respects, FE-type rules are just like Path-type rules. For instance, both can be feature-filling or feature-changing (i.e. they may include DELETE or not), and both can cause changes to a single segment (apply locally/non-iteratively) or multiple ones (apply iteratively).

The formulation of FE-type rules requires only two minimal changes to the SEARCH and COPY schema. We already saw the first change, namely that the direction of COPY is from ς to γ rather than the other way around. The new type of COPY is illustrated by the earlier example of placing a feature [F] on the final vowel in a word, which I repeat:

(135)   a. ς (initiator of SEARCH): [+F]

     b. γ (target of SEARCH): First V

     c. δ (direction of SEARCH): L

     d. β (beginning point of SEARCH): %

     e. Copy $ς_n$ to $γ_n$

To see the other modification which is necessary, consider again the Tonga data from the previous section. I already demonstrated how the H-tone spreading and delinking shown in these forms can be obtained via a Path-type rule. This will generate the following intermediate representations:

(136)   Tonga H-spread and deletion (Archangeli and Pulleyblank 1994: 292)

	Underlying	Intermediate	Surface	
a.	ìmakáni	ímákani	ímákànì	'news, affairs'
b.	imusimbí	ímúsímbi	ímúsímbì	'girl'

Now I will show how L tones—(at least some of) which cannot be present underlyingly since they will replace deleted H—fall into place. I will suggest that the low tone is the initiator of SEARCH into the string, and allow one small modification to the goal (γ) parameter of SEARCH: just as I introduced universal quantification in the standard (ς) parameter to yield 'iterative' Path-type rules, I will now introduce universal quantification in the γ parameter as well. This will allow SEARCH to identify all segments of a particular type (in this case, all vowels) and COPY to place low tone on all of them. (Since DELETE is not involved, this application of COPY will be feature-filling and not disrupt the H-tones.) The parameters for the L-insertion process are shown below, though note that β and δ could take any number of values; my selection of leftward search from % is arbitrary. (This underdetermination of parameters will play a large role in Ch. 6.)

(137)   a. ς (initiator of SEARCH): L (i.e. L tone)

     b. γ (target of SEARCH): ∀V

     c. δ (direction of SEARCH): L

d. β (beginning point of SEARCH): %

e. COPY s_n to γ_n.

This additional use of the universal quantifier and the reversal of the COPY operation appear sufficient to account for all the differences between Path-type and FE-type rules.

5.6 Quantification and Feature Algebra

Thus far, in this chapter I have primarily been concerned with how SEARCH and COPY eliminate the need for autosegmental notation, but I have not presented an alternative to an important partner of autosegmentalism, namely feature geometry. To this end, I will recap arguments made by Reiss (2003*a*, *b*) against feature geometry. These arguments will lead me to adopt Reiss's alternative, "feature algebra."

Early theories of generative phonology held all phonological features to be on a par, with no structure internal to the featural system. Since the mid-1980s (e.g. Clements 1985), though, many phonologists have argued for a hierarchically structured feature system (feature geometry). There are some ways in which groupings of features are obvious, either on articulatory or auditory bases. For example, many phonologists have posited a LARYNGEAL node. Avery and Idsardi (2001) give this internal structure for it:

(138)

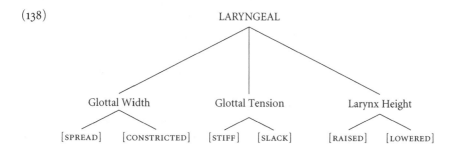

The evidence for feature geometry comes from two different places. First, there are such groupings as Glottal Width which are inevitable from an anatomical or acoustical standpoint: the glottis can either be spread or constricted, and but not both; the features associated with these properties must be in complementary distribution purely for physical reasons, so the node Glottal Width does not really do any work in phonology. There are several similarly opposed pairs of features used to describe vowel height, tongue root specifications, and backness: physically, no segment can be both [+HI] and

[−HI], or [ATR] and [RTR], or [FRONT] and [BACK] (put more starkly [+BACK] and [−BACK]). Encoding these non-co-occurrence restrictions in the feature system is merely a redundant restatement of biological fact.

More interesting to me is the evidence adduced in support of feature geometry which comes from the typology of sound patterns. For example, Odden (1991) noticed that [BACK] and [ROUND] often seem to pattern/spread together, and on this basis he proposed the node Color, subsuming these two features. This essentially creates a featurally natural class by brute force. But one of the major lessons which I take away from the massive survey of phonologically active classes by Mielke (2008) is that positing more and more features/nodes in order to make more phonologically active classes expressible in featurally natural terms is barking up the wrong tree: even after a half century of research into phonological feature systems, the *SPE* system remains the most effective at capturing attested patterns, but even that system still fails to express patterns in terms of featurally natural classes a quarter of the time. Trying to add more features to increase the empirical coverage will only result in a dramatic increase in ad hoc features/nodes. What would really help is a way to refer to any arbitrary group of segments. Reiss (2003*a*) makes this point in a different way. He focuses on the typology of rules which delete a vowel between certain consonants. There are some vowel deletion rules, such as the one in Biblical Hebrew which takes /kaːtab-uː/ to [kaːθvuː], which apply only when the flanking consonants are (underlyingly) non-identical: syncope does not occur in, for instance, /saːbab-uː/, which surfaces as [saːvavuː] after spirantization. "Anti-gemination" processes like this one have been explained in terms of blocking by a universal constraint called the Obligatory Contour Principle (OCP; Leben 1973).

But there is an alternative, which was raised and then rejected by Yip (1988): write the rule A → Ø/ B_C as per usual, and then add the condition that B ≠ C. Odden (1988) and Reiss (2003*a*, *b*) counter that Yip was too quick to dismiss this option. As Odden points out, antigemination is but one piece in the typological puzzle. Not only are there syncope rules which exhibit antigemination effects and those which apply blindly regardless of whether they create geminates, there is also a third type which applies *only* in the case where the flanking consonants are identical, producing what Odden dubs "antiantigemination." The same, Odden shows, is true of vowel insertion rules: there are some which apply only when the flanking consonants are identical, some which apply blindly, and some which apply only if the flanking consonants are non-identical. (We will see concrete examples of such processes shortly.)

The condition in which the two consonants must be identical can be described as a condition on rule application or (in autosegmental terms) as a constraint referring to structures like the one below, in which two segments are linked by sharing the same feature value:

(139) C_1 C_2

[+F]

While feature-value identity can be conveniently expressed in autosegmental notation as above, Reiss (2003*a*, *b*) makes the point that because the autosegmental/feature geometric approach does not use variables, it cannot account for rules which require that two segments differ by any arbitrary feature, or any from among a particular subset of features. In order to account for such rules, Reiss proposes a system of "feature algebra" which incorporates variables and quantifiers. The basis of this theory is that what we call a segment (here, C_1 or C_2) is an abbreviation for a feature matrix, represented in the following manner:

(140)   Segments as feature matrices (Reiss 2003 *b*: 222)

$$C_1 = \begin{bmatrix} (\alpha F_1)_1 \\ (\beta F_2)_1 \\ (\gamma F_3)_1 \\ \vdots \end{bmatrix} \quad C_2 = \begin{bmatrix} (\delta F_1)_2 \\ (\epsilon F_2)_2 \\ (\zeta F_3)_2 \\ \vdots \end{bmatrix}$$

F_i denotes a feature, such as [NASAL] and Greek letter variables denote the value ($\pm$) that feature F_i has for a given segment. The subscript outside of a pair of parentheses containing αF_i denotes the segment in question; thus, these subscripts are always 1 for C_1 and 2 for C_2.

With these representations, it is still possible to represent the equivalent of (139), where segments C_1 and C_2 have the same value for feature F_n:

(141) $[(\alpha F_n)_1] = [(\beta F_n)_2]$

The case in which two segments have different values for F_n can be represented in exactly the same fashion, substituting $\neq$ for =. This takes care of the case in which two segments must differ in their values for a *particular* feature, but it can also be extended to account for the non-identity condition: the case in which two segments must differ in terms of *some* feature value, but it does not matter which. This is expressed using the existential quantifier, as below, where $\mathbb{F}$ is the set of features.

(142)   NON-IDENTITY CONDITION (preliminary version)
$\exists\, F_i \in \mathbb{F}$ such that $[(\alpha F_i)_1] \neq [(\beta F_i)_2]$

This is actually a special case of a more general condition in which F_i belongs to some set of features $\mathbb{G} \subseteq \mathbb{F}$. Going back to the identity case, the same logic is applicable. The existential quantifier is not relevant here—it is never the case that a rule applies only when two segments share a value for any arbitrary feature—but if we use the universal quantifier instead, it becomes possible to require that two segments agree in their values for an arbitrary set of features. The requirement of total identity (segments must share *all* feature values) is the special case in which $\mathbb{G} = \mathbb{F}$.

(143)   IDENTITY CONDITION
$\forall\, F_i \in \mathbb{G}$ such that $[(\alpha F_i)_1] = [(\beta F_i)_2]$

In fact, Odden (forthcoming: 21–2 n. 16) points out that *all* the possible identity and non-identity conditions can reduce to variations of (143):

Reiss proposes that both universal and existential quantifiers are required, to formulate the Non-Identity Condition—$\exists F_i \in G$ s.t. $[(\alpha F_i)_1] \neq [(\beta F_i)_2]$—and the Identity Condition—$\forall F_i \in G$ s.t. $[(\alpha F_i)_1] = [(\beta F_i)_2]$. This formalism predicts two unattested conditions, Variable Partial Identity—$\exists F_i \in G$ s.t. $[(\alpha F_i)_1] = [(\beta F_i)_2]$ where at least one feature must be the same—and Complete Nonidentity—$\forall F_i \in G$ s.t. $[(\alpha F_i)_1] \neq [(\beta F_i)_2]$ where all features must be non-identical. Reiss proposes a functional explanation for the nonexistence of the latter two classes. It is worth pointing out that this can also be formally explained. Exploiting DeMorgan's Laws, the Identity Condition [*sic*; should be *Non*-Identity Condition—B.D.S.] can be equivalently expressed as $\neg\forall F_i \in G$ s.t. $[(\alpha F_i)_1] = [(\beta F_i)_2]$. Given that, Identity and Non-Identity are a single proposition $\forall F_i \in G$ s.t. $[(\alpha F_i)_1] = [(\beta F_i)_2]$ or its negation. If the formal theory only employs the notion of feature identity, not non-identity, and only employs universal quantifiers, not existential quantifiers, then all and only the attested classes of identity conditions can be formalized.

I will take Odden's suggested formulations of the Identity and Non-Identity Conditions as the starting point for my translation of the feature algebra approach into conditions on COPY.[21] The Identity and Non-Identity Conditions with universal quantification are repeated here:

---

[21] This reformulation of the Non-Identity Condition takes the force out of Baković's (2005) criticism of Reiss's proposal to the effect that the latter does not rule out the unattested Variable Partial Identity and Complete Non-Identity Conditions.

(144) IDENTITY CONDITION
       $\forall F_i \in \mathbb{G}$ such that $[(aF_i)_1] = [(\beta F_i)_2]$

(145) NON-IDENTITY CONDITION
       $\neg\forall F_i \in \mathbb{G}$ such that $[(aF_i)_1] = [(\beta F_i)_2]$

With this foundation in place, I can now discuss the importance of these two conditions for a SEARCH-and-COPY model of phonology. I will illustrate this with two examples: syncope in Afar, which is subject to the Non-Identity Condition, and syncope in Yapese, which is subject to the Identity Condition.

First, let us look at the Afar case. The data, originally from Bliese (1981), have been treated by McCarthy (1986), Yip (1988), Reiss (2003a, b), and Baković (2005). The alternations to be considered are:

(146) Afar syncope

	Underlying	Surface	
a.	digib-e	digbé	'he married'
b.	xamil-i	xamlí	'swamp grass'
c.	danan-e	danané	'he hurt'
d.	xarar-e	xararé	'he burned'

Descriptively, the second vowel in a word deletes, providing the flanking consonants are not completely identical (the vowel must also be unstressed). In order to restrict the deletion of the vowel, it is necessary to add a Non-Identity Condition which permits deletion only if, for flanking consonants γ_i and γ_j, $\neg\forall F_i \in \mathbb{F}$ such that $[(aF_i)_{\gamma_i}] = [(\beta F_i)_{\gamma_j}]$.

This will give the correct result for the forms in (146). However, more careful inspection of the Afar data reveals that the situation is a bit more complicated. Syncope does not happen when the second syllable is closed:

(147) a. digibté   *digbté   'she married'   (cf. digbé 'I married')
       b. wagerné   *wagrné   'we reconciled' (cf. wagré 'he reconciled')

One way to express this would be to initiate another subsidiary iteration of SEARCH and incorporate the target of this search, γ_k, into the identity condition, allowing for deletion only if γ_k is [−CONS] and $\neg\forall F_i \in \mathbb{F}$ such that $[(aF_i)_{\gamma_i}] = [(\beta F_i)_{\gamma_j}]$.

A similar approach can account for syncope in Yapese (Jensen 1977; Odden 1988; Reiss 2003a, b), which only applies if the flanking consonants are homorganic and the first consonant is word-initial;[22] this is a case which requires partial identity.

---

[22] Or postvocalic. Let us abstract away from this because it will add the unnecessary complication of potential self-bleeding. See Samuels (2009b), Ch. 4, for further discussion of this issue.

(148)   *Underlying*   *Surface*
    a. ba puw   bpuw   'it's a bamboo'
    b. ni teːl   nteːl   'take it'
    c. radaːn   rdaːn   'its width

In this case, the vowel deletes only if $\forall F_i \in \{\text{CORONAL, DORSAL, LABIAL}\}$ such that $[(\alpha F_i)_{\gamma_i}] = [(\beta F_i)_{\gamma_j}]$.

It so happens that the rules discussed in conjunction with the OCP, and therefore with the Identity and Non-Identity Conditions, are FE-type processes (namely epenthesis and syncope). However, it is quite possible that the feature-algebraic conditions discussed in this section may also be useful for describing Path-type processes. I leave this matter to future research and now turn to another application of the SEARCH and COPY procedure.

5.7 The Topology of Morphology

Recall that in Chapter 4 I presented a theory of the syntax–phonology interface developed by Idsardi and Raimy (forthcoming). One of the hallmarks of this theory is the idea that, when phonological material enters the derivation at spell-out, it is in the form of a directed graph which may be "looped" or non-asymmetric. Such loops then get unwound during serialization, as detailed in §4.2.3. But how and why do loops arise in the first place? That is the question I will try to answer in this section, and my answer will be a simple one: through SEARCH and COPY. This makes sense since the representations involved at spell-out (once non-phonological features have been traded in) and serialization are made of the same fundamental stuff as is manipulated by narrowly phonological operations—so, I think, it is reasonable to expect that the same operations would be at play in these processes as well. Let me begin with a bit more detailed summary of how morphological processes are viewed as adding precedence arcs to directed graphs in a Raimyan framework.[23]

Reduplication can be very informally defined as a process that causes some portion of a word to appear twice. A given instance of reduplication can be either total (encompassing the entire word) or partial (copying only part of the word); in many languages both appear, with different morphological functions. Just as the base may contain elements not found in the reduplicant (as in partial reduplication), the reduplicant may likewise contain elements not found in the base, and this is called "fixed segmentism." We have

---

[23] I will not discuss "templatic" or "copy-and-associate" approaches to reduplication here. See Poser (1982), Raimy (2000a) for arguments against these methods.

already seen that reduplication can be represented as a "backward" loop in the string:

(149)   Add (t, k):   # → k → æ → t → %

Serialization, as discussed in §4.2.3, turns that looped, non-asymmetric graph into an asymmetric linear string:

(150)   # → k → æ → t → k → æ → t → % = /kætkæt/

Note that there is no principled distinction between total and partial reduplication in this theory: total reduplication occurs when a loop just happens to establish precedence between the segment after # and the segment before %.[24]

We have also already seen that directed graph notation accounts for affixation in exactly the same way; the only difference is that the loop in (151) goes forward rather than backward.

(151)   Add (X, Z), (Z, Y):   # →   X →   Y → % = XZY

                                           Z

Recall that if the instructions regarding the placement of Z come from the morphology, these "m-links" are added to the top of the serialization queue and therefore prioritized ahead of their lexical counterparts. Thus, (151) produces a string XZY, or in other words, XY with an infix Z.

Prefixation and suffixation are the special cases in which a forward loop involves the addition of a forward loop between # and the first lexical segment, or between the last lexical segment and %.

Forward loops can also be used to account for "templatic" or "non-concatenative" morphology (a true misnomer), which on this view is simply multiple infixes (see discussion in Raimy 2000a: 32 ff.). It also provides a mechanism for subtractive morphology, which has been explored by Gagnon and Piché (2007); see also Gagnon (2008). Indeed, the possibility of having a "jump link" in which a forward loop skips one or more lexical segments, effectively deleting the skipped string, cannot be ruled out without additional stipulations. One case which can easily be accommodated using this approach is the Tohono O'odham perfective:[25]

---

[24] Admittedly, it is not clear how this could explain an implicational universal which was first noted by Moravcsik (1978), namely that the presence of partial reduplication in a language implies that it also has total reduplication. However, the answer may lie in the idea that the positions of all segments are encoded with respect to the ends of the string (recall the discussion of positional memory in Ch. 3). The ends themselves are thus easiest to locate.

[25] A few vowel-final stems do not conform to this pattern; in these cases, the imperfective and the perfective are identical. Following the literature, I assume these exceptional forms to be lexicalized.

(152)   Tohono O'odham perfective (Zepeda 1983; Gagnon and Piché 2007)

	Imperfective	*Perfective*	
a.	hiːnk	hiːn	'bark(ed)'
b.	ñeid	ñei	'see/saw'
c.	golon	golo	'rake'
d.	siːsp	siːs	'nail(ed)'
e.	ʔiːi̥	ʔiː	'drink/drank'
f.	moːto	moːt	'carry/carried'

From the above data it should be obvious that the final segment in the imperfective is not predictable from looking at the perfective forms, which suggests an analysis of the perfective in terms of subtraction from the imperfective. As Gagnon and Piché (2007) have argued, when viewed in this light, the rule for formulating the perfective is very simple: delete the final segment. In loop notation, this is represented as below:

(153) $\# \to g \to o \to l \to o \to n \to \%$

Since the m-link takes precedence over the lexical ones, the result will be deletion of the final segment. I would like to address one question which may be in the reader's mind: why should there be a primitive operation DELETE when SEARCH and COPY can create a jump link which has the effect during linearization of deleting a segment or string of segments? One way to think of this is as parallel to the difference in syntax between the deletion of uninterpretable features and the deletion of movement copies at the interfaces: one can delete a feature value only, while the other can delete an entire syntactic/phonological feature bundle (i.e. a segment or a word/phrase).[26] This is why I was vague in the previous section on feature algebra and did not provide SEARCH and COPY schemata for the epenthesis and deletion processes discussed there; I had not yet motivated this approach to whole-segment insertion and deletion. (Full details are provided in Samuels 2009*b*: §4.4.3.)

Halle (2008) adds metathesis to the list of processes which can be described along Raimyan lines. (The notation Halle uses is different; however, the result holds for loop notation as well.) For example, the string ABC can be transformed into BCA thus:

---

[26] Of course, one must be careful not to push this analogy too far—in recent Minimalist syntax it is typically thought that uninterpretable features are unvalued features, and therefore that valuation and deletion go hand in hand; moreover, a newly valued feature *must* delete in syntax whereas in phonology I am claiming that DELETE normally does *not* apply—but as a heuristic I believe the parallel has some value.

(154)

$$\# \rightarrow A \rightarrow B \rightarrow C \rightarrow \%$$

5.7.1 *From Strings to Loops*

Now that we have seen how adding precedence relationships in this way can account for a wide variety of morphophonological processes from reduplication to subtractive morphology, I would like to connect this to the SEARCH and COPY framework developed earlier in this chapter. This will address the questions of how, why, and where loops enter phonological representations.

If we take seriously Marantz's (1982) view that reduplication involves the introduction of a phonetically null morpheme, but depart from Marantz by not assigning any skeletal structure to that morpheme, it becomes possible to treat reduplication and affixation as initiating SEARCH in order to find a host for a newly introduced morpheme. In other words, each time a string enters the phonological workspace, before anything else happens, it must be combined with the string already present. The details of *when* this occurs have already been discussed in the context of Chapter 4: it happens at spell-out, on every phonological cycle (i.e. every phase). The SEARCH algorithm I will use is the same one which I used for phonology-internal processes, and I will show that the COPY mechanism can be used to integrate the precedence relationships carried by the new morpheme with the ones already present in the host word. We will now see how this works.

First, for the sake of concreteness, let us consider the case of suffixing *want* with the past tense *-ed*. I assume that what it means to be an affix is to lack one or both terminal elements, # and %. This means there is a "sticky end" on the affix which enables it to concatenate with another string. In more formal terms, the sticky end is a variable (which I label as ς for reasons that will soon become clear), and concatenation of the two strings is achieved by replacing that variable in the affix with information copied from the existing string— exactly how underspecified representations are repaired in the phonology. So in the lexicon, *want* and *-ed* are represented as:[27]

(155)   a. $\# \rightarrow w \rightarrow a \rightarrow n \rightarrow t \rightarrow \%$

       b. $\varsigma \rightarrow e \rightarrow d \rightarrow \%$

The role of ς is exactly the same as it was when it represented a segment with an underspecified feature value in the case of harmony; that is, ς is the

---

[27] In this section I represent example morphemes as they are spelled to keep things as simple as possible.

"standard" or the initiator of a search into the string (Σ) which is already in the workspace. The goal (γ) of SEARCH will ultimately replace ς via an application of COPY, eliminating the sticky end and integrating the two morphemes. It is desirable, then, for the values which γ can take to reflect the possible anchor points for affixation (and of course for reduplication and the other morphophonological processes), if the goal is to constrain the theory such that one cannot place loops just anywhere, but only in the places which attested morphological patterns demand. I have argued previously (Samuels 2010*d*) that these anchor points are the {first, second, stressed, penult, last} elements of type {X, C, V, foot} in the string.[28] As we saw earlier, the SEARCH algorithm has a direction parameter (δ) which allows it to traverse the string either to the left or to the right. This means there are really only three positions to consider, namely {first, second, stressed}. The "last" and "penult" are just the first and second from the right, respectively. (I will address a minor complication to this typology momentarily.)

Going back to the example of *want* + -*ed*, then, the parameters on the SEARCH specified in the lexical representation of -*ed* would be:

(156) a. Σ (string in the active workspace): # $\to$ w $\to$ a $\to$ n $\to$ t $\to$ %

 b. ς (initiator of SEARCH): $\varsigma_i \to$ e $\to$ d $\to$ %

 c. γ (target of SEARCH): First X

 d. δ (direction of SEARCH): L

 e. β (beginning point of SEARCH): %

Upon completion of this search, the target /t/ will be copied into the precedence statement which contained the initiating ς:[29]

(157)   # $\to$ w $\to$ a $\to$ n $\to$ t $\to$ %

                                    $\searrow$ e $\to$ d $\to$ %

The difference between a suffix like -*ed* and an infix is that the former contains %, while the latter has two sticky ends. I give an example from Tzeltal below. In this language, a verb is made intransitive by infixing -*h*- after the first vowel:

---

[28] Putting feet aside, since so few words have a large enough number of feet to see the pattern of attestation clearly (recall the discussion of Golston 2007 in §5.3.3; of the possible combinations of these two sets of parameters, only two—stressed C (for obvious reasons) and penult X—are completely unattested). Again, see Samuels (2010*d*) for further discussion.

[29] Note that Raimy (2000*a*) explicitly states that two morphemes which combine, such as *want* and -*ed*, actually come to share a single beginning/end marker (i.e. in any type of affixation there is one instance each of # and %). I show two tokens of % to emphasize that a prefix/suffix has only one sticky end as opposed to an infix which has two.

(158)   Tzeltal intransitivization (Yu 2007: 102)
      a. puk   'to divide among'   pu-h-k   'to spread the word'
      b. kuč   'to carry'   ku-h-č   'to endure'
      c. k'ep   'to clear away'   k'e-h-p   'to be clear'

There are a few important things to note about the way SEARCH proceeds for infixation. First and foremost, since there are two sticky ends, there must be *two* applications of SEARCH, which share the same search space (Σ) and direction (δ) but not the same standard (ς) or target (γ). Furthermore, an entire segment is being copied into the precedence statement in which ς acts as a placeholder.[30] Allow the COPY algorithm, then, to copy an entire segment.

Also, for all cases of (pure) infixation, the target identified in the first search is the *starting* point for the next search. That is to say, the value of β can be only one of the terminals or the target of the previous search (#, %, or γ_{n-1}). In this particular case, the first search is to the right from #, for the first vowel in the word. But rather than beginning at # again for the second search, the starting point is that first vowel in Σ which was just identified (i.e. the previous γ). The second search then proceeds to the right, looking for the first segment it encounters. This ensures that the two sticky ends are attached to adjacent segments, and thus the loop which is created does not have the effect of deleting anything in the base. (Though keep in mind that I am not stipulating that the second application of SEARCH is *always* "first X from previous γ." This is to allow a jump link to be created when the second search looks for some other target.) The end result is as desired, taking *puk* as our example:

(159)   # → p → u → k → %
                                   h

---

[30] This runs counter to Principle 6 of Chomsky (1967: 125):

(1)   PRINCIPLE 6: Two successive lines of a derivation can differ by at most one feature specification.

However, this generalization was clearly not meant to apply to morphological processes—and note that spreading of an autosegmental node subsuming multiple features also violates Principle 6. Nor is it obvious to me in light of, for example, epenthesis of segments other than schwa, which presumably have more than a single feature value, how one could maintain this generalization. It is particularly hard to do so when one assumes little underspecification. See Vaux and Samuels (2003) for relevant arguments concerning consonant epenthesis.

Formally, this can be expressed with these parameters:

(160)   a. Σ (string in the active workspace): $\# \to p \to u \to k \to \%$

      b. ς (initiator of SEARCH): $\varsigma_i \to h \to \varsigma_j$

      c. γ (target of SEARCH): $\gamma_i = $ First V; $\gamma_j = $ First X

      d. δ (direction of SEARCH): R

      e. β (beginning point of SEARCH): $\beta_i = \#$; $\beta_j = \gamma_i$

Now look at what happens in reduplication. It is helpful to distinguish between reduplication which does not add any material to the original string and reduplication with fixed segmentism. In both cases, the affix involved will enter with two sticky ends. However, this affix is extremely abstract if no fixed segmentism is involved: it consists only of the precedence relation (ς_i, ς_j). And unlike what we just saw for affixation, the second SEARCH in a case of reduplication can either begin fresh at one of the terminal nodes, *or* begin from the target of the first search. English *shm*-reduplication (here, *fancy-shmancy*) provides an example of the first type, where the two searches are totally independent (and in fact even have different settings for δ, which we have not yet seen up to this point).

(161)   a. Σ (string in the active workspace): $\# \to f \to a \to n \to c \to y \to \%$

      b. ς (initiator of SEARCH): $\varsigma_i \to sh \to m \to \varsigma_j$

      c. γ (target of SEARCH): $\gamma_i = $ First X; $\gamma_j = $ First V

      d. δ (direction of SEARCH): $\delta_i = $ L; $\delta_j = $ R

      e. β (beginning point of SEARCH): $\beta_i = \%$; $\beta_j = \#$

Note that the "backwardness" of the loop is an epiphenomenon resulting from the accidental fact that γ_i happens to precede γ_j. Nothing about the shape of the affix, or about any one particular parameter setting, guarantees this result. We can verify this by considering the case of a language with final stress where both searches begin at # and proceed to the right, but the first terminates at the stressed vowel and the second terminates at the second vowel. This produces a backward loop. Conversely, in a word with initial stress, the exact same SEARCH parameters will result in a forward loop:[31]

---

[31] Searching for the stressed vowel is always ambiguous as to direction; since there is only one primary stress in a word, the result will be the same either way. Which choice(s) from among the multiple possible parameter settings learners actually entertain is a different question entirely, and one I will begin to explore in Ch. 6.

(162)   From stressed vowel to second vowel (final stress)

   $\# \to C \to V \to C \to V \to C \to \acute{V} \to \%$

(163)   From stressed vowel to second vowel (initial stress)

   $\# \to C \to \acute{V} \to C \to V \to C \to V \to \%$

Kamaiurá presents an example from the opposite end of the reduplication spectrum: no fixed segmentism, but the target of the first search provides the beginning for the second search.

(164)   Kamaiurá aspectual reduplication (Yu 2007:111)

	Singular	*Plural*	
a.	omokon	omoko-moko-n	'he swallowed it (frequently)'
b.	ohuka	ohuka-huka	'he (kept on) laughing'
c.	jeumirik	jeumiri-miri-k	'I tie up (repeatedly)'

(165)   a. Σ (string in the active workspace):

   $\# \to o \to m \to o \to k \to o \to n \to \%$

   b. s (initiator of SEARCH): $s_i \to s_j$

   c. γ (target of SEARCH): γ_i = First V; γ_j = Second C

   d. δ (direction of SEARCH): $\delta_i = L$; $\delta_j = L$

   e. β (beginning point of SEARCH): $\beta_i = \%$; $\beta_j = \gamma_i$

There is one more issue which must be addressed, namely the difference between reduplicative patterns such as the kind exhibited by Diyari on the one hand and the one found in Oykangand (and Mangarrayi) on the other. In Diyari, the whole stem up to *and including* the second vowel is reduplicated, whereas in Oygankand, the whole stem up to *but not including* the second vowel is reduplicated. I repeat the data here:

(166)   Diyari reduplication (Poser 1982: 7)

	Stem	*Reduplicated*	
a.	ŋama	ŋama-ŋama	'to sit'
b.	wakari	waka-wakari	'to break'
c.	kanku	kanku-kanku	'boy'
d.	ŋankaṇṭi	ŋanka-ŋankaṇṭi	'catfish'
e.	ṭilparku	ṭilpa-ṭilparku	'bird (sp.)'

(167)   Oykangand reduplication (McCarthy and Prince 1986: 12)

	Stem	*Reduplicated*	
a.	eder	ed-eder	'rain'
b.	algal	alg-algal	'straight'
c.	igu-	ig-igun	'go'

The Diyari pattern is handled straightforwardly by the theory as it has been presented up to this point. Take *wakari* as an example:

(168) a. Σ (string in the active workspace): # $\rightarrow$ w $\rightarrow$ a $\rightarrow$ k $\rightarrow$ a $\rightarrow$ r $\rightarrow$ i $\rightarrow$ %

b. ς (initiator of SEARCH): $s_i \rightarrow s_j$

c. γ (target of SEARCH): γ_i = Second V; γ_j = First X

d. δ (direction of SEARCH): δ_i = R; δ_j = R

e. β (beginning point of SEARCH): β_i = #; β_j = #

The result will be as desired:

(169) # $\rightarrow$ w $\rightarrow$ a $\rightarrow$ k $\rightarrow$ a $\rightarrow$ r $\rightarrow$ i $\rightarrow$ %

However, to capture the reduplication in Oykangand which excludes the second vowel, the SEARCH procedure must establish a loop between the first segment in the string and the segment *to the left of* the second vowel. This has already been noted by Raimy (2005, 2009), who proposes a "Placement" parameter which can be set to establish a loop at, before, or after an anchor point. This could be formally implemented in my theory by a subsidiary SEARCH which searches from the segment identified in one iteration of SEARCH for the first X to its left or right, then establishes a precedence relation from that segment to one identified by another SEARCH. At the present time I have no choice but to stipulate that a subsidiary SEARCH in the context of reduplication is always for the first X—i.e. an adjacent segment. Without this restriction, it should be possible for SEARCH to identify the second vowel, then subsidiary SEARCH to find the first vowel after that; this would effectively yield a "third vowel" pivot, which is unattested. However, as Samuels (2009*b*) notes, subsidiary SEARCH for something other than "first X" is necessary as a condition on certain types of phonological rules.

Before moving on, I would like to discuss the differences between the theory presented here and the one developed by Raimy (2005, 2009), to which I have just alluded. Raimy also posits a system of parameters which constrain where loops can be created. The parameters Raimy proposes are:

(170) Anchor Point Theory parameters for structural description (Raimy 2009: 6)

a. Placement: {at/before/after}

b. Count: {first/last}

 c. Plane: {x-tier/metrical/syllable/consonantal}

 d. Target: {plain/stressed(head)/consonant}

Raimy's parameters do not correspond to the parameters on SEARCH in a neat way: for example, I consider {first, second, stressed} to be different settings of a single parameter γ, while for Raimy, reference to the penultimate element is obtained by setting the Placement parameter to "before" and the Count parameter to "last."[32] This method of deriving the second/penultimate elements does not seem to go far enough: I can see no way to find the segment before the second vowel (the Oykangand/Mangarrayi pattern) using Raimy's parameters. Another difference between my theory and Raimy's is that I obtain reference to elements defined relative to the tail end of a string by setting the δ parameter to L and the β parameter to %, whereas Raimy's mechanism always looks from the left. This may seem trivial, but if a search algorithm is truly at work, then it is undesirable to refer to the last item which is found, since the search will have to traverse the entire string in order to determine which this is. Searching from the opposite end for the first item will achieve the same results but in a more economical fashion. Additionally, not only in order to avoid requiring tiered representations but also for theory-independent considerations of symmetry, I prefer not to treat vowels and consonants differently, as in (170): for Raimy, consonants are accessed by setting the Target parameter to "consonant," whereas vowels are accessed by setting the Plane parameter to "metrical."

5.8 Operations in Evolutionary Perspective

To conclude the discussion of SEARCH and COPY, I return to the questions addressed in Chapter 3: are such abilities operative in other cognitive domains and/or in other species?

 Searching is ubiquitous in animal and human cognition. It is an integral part of foraging and hunting for food, to take but one example. The Ohshiba (1997) study of sequence-learning by monkeys, humans, and a chimpanzee is an excellent probe of searching abilities in primates because it shows that,

---

[32] Raimy achieves references to foot-like chunks in this fashion: setting one anchor to, for example, {after, first, metrical, plain} = peninitial vowel. Only these chunks, not true feet, are relevant to reduplication in Raimy's view. I find this unsatisfactory in light of the cases discussed in Samuels (2010d), which seem to involve true metrical feet. Apart from this, the two theories therefore make different predictions about words with lots of feet. I can refer to the first, second, stressed, penultimate, and final feet, but Raimy can only refer to initial, final, and possibly stressed pseudo-feet. Since I am not aware of data which shows the typology of foot-based reduplication clearly, I set this issue aside for the time being.

while various species can perform the multiple sequential searches required to perform the experimental task (touching four symbols in an arbitrary order), they plan out the task in different ways. Human subjects were slow to touch the first circle but then touched the other three in rapid succession, as if they had planned the whole sequence before beginning their actions (the "collective search" strategy). The monkeys, meanwhile, exhibited a gradual decrease in their reaction times. It was as if they planned only one step before executing it, then planned the next, and so forth (the "serial search" strategy).

Perhaps most interestingly of all, the chimpanzee appeared to use the collective search strategy on monotonic patterns but the serial search strategy when the sequence was not monotonic. That at least some chimpanzees employ collective searches is corroborated by the results of a similar experiment by Biro and Matsuzawa (1999). The chimp in this study, Ai, had extensive experience with numerals, and she was required to touch three numerals on a touchscreen in monotonic order. Again, her reaction times were consistently fast after the initial step. But when the locations of the two remaining numerals were changed after she touched the first one, her reactions slowed, as if she had initially planned all three steps but her preparation was foiled by the switch. Notice that the SEARCH mechanism proposed by M&R and adopted here operates in a manner consistent with the collective search strategy: scan the search space to find all targets of the operation to be performed, and then perform the operation to all targets sequentially.

One possible parallel to the COPY operation in phonology, particularly the copying of a string of segments as in reduplication, could be the patterns found in bird and whale songs. As we saw in §3.3, Slater (2000) shows that for many bird species, songs take the shape $((a^x)(b^y)(c^z))^w$: that is, a string of syllables a, b, c, each of them repeated, and then the whole string repeated. We also saw that whale songs are similarly structured (Payne 2000). Schneider-Zioga and Vergnaud (2009) question the parallel I suggest here, contending that human phonology (i.e. reduplication) exhibits repetition at the planning level, while birdsong exhibits repetition only at the level of execution. While this is a possible interpretation of the type of repetition found in bird and whale song, it is speculative; we do not know enough about the mental representations in these species to rule out the possibility that there *is* repetition at the planning level in their vocalizations. And regardless of the level at which repetition occurs, there must be a computational mechanism which makes it possible.

With respect to the copying of a feature from one segment to another (as in assimilatory processes), the relevant ability might be transferring a representation from long-term memory to short-term memory: retrieving a lexical representation (or extracting a feature from one) and bringing it into the active phonological workspace (Phillips and Lau 2004). This seems like a prerequisite for any task which involves the recall/use of memorized information, and perhaps can be seen as a virtual conceptual necessity arising from computational efficiency.

We should also keep in mind that one of the major applications of SEARCH and COPY is morphological: to concatenate strings. As I mentioned in Chapter 3, concatenation serves both the ability to group (assign to sets) and the ability to chain together sequential actions. Without the ability to assign objects to sets or combine multiple steps into a larger routine, neither grouping nor sequential planning is possible. We have already seen that bird and whale songs have the kind of sequential organization which is indicative of concatenated chunks, and primates can perform multi-step actions with sub-goals.

Concatenation may also underlie the numerical abilities common to humans and many other species as well (for an overview, see Dehaene 1997; Butterworth 1999; Lakoff and Nuñez 2001; Devlin 2005; Shettleworth 2010). This is perhaps clearest in the case of parallel individuation/tracking, or the ability to represent in memory a small number of discrete objects (< 4; see Feigenson and Halberda 2004 and references therein) and perform basic operations, such as comparisons of magnitude, over those representations. The connection between parallel individuation and concatenation is suggested by the fact that the speed of recognizing the number of objects in a scene decreases with each additional object that is presented within the range of capability (Saltzman and Garner 1948). This leads me to suspect along with Gelman and Gallistel (1978) (but contra Dehaene) that such tasks require paying attention to each object in the array separately, yet they must be represented as a set in order to be manipulated arithmetically. Lakoff and Nuñez (2001) also discuss a number of studies showing that chimpanzees (most notably Ai, who was also the subject of Biro and Matsuzawa's 1999 study), when given rigorous training over a long period of time, can engage in basic counting, addition, and subtraction of natural numbers up to about ten. Subtraction or removal of objects from a set could be seen as akin to the DELETE operation; the ability to subtract has also been shown in pigeons (Brannon *et al.* 2001). This and a number of other studies showing that species as diverse as primates, rats, and birds can both count and add with a fair degree of precision are summarized by Gallistel and Gelman (2005) and Shettleworth (2010).

In sum, searching, copying, and concatenation are far from unique to language or to humans. But there are several interesting questions to be asked regarding the relationship between these phonological operations and seeming parallels in other domains. For example, is there one SEARCH operation at work in the human mind, or are there several SEARCH-like operations in different cognitive modules? One avenue of research along these lines, suggested by Chomsky (2009: 34), would be to look into the differences between searches in language and in animal foraging behavior:

> In the case of language, [searching] is going to have very special properties, because language is apparently unique as a system of discrete infinity. So it is going to be totally different from foraging, let's say, which is a continuous system, unlike language which is a discrete system. But it would be nice to try to show that the differences that occur in the case of language ... are just due to the fact that it is uniquely a system of discrete infinity, which is then of course going to have different effects.

There is no reason to expect searching in language to be *exactly* the same as searching in other cognitive domains; nevertheless, it would be enlightening to know *how* it is different and *why* it is so. No answers can be offered at present. However, it is possible to probe these questions from several angles: behaviorally, via neuroimaging, and so on. We might also look deeper into linguistic deficits—problems with lexical retrieval, morphological production, and echolalias, to name a few—which could result from problems with the primitive operations.

6

Linguistic Variation

6.1 Introduction

In the previous chapters I have focused on the core of phonology which is shared by all languages. However, even the most naive observer notices that languages, dialects, and indeed, individual speakers vary widely in the phonological systems which they manifest. To steal a line from Otto Jespersen, no one ever dreamed of a universal phonology: all theories have to posit some kind of language-specific mechanisms, in the guise of learned rules, constraint rankings, and/or parameter settings.

It bears emphasizing that this type of variation, which is circumscribed by biology but not determined by it, "represents something interesting: the language capacity is a biological system that is open, consistent with a range of phenotypical shapes. This is not unique in the biological world—there are plants that grow differently above or below water and immune systems that develop differently depending on what people are exposed to (Jerne 1985)—but it is unusual" (Lightfoot 2006: 4). This leads me to ponder a question which has never received an adequate answer (nor, sadly, will I be able to answer it adequately here): where does phonological variation come from?[1] The short answer is easy: variation arises from some combination of primary linguistic data (different for every learner), the learning mechanisms the acquirer brings to the task, and the space of possible grammars. Simulations by Niyogi (2006) and Niyogi and Berwick (1995, 1997) show that, even within a population in which there is only a single grammar, if each child is exposed to a finite number of sentences, it only takes *one generation* for variation to emerge. As Roberts and Holmberg (2009) put it,

if we combine the hetereogeneity in any speech community, the random distribution of [the primary linguistic data] (poverty of the stimulus) and the limited time for learning (i.e. the critical period for language acquisition), change in grammatical sys-

---

[1] Here I mean variation in the sense that two phonological systems differ, not variation in terms of speech rate, register, and so on, although the latter ultimately may be represented in terms of the former.

tems is inevitable. If change is inevitable in the diachronic dimension, then variation is inevitable in the synchronic dimension.

But to identify the sources of variation in a less nebulous way will surely require deeper investigation into phonology and phonetics as well as studies of our perceptual and articulatory systems, our learning biases, and human cognition more broadly.

6.2 Phonological Poverty of the Stimulus

I will start this chapter by providing justification for my approach to phonological acquisition and therefore variation, which depends on there being an argument from the poverty of the stimulus in phonology. This issue is rarely discussed; the classical arguments are typically formed in terms of the learning of structure-dependent syntactic rules. One typical argument, here as presented by Lasnik and Uriagereka (2002), goes as follows. English has a rule of auxiliary fronting in yes/no questions which produces sentences such as the one below:

(171)   Is the dog *t* hungry?

From observing monoclausal sentences of this type, and armed with the knowledge that "is" is an auxiliary, a child may entertain a number of hypotheses about auxiliary fronting which are consistent with the observed data. For example:

(172)   a. Hypothesis A: Front the first auxiliary in the sentence.

          b. Hypothesis B: Front the auxiliary in the matrix clause.

Nevertheless, children do not in fact ever seem to posit Hypothesis A (Crain and Nakayama 1987)—a curious fact considering that Hypothesis A requires less prior knowledge about possible sentence structures than Hypothesis B. In the original formulation of the argument, Chomsky (1965) emphasized the dearth of positive evidence for Hypothesis B, which would have to come from sentences like (173):

(173)   Is the dog who is hungry *t* in the backyard?

The conclusion that children must be innately primed to favor structure-dependent analyses such as Hypothesis B is taken to follow from the unavailability of (173) in the child's experience. The premise upon which this conclusion rests—that sentences such as (173) are rare—has been questioned by skeptics including Pullum and Scholz (2002) and Sampson (2005), who provide corpus statistics showing that between 0.1 percent and 1 percent of sentences which children hear may be of the relevant type.[2] But, as Legate and Yang (2002) argue, this by no means proves that such evidence is *sufficient* for children to learn the correct auxiliary-fronting rule.

Moreover, many hypotheses beyond A and B exist, several of which are consistent with both the garden-variety monoclausal yes/no question and (173). I give a brief sampling of these hypotheses here, synthesizing Legate and Yang (2002) and Lasnik and Uriagereka (2002):

(174)   Auxiliary-fronting hypotheses

  a. Front the last auxiliary

  b. Front the first auxiliary following the first NP

  c. Front the first auxiliary preceding some VP

  d. Front the auxiliary whose position in the sentence is a prime number

  e. Front the auxiliary which most closely follows a noun

  f. Front any auxiliary

  g. Front any finite auxiliary

  h. Front the first auxiliary that comes after an intonational break

  i. Front the first auxiliary that comes after the first complete constituent

  j. Front the first auxiliary that comes after the first semantic unit you parsed.

The child must rule out not only Hypothesis A, but also a list of alternatives which is, in principle, infinite. And, as Lasnik and Uriagereka (2002) point out, hearing (173) does not help the situation much; that type of sentence is still consistent with many of the hypotheses in (174), such as "front any auxiliary" and "front the last auxiliary." But again, children do not appear to consider any of these alternatives. This underscores the point made by both Lasnik and Uriagereka (2002) and Legate and Yang (2002) (see also Yang 2002, 2004) that the child simply *must* be equipped with some biases which constrain the hypothesis space. Halle (1978) makes several phonological arguments which run parallel to the auxiliary-fronting example. One is the fact that we have untaught phonotactic knowledge of our native languages. Consider the following list from Halle (1978: 95), which is comprised of words from actual

---

[2] This statistic includes *wh*-questions such as *How could anyone that was awake t not hear that?* in addition to yes/no questions.

languages (including English, though Halle purposely selected English words uncommon enough that the average reader will not know them):

(175)   ptak thole hlad plast sram mgla vlas flitch dnom rtut

Even without encountering any of these words before, a native speaker of English will correctly guess that *thole, plast,* and *flitch* are English words but the rest are not. Only negative evidence supports this conclusion, and phonotactic restrictions are not explicitly taught, but children acquire them nevertheless.

Another of Halle's arguments concerns regular plural formation in English. If learners simply listed the allomorphs of the plural and the sounds they follow, they would arrive at a rule such as the following (Halle 1978: 101):

(176)   a. If a noun ends with /s z š ž č ǰ/, add /ɨz/;

        b. Otherwise, if the noun ends with /p t k f θ/, add /s/;

        c. Otherwise, add /z/.

An alternative feature-based rule would distribute the plural allomorphs as described here (Halle 1978: 102):

(177)   a. If the noun ends with a sound that is [coronal, strident], add /ɨz/;

        b. Otherwise, if the noun ends with a sound that is [non-voiced], add /s/;

        c. Otherwise, add /z/.

As in the auxiliary case, the sound-based rule (176) is less abstract and requires less linguistic knowledge than the feature-based (177). In fact, this case provides an even stronger argument for innatism than the syntactic example because there is *absolutely no* evidence for (177) which does not also support (176), or vice versa. Nevertheless, we can distinguish between the two rules by asking what happens when native English speakers are forced to pluralize a word which ends with a sound that does not exist in English, such as *Bach* (i.e. /bax/). If they choose the sound-based rule, since /x/ is not listed in (176a) or (176b), the plural of *Bach* ought to be /baxz/. But if they choose the feature-based rule (and assuming they also know that /x/ is unvoiced), they will form /baxs/. Since native English speakers' intuitions converge on /baxs/, they must choose (177) despite the attractive competing hypothesis, for which they have no counterevidence. Again, this is taken to be evidence that langauge learners are biased in favor of the feature-based analysis—which is to be expected if features (rather than segments) are really the building blocks of phonological representations all the way down to the neural level, as the data from ferrets seems to suggest; recall the discussion of Mesgarani *et al.* (2008)

in Chapter 3, in which I suggested that this may be rooted in a basic fact about how mammalian auditory processing works.

Despite the availability of these and similar arguments in the literature since the earliest days of generativism (and see Idsardi 2005 more recently), authors such as Blevins (2004) and Carr (2006) have stated that arguments from the poverty of the stimulus do not exist in phonology. Blevins (2004: 219–20), building on Pullum and Scholz (2002), makes this assertion based on a contrast between two types of learning, the latter of which she claims is not present in phonology:

(178) a. *Data-driven learning*
       Data-driven learning is knowledge of language structure which relies on attention to evidence, specifically, the corpus of utterances to which the child is exposed when they happen to come up in everyday contexts and are uttered in the child's presence. The general conditions on correct reasoning that are germane to learning anything else from evidence are deployed in data-driven language acquisition, but crucially, the learner is assumed *not* to be in prior possession of any information about what languages are like.

       b. *Hyperlearning* (aka '*Innately primed learning*')
       Hyperlearning is knowledge of language structure which is acquired by children without evidence. Innately primed learning calls upon inborn domain-specific linguistic information.

Based on these criteria, it should be obvious that the examples I just discussed (and the ones which will be discussed throughout the rest of this chapter) are examples of hyperlearning. In order to come up with the same generalization consistently, learners must be equipped with some prejudice that says things *must* be so. To quote Sober (1994: 237, emphasis his), "The slogan for scientists is: NO MODEL, NO INFERENCE. This entirely familiar point from the practice of science should not be forgotten when we investigate the theory of that practice."

It is simply impossible to use induction unless the hypothesis space is constrained somehow. I therefore concur with Idsardi (2005) that it is only for historiographical reasons, and also owing to an overly narrow focus on the empirical (rather than conceptual and philosophical) side of the argument, that the poverty of stimulus has been ignored and even denied in phonology. It is true, as Blevins (2004: 235) notes, that "[s]ounds surround us, and if anything, there is too much information to process, not too little." But it is precisely for this reason that it is of the utmost importance to recognize the amazing inductive leaps that children make and the priors which must underlie that type of hypothesis formation. The argument from the poverty of the stimulus *is not about lack of data simpliciter*. It is about a lack of data on the basis of which learners may definitively choose one hypothesis from among a potentially infinite number.

6.3 The Locus of Variation

Investigating phonological variation is particularly important since linguistic variation may in fact be confined entirely to (morpho)phonology and the lexicon, if recent biolinguistic work is correct to suggest that (*a*) narrow syntax is itself invariant, consisting only of Merge, and (*b*) the mapping from narrow syntax to LF is optimized (recall discussion of Chomsky 2008 in Ch. 2)— hence the title of this chapter, "Linguistic Variation," rather than "*Phonological Variation.*" Even independently of this asymmetry, the confinement of variation to the PF side is exactly what we should expect, as Uriagereka (2007: 110) reminds us:

Such state of affairs is not even surprising, if the language faculty exists on an internal domain (leading to LF) and an external one (leading to PF). We don't expect genuine internal variation, for it would be virtually impossible for infants to acquire it. What crucial information would set it? But by the very same reasoning, variation in the external domain is expected, indeed even natural if the system, like much else in basic biology, doesn't specify its full structural details. The only issue is what the nature of that variation ultimately is, and how connected it is to the internal conditions.

This goes hand in hand with what Baker (2008) dubs the Borer–Chomsky Conjecture (introduced briefly here in an earlier chapter), which originates in Borer's (1984: 3) hypothesis that "the availability of variation [is restricted] to the possibilities which are offered by one single component: the inflectional component," or as Baker (2008: 353) states the Conjecture, "all parameters of variation are attributable to differences in the features of particular items (e.g. the functional heads) in the lexicon." Roberts and Holmberg (2009) describe an advantage of this view which Borer (1984: 29) had already noted, which is that

associating parameter values with lexical entries reduces them to the one part of a language which clearly must be learned anyway. Ultimately, on this view, parametric variation reduces to the fact that different languages have different lexica, in that sound-meaning pairs vary arbitrarily: the most fundamental and inescapable dimension of cross-linguistic variation. The child acquires the values of the parameters valid for its native language as it acquires the vocabulary (more precisely, as it acquires the formal features associated with the functional categories of its native language).

Boeckx (forthcoming *a*) identifies three branches of support for a related conjecture which he calls the Strong Uniformity Thesis (building on Chomsky's 2001 Uniformity Thesis and consonant with statements as early as Chomsky 1991), that "narrow syntax is not subject to variation, not even parametric variation. In other words, there is only one syntax, fully uniform, at the heart of the faculty of language, underlying all languages." Boeckx's arguments for such a view are closely tied to Chomsky's (2005) "Three Factors in Language Design," from which I quote p. 6:

Assuming that the faculty of language has the general properties of other biological systems, we should, therefore, be seeking three factors that enter into the growth of language in the individual:

1. Genetic endowment, apparently nearly uniform for the species, which interprets part of the environment as linguistic experience, a nontrivial task that the infant carries out reflexively, and which determines the general course of the development of the language faculty. Among the genetic elements, some may impose computational limitations that disappear in a regular way through genetically timed maturation. [...]

2. Experience, which leads to variation, within a fairly narrow range, as in the case of other subsystems of the human capacity and the organism generally.

3. Principles not specific to the faculty of language.

The third factor falls into several subtypes: (a) principles of data analysis that might be used in language acquisition and other domains; (b) principles of structural architecture and developmental constraints that enter into canalization, organic form, and action over a wide range, including principles of efficient computation, which would be expected to be of particular significance for computational systems such as language. It is the second of these subcategories that should be of particular significance in determining the nature of attainable languages.

Of course, the Three Factors are inextricable. The genetic endowment is governed by principles not specific to the faculty of language, and experience is filtered through physiology which is created by the interaction of genes and the environment, again constrained by general principles of biology and physics at the very least. But it is possible to highlight certain contributions of each factor to linguistic variation.

Concerning the First Factor, there is little evidence to suggest that—among the non-language-impaired population—genetic variation is correlated with linguistic variation. The simple fact that any infant can learn the language of her environment, no matter whether it is the language her biological parents spoke or one from an adoptive home halfway across the world, shows that this must be the case. That notwithstanding, Dediu and Ladd (2007), in the first study of its type, found a correlation between the geographical distributions of certain alleles of the genes *ASPM* and *Microcephalin* (both of which are implicated in brain development) and that of tonal languages. They suggest that "[t]he relationship between genetic and linguistic diversity in this case may be causal: certain alleles can bias language acquisition or processing and thereby influence the trajectory of language change through iterated cultural transmission" (p. 10944). But at present, this potential causation remains conjectural.

I do, however, want to emphasize that the First Factor need not be so narrowly construed. Uriagereka (2007) and others highlight the role of epigenetics, which taken together with the genetic portion of the First Factor would constitute a significant locus of variation. Uriagereka finds the definition of the First Factor as simply "genetic endowment" to be misleading for this reason:

> These [three factors] invite the inference, explicit in Chomsky (2005), that variation is restricted to the second factor. In my view, in contrast, variation starts actually in the very first factor, the genetic endowment—and following [Vercelli (2009)]—I take this variation to be quite literally of an epigenetic sort. It is slightly misleading to think of it as fixed by experience, in any classical sense of the term "experience." This parametric fixation is as structurally fateful and blind as whatever happens to a bee larva being fed on the crucial protein that royal jelly involves, thereby growing, structurally and behaviorally, into a queen-bee.   (ibid. 107)

This foregrounds the role of cognitive mechanisms which give structure to data, allowing for the process of language acquisition to unfold. Along these lines, I concur with Hayes and Steriade (2004: 6) that UG is properly viewed as "a set of abstract analytical predispositions that allow learners to induce grammars from the raw facts of speech, and not as a—dauntingly large— collection of a priori constraints" or, I would add, a massive switchboard of parameters.

The Minimalist Program gives elevated status to the Third Factor, particularly where narrow syntax is concerned. The import of this for present purposes is that the principles of efficient computation (or more generally, "good design") subsumed under the Third Factor cannot be parameterized (see Chomsky 2001 et seq.). That is to say, there is no language which does not adhere to the Phase Impenetrability Condition, or which does not exhibit locality/minimality effects (whether formulated in terms of SEARCH or however else), or in which Merge is not binary, and so forth. Moreover, if narrow syntax consists only of Merge, then there is simply no room for variation in that component. Instead, variation must be attributed to the interplay of the Second Factor with the parts of the First and Third Factors which serve to constrain the learner's hypothesis space and structure the data to which he is exposed.

The hypothesis that narrow syntax cannot be a locus of variation gains strength if the "free" or "wild-type" Merge view of narrow syntax (Chomsky 2004; Boeckx 2008) turns out to be correct: in such theories, Merge is not subject to Last Resort or triggered by the need to check features, but rather simply applies freely to any objects endowed with an "Edge Feature."[3] It is as if, bearing the Edge Feature, all lexical items—like all electrons in physics—are indistinguishable by Merge. At PF and LF, however, some featural content is visible, and derivations in which those features' requirements go unsatisfied are filtered out; we say a derivation "fails to converge" if it is ill-formed at one (or both) of the interfaces. I will not review the evidence here, but see already Chomsky (1993) and especially Chomsky (2007, 2008) on the asymmetry between PF and LF in this regard: while the requirements posed by LF seem to be uniform across all languages, every language has its own set of requirements at PF. This forces the lexicon to be the primary source of the rich linguistic variety that we observe.

Boeckx (forthcoming *a*), in line with Fukui (1995), Fukui and Takano (1998), and more recent works such as Fortuny (2008) and Gallego (2008), proposes two sources for what was traditionally thought to be syntactic variation: differences in linear order and differences concerning features which LF does not interpret. Within the latter category, there can be differences in how a given set of features are bundled (as opposed to being expressed separately); additionally, a given feature may have an uninterpretable variant uF or not, and a given phase head may bear uF or not.

At PF, Boeckx suggests, there are a number of other points of variation: whether a given head requires an overt specifier, which end(s) of a chain are pronounced, whether a given head is an affix, and whether a given head comes before or after its complement. Note that shifting this second set of options to the interface is by no means an arbitrary move: in point of fact, it is impossible to formulate them in terms of syntactic parameters given now-standard assumptions about the architecture of grammar, namely (*a*) late insertion of vocabulary items, (*b*) a syntax which expresses only hierarchical (not linear) relations, and (*c*) a copy or re-Merge theory of movement. I would add that there are at least three additional types of variation with which the phonologist

---

[3] In my opinion, the name "Edge Feature" is an unfortunate misnomer which has engendered a considerable amount of confusion in the field. In Chomsky's original conception, which I adopt here, the Edge Feature is quite unlike, for example, a ϕ-feature which can take on different values; it might better be called an "Edge Property" which simply signals mergeability. Such a property can be identified with the "lexical envelope" which I discussed in Ch. 3, and which is potentially unique to humans.

must be concerned. First, heads which are affixal vary as to *how* and *where* they affix: as a prefix, suffix, infix, circumfix, reduplicant, or whatnot—recall Chapter 5. Second, we must account for the fact that every phonological system has a different set of rules. Third, there is the issue of phonological features, the use of which appears to vary across languages, both in terms of which features are active and how they are phonetically implemented. I will address features first, then turn to affixation as a means of approaching variation in rule systems.

6.4 Variation in Feature Systems

In the previous section, we saw that "syntactic" variation is now increasingly being viewed as a manifestation of differences in the distribution of features and feature values on various heads. Van Gelderen (2007; 2008) suggests that a principle of feature economy (179) may bias acquisition in this domain.

(179)   Principle of feature economy (van Gelderen 2007: 286)
        Minimize the semantic/interpretable features in the derivation

Adjunct		Specifier		Head		Affix
Semantic	>	[iF]	>	[uF]	>	–

Children acquire interpretable features before uninterpretable ones, but may subsequently reanalyze them (Radford 2000); viewed diachronically, this change from semantic to interpretable to uninterpretable features and finally to affixhood defines grammaticalization, which can be seen as a change towards a more economical system; see also Lohndal (2009*a*) in support of this view. Note that although this principle is stated in terms of formal features, it has been known even since Humboldt, Meillet, and Kuryłowicz that grammaticalization has consequences which extend into phonology, such as phonetic reduction or "erosion" of the grammaticalized element. I will discuss more acquisition biases which give rise to variation and change in phonological systems throughout the remainder of this chapter.

I argue here that paying attention to phonological features is also worthwhile, with an aim towards explaining one type of variation for which any theory of phonology must account: large-scale studies such as Maddieson (1984) have shown that most languages use but a tiny fraction of the sounds which are attested cross-linguistically.[4] I must be careful here not to make a

---

[4] Another vein of research on variation in phonological feature systems, namely cross-linguistic differences in the feature-geometric hierarchy, goes back to Halle (1959) and is emphasized in recent literature on contrastive underspecification (see e.g. Dresher 2003, 2009). I will not discuss this issue here since I reject both feature geometry and contrastive underspecification; recall §5.2.1, 5.6 and see Samuels (2009*b*, §3.2.3, 4.4.3) for discussion.

specious argument like the one made regarding factorial typology in Optimality Theory—I certainly do not want to claim that the full range of possible feature systems should be attested—but it is curious that so much of the potential feature-system morphospace is underused (see also Pulleyblank 2006). It is also interesting to consider what signed languages imply for thinking about variation in phonological feature systems. Since Stokoe (1960), it has been widely recognized that sign languages have phonology, and have phonological features. This underscores the modality-independence of phonology, and therefore the necessity of divorcing phonological representations and operations from phonetic substance. But features are an important point of contact between form and substance: they are the currency of abstract phonological computation, and they are also the elements which are transduced and interpreted phonetically. In light of the need to accommodate sign in the feature system, there are three options (modified from Mielke 2008: 16):

(180)   a. Maintain that features are innate, but give each feature two separate phonetic interpretations: one for spoken language and the other for sign.

          b. Maintain that features are innate and that their phonetic interpretation is always the same, but posit two sets: one for spoken language and the other for sign

          c. Allow for features and their phonetic interpretations to be learned, depending on the modality of the linguistic input.

Adopting option (a) or (b) makes a strong prediction, namely that we should find a high degree of parallelism between signed and spoken language features/featural organization. But the evidence actually supports (c): studies of sign language phonology have shown that sign language features are very different from the ones posited from spoken language in several ways. First, there seem to be far more features in signed language: for example, Stokoe (1960) makes use of twelve place distinctions, and even the very conservative feature set posited for sign by Sandler and Lillo-Martin (2005) has nearly twice as many features as the *SPE* system. Secondly, the organization of these features appears to be quite distinct from geometries posited for spoken languages (see Corina and Sagey 1989; Brentari 1998; Mielke 2008, *inter alia*). Furthermore, the features utilized in signed language seem to be learnable from facts about the articulators that are independent of language. For this reason, Corina and Sagey (1989) conclude that UG is not necessary to explain the properties of sign language features.

This leaves an uncomfortable paradox: if some feature systems can be learned, why can't they all be? This led to the hypothesis entertained by

Christdas (1988) that a small number of core features are universal while non-core features are learned. But again, if some features can be learned, why not all of them? Or if they are all universal, why are so few typically used? The emergentist position answers these questions by saying that "categories/features emerge as a result of contact with language data, and they naturally reflect the modality of the language being learned.... [T]he formal role of distinctive features and other primitives is the same for both modalities" (Mielke 2008: 18; see also Brentari 1998).

Previously, I argued (Samuels 2009*b*: §3.2.1) along with Mielke (2008) that an emergent feature set ought to be the null hypothesis, despite conceptual arguments from Hale and Reiss (2008) that this cannot be so. As more data concerning auditory processing and cortical representations in both humans and other mammals comes to light, I would like to revise that statement, since I think we are beginning to be able to make more informed arguments and take a more nuanced position. The debate over whether features are innate or emergent, which has taken on a rather black-and-white character, is increasingly misleading. One way in which this debate has been cast is as a top-down versus a bottom-up one: either features are primary and phonetic categories take shape based on these pre-existing phonetic/phonological features (the innatist view; see for instance Hale and Reiss 2008), or else features are abstracted away from categories, taking phonological patterns into account (the emergentist view; see for instance Mielke 2008). But even if features are innate in some sense, they may not be specific to humans or to language—it would stand to reason that the auditory system did not evolve a whole new set of sensitivities solely for human phonology with zero basis in the inherited mammalian perceptual system. A new method which is now being used to try to understand this inherited perceptual system involves taking single-neuron recordings from the auditory cortex in ferrets while they are listening to human speech (Mesgarani *et al.* 2008). Using this technique, it is possible to look at every instance in which a particular neuron fired and then determine what properties of the acoustic stimulus are common to each of those instances. For instance, some neurons respond best to the vowels / i ɪ i/; these neurons are tuned to a frequency band where this group of vowels has a formant (a strong energy peak). Other neurons are more broadly tuned in terms of frequency but respond best to a fast transition between silence and a burst of noise, as in the plosives. In short, it looks as though ferrets have neurons which detect acoustic properties that correlate with phonological features. These neural measures stand alongside a number of behavioral studies on a variety of species (since Kuhl and Miller 1975 on chinchillas) showing categorical perception of voicing contrasts, among others.

It certainly seems to be the case, then, that features (or put more neutrally, neural detectors which reflect distinctions we typically cast in terms of features) have an inherited existence independent of phonology. This in some sense tips the scales in favor of those who, like Hale and Reiss (2008), see features as necessary precursors to the acquisition of phonology. But at the same time, the emergentist story answers questions about the acquisition of sign systems, the (absence of a) relationship between features in signed and spoken phonology, the uneven distribution of features across phonological systems, and the disconnect between featural natural classes and phonologically active classes (see Mielke 2008 for further discussion). Attempting to reconcile these positions with an aim towards characterizing the possible range of variation in featural systems remains an area in need of much further research.

6.5 Underspecification and Underdetermination

Stepping back, a logical question which follows once we have determined the loci of variation is how to capture the range of options from which languages choose. In some sense, featural variation of the type discussed in the previous section is one of the easiest types to characterize: it is very simple to say that languages vary according to whether a given feature is present or absent, or (in syntax) whether it comes in an uninterpretable form or not. But it is not always possible to characterize variation in featural terms. I will illustrate this first with a familiar syntactic example, then turn to less familiar morphophonological ones. Consider the following facts about word order:

(181)   • For a given head H, a language must exhibit either H-complement or complement-H order.
   • There exist languages which exhibit H-complement order for some categories but not for others (call these "mixed languages").
   • Mixed languages are rarer than languages which exhibit a single order across all categories.

One approach would be to say that there is a single "macroparameter" which fixes the position of all heads relative to their complements in one fell swoop, and then admit exceptions on a case-by-case basis. Another approach would be to say that there are as many "microparameters" as there are heads, and that the settings of these parameters somehow cluster in most languages.[5] I will

---

[5] A third approach, which I set aside here, is that of Kayne (1994): deny that linearization is parameterized, arguing instead that H-complement order is universal and that complement-H order must be derived by syntactic movement. Such an account is inconsistent with the fact that linear order seems to play no role in the core syntactic computation or at LF; thus, we do not expect

return to this choice momentarily, but I would first like us to consider how, regardless of whether one picks the macro or micro option, such a parameter could be formalized. How is it possible to explain the statistical regularities while still admitting exceptions?

Along with authors such as Boeckx (forthcoming *a*), Richards (2008), and Fujita (2007), I view the original conception of parameters as a switchboard— with the switches and their possible settings constituting innate knowledge— as unrealistic because it attributes so much to UG, against the Minimalist ideal of approaching UG from the bottom up:[6] "acquisition theories under a [traditional Principles and Parameters] approach ... ascribe remarkable bio- logical redundancy to UG, for the brain must contain a number of parametric variations that are to be eliminated (i.e. unexpressed as an I-language) in the end" (Fujita 2007: 88). M. Richards (2004 et seq.) argues instead that variation in word order results from *underdetermination*: there is only the PF-interface requirement that the head and complement must end up in *some* linear order, and both options for doing so are exploited cross-linguistically. In order to account for the fact that there can also be variation in head-complement order within a language, but mixed languages are rarer than ones which obey the same order across all heads, Roberts and Holmberg (2009) propose that learners are conservative in a specific way: they first determine whether *v* comes before or after its complement, then extend this value to other heads, unless and until they receive evidence to the contrary. In this fashion, they resolve the tension between the coarse-grained macroparametric approach, which is overly restrictive, and the highly specific microparametric approach, which fails to account for the scarcity of mixed languages.

This combination of underdetermination plus learning biases is certainly a part of the picture when it comes to phonological variation as well. This is essentially the core of the substance-free view: Universal Grammar provides only the barest of templates—in the manifestation proposed here, SEARCH, COPY, and DELETE—and the specifics must be filled in by the learner on the basis of the primary linguistic data. To make it more concrete, UG provides an algorithm of the type:

(182)   Identify αF on γ_i and assign αF to s_i if the set of conditions C on γ_i are satisfied

---

linear order outside phonology. See Chomsky (1995*b*) *inter alia* for discussion. Yet another approach, that of Fukui and Takano (1998), takes complement-H order to be universal, with H-complement order derived by head movement. Again, I will not discuss this option further.

[6] See Lasnik and Lohndal (2010) for an excellent overview of Principles and Parameters theory from its inception to the present day.

But such statements do not refer to any features in particular—or indeed to phonology at all, if the variables can stand for any objects, not just phonological ones. That is, I contend that UG does not contain specific statements such as:

(183)   Identify [αROUND] on γ_i and assign [αROUND] to s_i if γ is [−BACK].

This runs counter to the mainstream, since it precludes markedness from taking an active role in phonological explanation (recall Ch. 2); there is nothing to prevent a learner from acquiring an unnatural rule—final voicing instead of final devoicing, for example—if there is sufficient evidence for it.

Nevertheless, even if there are no specific statements such as (183) in UG, a Kirghiz child must learn that statement in order to perform the vowel harmony in his language correctly. This means there is quite a lot of room for error, as is particularly clear when we probe the margins of speakers' intuitions. One of my favorite examples comes from the investigation of shm-reduplication undertaken by Nevins and Vaux (2003). When presented with simple words, speakers typically agree on the shm-reduplicated form of a word: *table-shmable, easy-shmeasy*, and so on. This pattern conforms to the schema:

(184)   a. Σ (string in the active workspace): # → f → a → n → c → y → %

  b. s (initiator of SEARCH): s_i → sh → m → s_j

  c. γ (target of SEARCH): γ_i = First X; γ_j = First V

  d. δ (direction of SEARCH): δ_i = L; δ_j = R

  e. β (beginning point of SEARCH): β_i = %; β_j = #

This creates exactly what we need for these simple cases:

(185)   # → f → a → n → c → y → %

m ← sh

But there are a number of generalizations which may be made on the basis of simply hearing tokens such as *fancy-shmancy* which are massively ambiguous. For example, one learner might hypothesize that the reduplication begins at the first vowel of the word, thus arriving upon the schema shown above, while another might think that the reduplication begins at the first stressed vowel. Upon testing a wider range of words, a range of variation is observed:

(186)   Variation by anchor point in shm-reduplication (modified from Nevins and Vaux 2003)

a. Reduplicate first syllable vs. stressed syllable
   Obscene shmobscene vs. *obscene obshmene*

b. Full reduplication vs. reduplication beginning with *shm* at stress
   Confusion conshmusion vs. *confusion shmusion*

c. Target material in first consonant vs. first onset
   Breakfast shmreakfast vs. *breakfast shmeakfast*

All these patterns are generable using SEARCH and COPY, but the schemata necessary to generate some of them are more complicated than others. For example, consider the case of *confusion-conshmusion*. This would require the following loops to be established:

(187) $\# \to c \to o \to n \to f \to u \rightleftharpoons s \to i \to o \to n \to \%$

                    sh $\to$ m

Note here that there is also a critical ordering for (n, sh) and (n, f): the latter has to be *lower priority* than the former (or else the result would be *conshmusion-confusion*), which runs counter to the principle that new precedence relations are always added to the top of the queue. This may be an option only available in language games like this one, which are widely acknowledged to "extend, modify, or exaggerate recognizable natural language processes" (Bagemihl 1989: 492).

Nevins (2010), building on Bagemihl (1989), provides another set of examples from ludlings (language games) which involve the reordering of syllables. The genre of games in question provides a useful illustration of ambiguity. For example, consider a game which turns a string $\sigma_1\sigma_2$ into $\sigma_2\sigma_1$. This pattern is consistent with a number of different analyses, at least five of which are attested ludlings:

(188)   Extensions of disyllabic inversion in ludlings (modified from Nevins 2010)

a. Move first σ to end   Fula: *pii.roo.wal* $\to$ *roo.wal.pii*
b. Move final σ to beginning Tagalog: *ka.ma.tis* $\to$ *tis.ka.ma*
c. Transpose first two σ Marquesan: *nu.ku.hi.va*
                                     $\to$ *ku.nu.hi.va*
d. Transpose final and penult σ Luchazi: *ya.mu.nu.kwe*
                                        $\to$ *ya.mu.kwe.nu*
e. Invert order of all σ Saramaccan: *va.li.si* $\to$ *si.li.va*

Even despite the apparent ability of ludlings to go beyond the range of normal linguistic operations, the range of hypotheses which learners construct is nevertheless constrained, as Nevins and Endress (2007) show. They created a controlled poverty-of-stimulus situation by training subjects on a rule that inverted three CV syllables, $\sigma_1\sigma_2\sigma_3 \rightarrow \sigma_3\sigma_2\sigma_1$. (Note that this reversal pattern is unattested in natural language metathesis processes; see Halle 2008.) Such a rule is consistent with at least four possible analyses which cannot be disambiguated based on trisyllabic data, but each hypothesis makes a unique prediction when it comes to tetrasyllabic forms, as shown:

(189)   a. Invert the order of syllables: 1234 → 4321

       b. Exchange the first and last syllables: 1234 → 4231

       c. Exchange the final and antepenultimate syllable: 1234 → 1432

       d. Exchange every other syllable: 1234 → 3412

The subjects of Nevins and Endress's study were asked during the training phase of the experiment to listen to a "Martian rite" which involved one synthesized voice (the "chief Martian") producing the original trisyllabic sequence (123) and a second voice (the "subordinate Martian") repeating back the inverted sequence (321). In the test phase, they again heard both Martian voices, this time with tetrasyllabic sequences, and were asked to rate on a scale of 1–9 whether the subordinate Martian had performed the rite correctly. Subjects rated the (a) and (b) transformations (1234 → 4321 and 4231, respectively) significantly higher than the (c) and (d) transformations (1432 and 3412, respectively) and there was no significant difference between their ratings of the (a) and (b) transformations. This is a striking result considering only (a) and (b) are attested in ludlings. The evidence thus converges to suggest that learners consider only hypotheses (a) and (b) and choose between them roughly at chance.

It is not always the case, though, that subjects show no preference for one licit variant over another: in the *shm*-reduplication situation described in (186), a survey revealed a very uneven distribution. For example, for the input *breakfast*, 87 percent of subjects preferred *breakfast shmeakfast* while only 10 percent preferred *breakfast shmreakfast*. And for *obscene*, while roughly the same proportion of respondents preferred *obscene shmobscene* (30%) and *obscene obshmene* (28%), fully 37 percent preferred no output at all. I will resist the temptation here to speculate in the direction of a derivational theory of complexity for *shm*-variation, but the interplay of multiple possible variants along with ineffability raises questions for any theory (see C. Rice 2005 et seq.

for lucid discussion of this issue, centering on ineffability in verbal paradigms in certain dialects of Norwegian).

Though these are admittedly humorous paralinguistic examples, the problem is pervasive throughout phonology. The input is rife with patterns which may be analyzed in multiple ways, with subtle consequences for variation in phonological systems. Such examples also serve to illustrate the fact that the seemingly non-deterministic nature of choosing between extensionally equivalent analyses is not merely an illusory problem encountered only by linguists (and not real children). Here I disagree with Hale and Reiss (2008: 19), who define "The Linguist's Problem" and "The Human's Problem" thus:

(190)   *The Linguist's Problem*: In modeling a mental grammar, a specific, physically instantiated knowledge state, a linguist may be faced with choices which cannot be determined from the available data. Since scientific models are always somewhat incomplete, this should be seen as a normal state of affairs. However, it should not be assumed that the indeterminacy can never be overcome more data may be forthcoming or indirect forms of reasoning may be applied.

(191)   *The Human's Problem*: Since the learner acquires *some* particular grammar, he or she must have an algorithm for selecting specific representations and rules among a range of extensionally equivalent ones. We assume a deterministic learning algorithm, so that the learner is not faced with a choice, in any meaningful sense—the choice is part of the Linguist's Problem.

This belies the fact that children learning language are, in a sense, little scientists. They cannot wait an infinite amount of time for data which may or may not be forthcoming, and there is no reason (other than idealization) to suggest that "indirect forms of reasoning" must be deterministic, or that they guarantee the correct learning result. Roberts (2007: §2.1) discusses this issue at length, following Andersen (1973) in arguing that linguistic change results from flawed logic employed during acquisition, namely abduction. I summarize the differences between abduction and other forms of reasoning:

(192)   Modes of reasoning (adapted from Roberts (2007: 123–4))

    a. **Deduction**: law + case → result
       All men are mortal (law); Socrates is a man (case)
       ∴ Socrates is mortal (result)

    b. **Induction**: case + result → law
       Men (cases) eventually die (result)
       ∴ all men are mortal (law)

c. **Abduction:** law + result → case
   Socrates is mortal (result); all men are mortal (law)
   ∴ Socrates is a man (case)

It is necessary to learn through abduction since the child only has access to the output of a grammar, not the grammar itself. I schematize this in this diagram, adapted from Andersen (1973: 767):

(193)

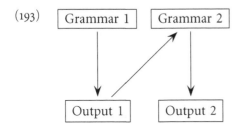

From this example it should be clear that abductive reasoning is particularly susceptible to converse error, or affirming the consequent. (That is, just because "If P, then Q" holds and Q is true, it does not mean that P is also true.) However, deduction is also subject to the fallacy of converse accident (destroying the exception), and induction can also lead to hasty generalizations. The result of such overgeneralizations is another hallmark of child language (think of common child errors such as "goed" rather than "went" or "foots" instead of "feet"). Note further that, although induction serves as a check on abductive errors, nevertheless induction cannot occur without prior abduction: "the mere process of joining one particular with another as result and case—the procedure which is usually called 'induction'—implies the previous existence of a hypothesis, viz. that the two particulars may belong together as case and result. In this way abduction necessarily precedes induction" (ibid. 775 n. 12).

Language acquirers organize and analyze input (the Second Factor, experience) using tools—including the above, potentially faulty, modes of reasoning—provided for them by the First and Third Factors; these heuristics are demonstrably *not* deterministic, as the variation uncovered by studies such as Nevins and Endress's make clear. Unfortunately, when it comes to identifying the biases which urge learners toward one analysis or another, we are only beginning to scratch the surface. Concerning the ambiguity in reduplication/affixation patterns discussed earlier in this section, Raimy (2009) proposes two biases which speak specifically to this issue:

(194)   Biases for reduplicative learning (Raimy 2009: 397)

a. *Be conservative:* favor anchor points with more general parameter settings.

Placement:	at	>	before/after
Plane:	x-tier	>	metrical/syllable/consonantal
Target:	plain	>	stressed (head)/consonant

b. *Be different:* if the anchor points, X and Y, that define a precedence link are not identical (X = Y), then favor pairs of anchor points that are distinct with respect to (a).

The first principle, *be conservative*, is easily translatable into the terms of the theory which I advocated in Chapter 5, and indeed this theory permits collapsing two of the principle's conditions:

(195)   *Be conservative* (revised version)

   a. Avoid subsidiary SEARCH.

   b. Prefer $\gamma = X$ over $\gamma = \{C, V\}$

Be conservative also potentially yields a rubric by which to measure the likelihood of a given analysis—or at least, if the principle is correct, its predictions ought to align with the frequencies with which various analyses are chosen for an ambiguous pattern, all else being equal. Raimy (2009: 397) invites us to consider the hypothetical case of *tago → tago-tago*, which can be analyzed in any of the following ways[7] (I have translated the anchor point descriptors from Raimy's system to the one from Ch. 5 of the present work):

(196)   # → t → a → g → o → %

   a. Anchor point descriptors for /t/

      i. First segment (from the left)

      ii. First consonant (from the left)

      iii. First vowel (from the left) + subsidiary SEARCH for the first segment (to the left)

   b. Anchor point descriptors for /o/

      i. First segment (from the right)

      ii. First vowel (from the right)

---

[7] Among others: /t/ could be the second consonant counting from the right, /o/ could be the second vowel counting from the left, and so on. Allowing subsidiary SEARCH for elements other than "first X" would allow for constructing even more hypotheses.

    iii. First consonant (from the right) + subsidiary SEARCH for the first segment (to the right)

An ordering of hypotheses, from most preferred (197a) to least preferred (197d), emerges when *be conservative* is applied to these options. Again, I have translated the list which Raimy (2009: 398) provides into terms which are more familiar from Chapter 5.[8]

(197) a. First segment (from the right) → First segment (from the left)

    b. • First segment (from the right) → first consonant (from the left)
        • First vowel (from the right) → first segment (from the left)

    c. • First vowel (from the right) → first consonant (from the left)
        • First segment (from the right) → first vowel (from the left) + subsidiary SEARCH for the first segment (to the left)
        • First consonant (from the right) + subsidiary SEARCH for the first segment (to the right) → first segment (from the left)

    d. • First vowel (from the right) → first vowel (from the left) + subsidiary SEARCH for the first segment (to the left)
        • First consonant (from the right) + subsidiary SEARCH for the first segment (to the right) → first consonant (from the left)

    e. First consonant (from the right) + subsidiary SEARCH for the first segment (to the right) → first vowel (from the left) + subsidiary SEARCH for the first segment (to the left)

Whether this ordering of hypotheses matches with the range of hypotheses made by language learners is, of course, an empirical question which ought to be put to the experimental test. It seems quite plausible, at the very least, that hypothesis (197a) is entertained quite frequently while (197e) is rarely, if ever, considered. Applying (197e) to a case like *spry*[9] would yield /spra-ra-i/ by the following:

(198) # s → p → r ⇄ a → i → %

    The status of *be different* as a principle of data analysis is less clear. It is easy to see what this principle means in practice, but it is not obvious that

[8] I also recognize one more distinction than Raimy, between the least and next-to-least preferred analyses, since the former requires two subsidiary searches while the two patterns which fall under the latter require only one.

[9] Assuming underlying /sprai/. Assuming underlying /spraj/ would potentially be problematic, since the subsidiary SEARCH for the first anchor point would fail: there is no segment to the right of the last consonant. This could yield /spraj-raj/ or perhaps even lead to ineffability for all consonant-final words.

it is a necessary or desirable bias from an empirical point of view. Raimy (2009: 397) states that *be different* "can be understood as … similar to the Obligatory Contour Principle, where the learner knows that sequences of extremely similar but not identical elements are generally disfavored." This appears to give the wrong result for total reduplication, which is the most common type (Moravcsik 1978). A reduplicative pattern like *tago* → *tago-tago* is formally quite ambiguous, as we noted above, and *be conservative* favors the analysis which produces total reduplication for all input forms. *Be different*, in contrast, favors literally every combination of parameters *except* the correct one, assuming that the two anchors taking different values for the direction (δ) parameter does not count as being "different" in the relevant sense (as Raimy's formulation of *be different* would suggest, since it refers back to the clauses in the original formulation of *be conservative*, which are silent concerning his Edge parameter, which encodes direction). And if directionality were relevant, the principle would fail to have utility, since all the possible analyses would satisfy it: all the descriptors of /t/ involve searches to the right while all the descriptors of /o/ involve searches to the left.

For infixation, *be different* is also of dubious import. Regardless of the identity of the first anchor point (γ_i) that is selected, nevertheless the second anchor point (γ_j) needs to be "first X." *Be different* would disfavor such an analysis if the first anchor selects X. In Samuels (2010d) I observe that infixation patterns tend to select for a particular consonantal or vocalic position, and in fact there do not appear to be any cases of infixation after the first segment, before the last segment, or around either the second or penult segments (the only segment-based parameter settings which are formulable in my system). For this reason, the anchor points for infixation will always satisfy *be different*. I therefore reject this principle, though I accept the revised version of *be conservative* stated above in (195).

Much work remains to be done in investigating analytic bias, particularly in phonology. So far, it is apparent that biases in phonological learning such as *be conservative* stand alongside a number of analytical tendencies which have been uncovered in other linguistic domains, such as the principle of conservativity in head-complement linearization proposed by Roberts and Holmberg (2009) and discussed earlier in this chapter, the whole object bias (when determining the referent of a new word, assume the label refers to a whole entity) and the mutual exclusivity bias (assume that each object has one and only one label); see Markman (1990). Investigations with the aim of uncovering other biases involved in the acquisition of phonological patterns would lead to improved understanding of the role of underdetermination and hypothesis-formation in phonological variation, both across time and across speakers.

6.6 Phonologization: Diachrony Revisited

There is a good reason why linguistic variation is often treated in works with a diachronic bent: for example, in *The Handbook of Language Variation & Change* (Chambers, Trudgill, and Schilling-Estes 2002). The observation that "historical change is variation in time" (Roberts 2007: 7) dates back to the Neogrammarians, most notably Hermann Paul (Paul 1880). This brings us full circle to the discussion of Evolutionary Phonology in Chapter 2, which I will briefly revisit in this section. In this vein, I would like to discuss "phonologization," or the birth of a phonological rule from a previously purely phonetic phenomenon.[10] Hale (2007: 110 ff.) gives a thorough discussion of phonologization based on the example of vowel nasalization in English, which I will recap here.

It is well known that, across languages, vowels before nasal consonants tend to be a bit nasalized. This is assumed to be an automatic process, stemming from properties of our articulatory system. As Ortony (1993: 44–5) writes,

> the tendency toward nasalization is universal. But is it a *linguistic* universal? I think not. An accurate ballistic description of the organs of speech, and particularly of the tongue and velum, would predict allegro nasalization *whether there was speech or not*. It seems, therefore, to be a grave error to write a specifically linguistic universal nasalization rule or rule schema, as Chomsky and Halle's (1968) do. There is, to be sure, a universal tendency toward vowel nasalization, but it is no more a reflection of our specifically linguistic makeup than the fact that people will stumble if they dance the polka too fast is a fact about our specifically terpsichorean abilities.

Nevertheless, it is also the case that English speakers nasalize vowels before nasal consonants more than the usual amount. Phonologists conclude from this that there is a language-specific phonological rule of nasalization which is operative in English. How did it come to be so? To paraphrase Hale (2007: 111), it is because learners of English at some stage misinterpreted the automatic, universal nasalization as being the result of an explicit command to the articulatory system—and they constructed a phonological rule to implement it (see also Bermúdez-Otero 2010 on "rule scattering"). This shift from phonetic tendency to phonological rule is a prime case of phonologization. It is interesting to note here that, though phonologization and grammaticalization (the change of a lexical item to a grammatical one; for instance, from a verb to a modal) are often viewed as being parallel to one another, phonologization goes against Faarlund's (2008: 234) proposed condition on

---

[10] Andersen (2008) expands this notion beyond phonology to any instance of an element entering a grammatical paradigm, which he calls "grammation."

acquisition, namely that it is much more common for a grammatical element to be ignored and omitted by a learner than for a new element to be added, which he takes to explain the unidirectional, reductive character of grammaticalization.

Of course, the next thing the curious reader will want to know is *why* phonologization happens, and why all languages have not become like English as far as nasalization and hundreds of other phonetic tendencies are concerned. Here the story is much less clear, since it is seldom possible to identify either necessary or sufficient conditions for a given change. Anyone wishing to answer this question immediately runs up against three problems identified by Coseriu (1958): the "rational" problem of why languages must change, the "general" problem of identifying the conditions under which certain changes occur, and the "historical" problem of explaining changes that have already taken place. To this list, Weinreich, Labov, and Herzog (1968) add the "actuation" problem: why does a particular change occur in one language at a given time, but not in other languages with the same feature, or in the same language at a different time? Lass (1976) calls attention to yet another question, the "inception" problem of determining the initial impetus for a given linguistic change. These five problems are little discussed in the generative literature (though see Lightfoot 1999, 2006), but they constitute one of the main avenues of inquiry in historical linguistics. Uncovering the factors and mechanisms behind them—in phonology as well as morphology, syntax, and semantics— has proven quite difficult indeed. After all, there is no reason in principle why a child cannot learn the *exact same* grammar as his father, since that grammar was obviously itself learnable. The difference must, of course, be attributed to an interplay of learning principles (be they specific to language or not) with the unique linguistic experience of each child.

It bears repeating that variation, and the changes which give rise to variation, are constrained only by the range of possible synchronic grammars allowed by UG. That is to say, there is no such thing as a diachronic constraint (Lightfoot 1979; Lohndal 2009*b*), as should be obvious[11]—how would one even formulate such a constraint, and in whose mind could it exist?— given that change is simply the acquisition of an i-language differing from the one that produced the input to the learner. As Lightfoot (1979: 391) puts it, "languages are learned and grammars constructed by the individuals of each generation. They do not have racial memories . . . ." Thus, anyone who seeks a

---

[11] But, as Lightfoot (1979: 407) also remarks, "it is nonetheless not the case that a grammar can be changed into *any* other grammar by each successive generation."

deterministic theory of language change is doomed to disappointment: the best we can do is point toward cognitive (though not necessarily or solely linguistic) biases which humans bring to bear on the problem of acquiring a language.

Among these biases is the tendency to seek patterns, or to make inductive generalizations, as I discussed in Chapter 3. This certainly contributes to the prevalence of phonologization in general. Another bias is the Feature-to-segment Mapping Principle, which drives CHANCE-type reanalysis in the Evolutionary Phonology model:

(199) FEATURE-TO-SEGMENT MAPPING PRINCIPLE (Blevins 2004: 152)
In the learning algorithm which allows listeners to interpret the phonetic string as a sequence of segments, a phonetic feature, F_p, whose domain overlaps with other segment-defining phonetic features is assumed to have a unique featural source $/S_F/$ in the phonological representation (where F may be a feature or feature-complex).

Specifically for the nasalization case, the Feature-to-segment Mapping Principle would bias learners in favor of an analysis with an oral vowel followed by a nasal consonant (i.e. automatic nasalization only) or perhaps an underlyingly nasalized vowel and loss of the conditioning consonant (i.e. what happened in several Romance varieties). Remember also that there are several ways in which a listener's analysis of a given signal may come to differ from the speaker's, of which phonologization is just one (below modified from Blevins 2004: 32–3):

(200) Evolutionary Phonology typology of sound change
a. CHANGE: The phonetic signal is *misheard* by the listener due to perceptual similarities of the actual utterance with the perceived utterance.
Example: speaker produces [ampa] for /anpa/; hearer posits /ampa/
b. CHANCE: The phonetic signal is accurately perceived by the listener but is intrinsically phonologically ambiguous, and the listener associates a phonological form with the utterance which differs from the phonological form in the speaker's grammar.
Example: speaker produces [ʔa̰ʔ] for /ʔa/; hearer posits /aʔ/, /ʔaʔ/, /ʔa̰ʔ/, or /a̰/
c. CHOICE: Multiple phonetic signals representing variants of a single phonological form are accurately perceived by the listener, and

due to this variation, the listener acquires a prototype or best exemplar of a phonetic category which differs from that of the speaker; and/or associates a phonological form with the set of variants which differs from the phonological form in the speaker's grammar.

Example: speaker produces [kǎkáta] and [kkáta] for /kakáta/; hearer posits /kkáta/

This can be read not only as a typology of sound change, but also of the sources of phonological variation. Let us revisit the examples of each of the above types of change, this time focusing on the different underlying representations which could exist among the pool of variants.

(201)   a. Input: [ampa]
             Variant 1: /anpa/
             Variant 2: /ampa/

         b. Input: [ʔa̰ʔ]
             Variant 1: /ʔa̰ʔ/
             Variant 2: /ʔa̰ʔ/
             Variant 3: /ʔa/
             Variant 4: /aʔ/
             Variant 5: /a̰/
             Variant 6: /ʔa̰/
             Variant 7: /a̰ʔ/

         c. Input: [kǎkáta] ∼ [kkáta]
             Variant 1: /kakata/
             Variant 2: /kǎkata/
             Variant 3: /kkata/

Even above and beyond the different possibilities for underlying representations, there is also another level of variation when it comes to processes by which these underlying forms and the associated surface forms are related. Take the [ampa] case, for instance: parallel to the case of vowel nasalization, some individuals who posit underlying /anpa/ may also construct a rule of nasal assimilation (i.e. the phonologization option), while others may simply attribute the assimilation to phonetic coarticulation.

Hale and Reiss (2008: 86) provide another means of categorizing ambiguity, which they illustrate with the /s/∼/š/ merger in child speech. There are three ways a child might produce merged output:

(202)

	A		B		C		
	'Sue'	'shoe'	'Sue'	'shoe'	'Sue'	'shoe'	
underlying rep.	s	s	s	š	s	š	
	⇓	⇓	⇓	⇓	⇓	⇓	phonology
grammar output	s	s	s	s	s	š	
	⇓	⇓	⇓	⇓	⇓	⇓	performance
body output	s	s	s	s	s	s	

Situation A, which Hale and Reiss call lexical ambiguity, results from identity in underlying representations. Situation B, structural ambiguity, results from the grammar neutralizing distinct underlying representations. Situation C, production ambiguity, results from the performance system neutralizing a phonological distinction. Looking only at the rightmost column in each situation, A corresponds to /ampa/ → [ampa], B corresponds to the phonological transformation of /anpa/ → [ampa], and C as the purely phonetic transformation of /anpa/ → [ampa]. It is easy to see how variation can proliferate, when there are so many types of ambiguity and so many places where the correct hypothesis is underdetermined: Andersen (1973: 780) notes that 'abductive innovations' which give rise to variation "can be entirely explained as motivated by ambiguities in the corpus of utterances from which the system has been inferred." This highlights the fact that change cannot simply be equated with "unsuccessful" acquisition. A child may succeed in the sense of learning a grammar which matches with the input she receives, but which nevertheless differs from the grammar(s) which produced that input, and which may result in outputs that those other grammars would not produce. Lightfoot (2006: 11) is explicit about the relationship between primary linguistic data and grammars as being many-to-one (two children receiving differing input can converge on the same grammar), but it works both ways: the same ambiguous, impoverished input can provide support for multiple grammars (see also Niyogi and Berwick 1995: 17 on this point).

If I am correct to go along with the Minimalist approach to UG, positing only as much as necessary, then language learners are operating within a hypothesis space which is constrained enough to make induction (and abduction) possible, and which results in language learning which is successful, even if it does not result in a perfect copy of any one grammar in the child's input. Still, particularly given the inherently and massively ambiguous nature of the primary linguistic data, that hypothesis space is also large enough that we should expect a great deal of variation among speakers, and that is exactly what we find.

7

Conclusions

In the present text, I sought the answer to a very open-ended question posed by Chomsky:

> Throughout the modern history of generative grammar, the problem of determining the character of [the faculty of language] has been approached 'from top down': how much must be attributed to UG to account for language acquisition? The [Minimalist Program] seeks to approach the problem 'from bottom up': How little can be attributed to UG while still accounting for the variety of I-languages attained[...]?
>
> (Chomsky 2007: 3)

I first discussed methodological issues which concern my pursuit of an answer to this question, introducing Minimalism, the substance-free approach to phonology, and Evolutionary Phonology, the three major underpinnings of a Galilean research program for phonology that strives to go "beyond explanatory adequacy" (Chomsky 2004) in Chapter 2. The conclusion of this chapter was essentially that, if the goal of a phonological theory is to characterize the properties of possible synchronic phonological systems, the role of diachrony must be factored out: what is *diachronically* possible must be separated from what is *computationally* possible, which is still different from what is *learnable*.

In Chapter 3, I attempted to break phonology into its constituent parts in order to investigate what abilities underlie phonological competence. After taking an inventory of these components, I demonstrated on the basis of behavioral and physiological studies conducted by other researchers on primates, songbirds, and a wide variety of other species that the cognitive abilities necessary for human phonological representations and operations are present in creatures other than *Homo sapiens* (even if not to the same degree) and in domains other than phonology or, indeed, language proper. I therefore rejected the claim made by Pinker and Jackendoff (2005: 212) that "major characteristics of phonology are specific to language (or to language & music), [and] uniquely human," and their conclusion that "phonology represents a major counterexample" to the hypothesis proposed by Hauser, Chomsky, and Fitch (2002), namely that the faculty of language in the narrow sense consists of only recursion and the mapping from narrow syntax to the interfaces. This discussion had two complementary purposes: to give a plausibility argument for the following chapters as a biologically viable theory, and to situate phonology within the faculty of language.

Chapter 4 took us to the syntax-phonology interface, and was mostly concerned with issues of timing (i.e. derivational cyclicity). This chapter provided proof of concept for "phonological derivation by phase" (PDbP), which combines elements of Lexical Phonology (Kiparsky 1982), Distributed Morphology (Halle and Marantz 1993), and Derivation by Phase (Chomsky 2001). PDbP provides for isomorphism between syntactic and phonological domains via the phase system, harking back to the direct reference conception of the syntax–phonology interface (Kaisse 1985; Odden 1990; Cinque 1993). The basis for this theory is the notion that phonology is cyclic, and moreover that this is the *direct consequence* of cyclicity (i.e. phasality) in syntax. Such a theory has numerous benefits, including computational efficiency and the ability to account for large amounts of data which can only be handled by a cyclic model of the grammar.

With this model in place, I presented arguments that the domains of phonological rule application, both above and below the word level, come for free when one assumes Distributed Morphology and a phasal syntax. Specifically, phonological processes and operations are restricted by the Phase Impenetrability Condition. The overarching claim supported in Chapter 4 was that morpheme-level phases can replace Lexical Phonology's hierarchy of strata, and that phrase-level phases can replace the prosodic hierarchy. These arguments were supported with analyses of segmental and suprasegmental processes including several case studies of each. Though the specifics of the model presented in Chapter 4 will surely require change as syntactic theory evolves—such is the nature of an interface theory—I hope that the discussion will stand the test of time, at least as a guide to how one might go about pursuing this type of analysis, and as a skeleton to be fleshed out in the coming years.

In Chapter 5 I turned to the task of defining the representations and operations which, I argue, are at play in narrow phonology and at the syntax–phonology interface. The discussion began with a survey of phonological features, including the issue of underspecification. I argued for a theory of "archiphonemic" underspecification along the lines of Inkelas (1995), as opposed to "radical" or "contrastive" underspecification, and further argued in favor of a distinction between perseverant underspecification, which persists throughout phonological computation, and underspecification which is repaired by application of the SEARCH and COPY operations specified later in the chapter. A significant portion of Chapter 5 was concerned with how segmental and suprasegmental material is organized into strings, and the idea that phonological representations are "flat" or "linearly hierarchical." I engaged in a comparison of phonological syllables and syntactic phrases and argued that the analogies which have been made between these two objects are false. I provided evidence that the properties commonly attributed to syllabic structure can be explained as well or better without positing innate structure supporting discrete syllables in the grammar.

In the second half of the chapter, I began to put these representations to use. I established the formalisms for the repertoire of primitive operations which, I argued, account for all (morpho)phonological processes. These three operations are:

- SEARCH provides a means by which two elements in a phonological string may establish a probe–goal relation.
- COPY takes a single feature value or bundle of feature values from the goal of a SEARCH application and creates a copy of these feature values to the probe.
- DELETE removes an element from the derivation.

I illustrated the application of these operations with analyses of data from domains such as vowel harmony, reduplication, affixation, syncope, tone sandhi, and subtractive morphology, showing that these three parameterized operations yield a restricted typology of possible phonological processes and can achieve the necessary empirical coverage without positing any additional structure to representations or constraints on operations.

The deeper question underlying the talk of linguistic variation in Chapter 6 could be stated as follows: why is there phonology in the first place? Is it possible to have a language without phonology, and what would such a language sound (or look) like? Hyman (2008: 87) invites us to ponder this question, concluding that "It is hard to imagine what a language without a phonology might look like," but it might, in the "extreme characterization," "lack...a fixed inventory of distinctive segments [and] any sequential constraints on segments."

There is one particularly interesting language now being studied in the Negev Desert which may be a real example of a language with no phonology. This is Al-Sayyid Bedouin Sign Language (ABSL), which emerged during the past century among an isolated community with a high percentage of hereditary deafness: out of 3,500 individuals in the community, approximately 100 people across three generations are deaf (Aronoff *et al.* 2008). Wendy Sandler (2008*a, b*), one of the leading experts on this language, has argued that not only does ABSL lack a discernible segment inventory and phonotactic restrictions, thereby meeting Hyman's criteria, it also displays a much higher rate of lexical variation than do other sign languages. Where one would typically expect only a small amount of variation (think *tom[ej]to* ~ *tom[a]to*), instead Sandler finds many more than a handful of signs—and quite common ones at that—with many more than a handful of variants. Furthermore, researchers report an absence of minimal pairs in the language:

> In ABSL, we have as yet not found clear-cut pairs distinguished by a meaningless formational element. We have found some signs with different meanings that are formationally similar to one another, but the difference between them is transparently attributable to iconicity rather than to substitution of meaningless contrastive formational elements.   (Aronoff *et al.* 2008: 137)

This supports the conclusion that, particularly among older speakers of ABSL, no true phonological system is in place.[1] It is particularly striking that this lack of phonology correlates with a distinct lack of derivational and inflectional morphology, and that only in the one type of complex words found in ABSL—compounds such as LONG-BEARD+THERE 'Lebanon' and HEAD-SCARF+THERE "Palestinian Authority"—do we see a phonological process, namely assimilation. Note that in the theory of phonological domains which I presented in Chapter 4, this is exactly what is to be expected: no lexical phonology in the absence of morphology.

Putting the extraordinary case of ABSL aside, why do all (other) languages have phonologies, or in other words, why aren't lexical representations simply pronounced the way they are stored? This, again, is a question which is not likely to have an easy answer. When we discussed resolvable underspecification and in particular harmony systems, I hinted at one avenue of explanation, namely that some representations are not memorizable since they depend on information (i.e. a feature specification) from other morphemes. How such situations come to be is a different question, probably rooted in the systematization of phonetic tendencies owing to coarticulation, various properties of the acoustic signal, the limitations of our articulatory apparatus, and so forth, as we touched on in Chapter 6. It would take us well into the realm of articulatory and acoustic phonetics to treat this matter thoroughly, and this is not the place to do so. However, stepping back, what I am trying to stress here is that phonological rule systems are created when phonetic tendencies are combined with the overwhelming human drive to find and figure out patterns (recall Ch. 3) and a society in which such patterns are learned and reinforced

---

[1] Speakers do, however, signal prosodic breaks with eyebrow and head/body position changes (Aronoff *et al.* 2008: 140).

by other individuals (or to put it in more biological terms, epigenetically transmitted).

My colleague Dennis Ott has suggested that this view might be character-ized by the slogan "phonetics plus culture equals phonology," and this seems to me a rather accurate label. I will conclude with one final animal study which underscores this point. Fehér *et al.* (2009) set out to test whether zebra finch isolates—birds who were deprived of the proper tutoring from adults during development—could evolve wild-type song over the course of generations in an isolated community (Fitch, Huber, and Bugnyar 2010 also draw parallels between this process, the creation of sign languages, and creolization). The experiment succeeded: the community of isolates, after only three or four generations, spontaneously evolved a song which approached the wild-type song of their species. Out of the chaos of stunted song, a well-behaved system emerged, stemming only from the birds themselves and the input they received from other individuals in the isolate colony. The Al-Sayyid Bedouin Sign Language community is approximately the same age, generationally speaking, as the zebra finch colony. What might we find ABSL phonology looks like in a few more decades? Phonology may not be necessary for language, but all signs point to its development being inevitable once the magical combination of the Three Factors—genetics, primary linguistic data, and principles of good design—are steeped in culture for enough time.

Glossary

Affix A morpheme which modifies a root, either by changing its category (for instance, *-ment* changes a verb to a noun) or by expressing inflectional properties such as person, number, and gender.

Allophone A variant of a phoneme which occurs in a particular context. For example, in English allophones of /t/ include [tʰ] (as in *tap*) and [ɾ] (as in *butter*).

Ambisyllabicity Simultaneous membership of a consonant in two syllables, permitted in certain phonological theories. The /m/ in *lemon* is often considered to be ambisyllabic.

Apocope Loss of a segment at the end of a word.

Assimilation One segment becoming more like another segment (which may, but need not, be adjacent to it).

Autosegmental Phonology A theory of phonology beginning with Goldsmith (1976) which treats phonological objects as consisting of a number of parallel tiers upon each of which only a subset of features is present.

Biolinguistics An interdisciplinary approach to linguistics from a biologically informed perspective.

Coda The consonants in a syllable which come after the nucleus. In some languages, having a coda is non-obligatory or banned altogether.

E-language External language. Language as seen from a social or cultural perspective.

Encyclopedia In Distributed Morphology, the Encyclopedia is the component which lists relations between vocabulary items (or idioms) and their meanings.

Epenthesis Addition of a segment to a word.

Event-Related Potential A brain response evoked by an internal or external stimulus, measurable as a spike in electrical activity on an electroencephalogram (EEG); the magnetic counterpart, an event-related field, can be detected using magnetoencephalography (MEG).

Faculty of Language—Broad Sense All the systems that are recruited for language but need not be unique to it, or to humans.

Faculty of Language—Narrow Sense The subset of the Faculty of Language—Broad Sense that *is* unique to humans and to language.

Feature A component of a segment which typically correlates with an acoustic or articulatory property: for example, a segment which involves air flowing through the nasal cavity bears the [nasal] or [+nasal] feature.

Harmony A property which obligates that certain segments have the same value for a particular feature. For instance, all vowels within a given word may be required to be made with rounded lips.

Head parameter The property of a language that specifies whether the head or complement of a given syntactic phrase is linearized first.

I-language Internal language. Language in an individual, as seen from a cognitive perspective.

Lexicon Loosely speaking, one's mental dictionary. Strictly speaking, in Distributed Morphology there is no lexicon; rather the role of the lexicon is "distributed" across components and the Encyclopedia takes over the basic function of the traditional lexicon.

Linearization The process, which likely proceeds in several stages, which transforms the hierarchical relations expressed in a syntactic tree into the precedence relations expressed in a linear phonological object.

Markedness An abstract measure of how unusual a particular linguistic structure is.

Metathesis Two (or more) segments in a word that switch positions. For example, metathesizing the [sk] sounds in *ask* yields something which sounds like *axe*.

Mismatch Negativity A component of the event-related potential evoked by a deviant stimulus interleaved within a sequence of other stimuli which are similar to one another.

Morpheme The smallest meaningful unit of language. For example, the word *meaningful* consists of the morphemes *mean*, *ing*, and *ful*.

Morphology (The study of) how morphemes are put together into words.

Natural class A group of segments which share one or more phonological features. A natural class typically acts as a group for the purpose of phonological rule application.

Nucleus Typically a vowel, the only mandatory part of a syllable and the part which bears stress. Also called the peak.

Onset The consonants in a syllable which come before the nucleus. In some languages, having an onset is non-obligatory.

PF Phonological Form, the stage at which linguistic objects obtain phonological features. This is often used as a cover term for the syntax/phonology interface.

Phase Impenetrability Condition From Chomsky (2001), a locality condition on syntactic operations which states: "For [ZP Z ... [HP α [H YP]]]:

The domain of H is not accessible to operations at ZP, but only H and its edge."

Phoneme A segment which can bear a meaning contrast. For instance, /b/ and /p/ are phonemes in English because words like *bad* and *pad* are differentiated by the /b/-/p/ distinction.

Phonetics (The study of) the acoustic and articulatory properties of speech sounds.

Phonology (The study of) the systematic relationships among features/segments in a linguistic system, as well as the component which manipulates those objects.

Phonotactics Rules which govern the possible sequential positions and co-occurrence relations among the phonemes in a language.

Prosodic Hierarchy A hierarchy of phonological domains which typically includes at least (from smaller to larger) the word, phonological phrase, intonational phrase, and utterance.

Prosody The stress and intonation pattern of a language.

Reduplication Repetition of all or part of a word. This typically serves a morphological function, for instance to indicate plurality.

Segment A bundle of features which acts as a discrete phonological unit; all (but not only all) the phonemes in a language are segments.

Sonority A property difficult to define which correlates roughly with the loudness or "singability" of a sound. Among the most sonorous sounds are vowels, while the least sonorous are stops.

Sonority Sequencing Generalization Also called the Sonority Sequencing Principle, the idea that the segments in a syllable should rise through the onset to the nucleus.

Spell-out The process by which a syntactic object becomes a phonological one. Sometimes used to refer only to the stage of this process during which phonological content is added.

Subtractive morphology A rare process in which a morphological function is indicated by deleting part of a word. In other words, when a more semantically complex notion bears a phonologically smaller form than a less semantically complex notion built off the same root.

Suprasegmental Dealing with properties such as stress and tone.

Syncope Loss of a segment in the middle of a word.

Syntax Narrowly construed, (the study of) the structures of language at the sentential level. More broadly, simply the computational/combinatoric properties of a system which need not even be linguistic.

Underspecification When a segment does not bear values for all possible features.

Universal Grammar The initial state of the language faculty or acquisition device with which human children are innately endowed.

Vocabulary item A Distributed Morphology term for a phonological expression which is inserted in a particular context.

References

Abels, Klaus (2003). 'Successive Cyclicity, Anti-locality, and Adposition Stranding.' Ph.D. thesis, University of Connecticut.

Abney, Steven (1987). 'The English Noun Phrase in its Sentential Aspect.' Ph.D. thesis, MIT, Cambridge, Mass.

Addessi, E., Mancini, A., Crescimbene, L., Padoa-Schioppa, C., and Visalberghi, E. (2008). 'Preference Transitivity and Symbolic Representation in Capuchin Monkeys (*Cebus apella*).' *PLoS ONE*, 3(6): e2414.

Akinlabi, Akinbiyi, and Liberman, Mark (2000). 'The Tonal Phonology of Yoruba Clitics.' In B. Gerlach and J. Grijzenhout (eds.), *Clitics in Phonology, Morphology, and Syntax*. Amsterdam: John Benjamins, 31–62.

Alexiadou, Artemis, and Anagnostopoulou, Elena (1998). 'Parametrizing AGR: Word Order, V-movement, and EPP-checking.' *Natural Language and Linguistic Theory* 16: 491–539.

Andersen, Henning (1973). 'Abductive and Deductive Change.' *Language* 49: 765–93.

—— (2008). 'Grammaticalization in a Speaker-Oriented Theory of Change.' In T. Eythórsson (ed.), *Grammatical Change and Linguistic Theory: The Rosendal Papers*. John Benjamins, Amsterdam: 11–44.

Anderson, John M. (2006). 'Structural Analogy and Universal Grammar.' *Lingua* 116: 601–33.

Anderson, Stephen R. (1981). 'Why Phonology Isn't "Natural".' *Linguistic Inquiry* 12(4): 493–539.

—— (1985). *Phonology in the Twentieth Century: Theories of Rules and Theories of Representations*. Chicago: University of Chicago Press.

—— (2004). *Dr. Dolittle's Delusion: Animals and the Uniqueness of Human Language*. New Haven: Yale University Press.

—— (2009). 'The Logical Structure of Linguistic Theory.' *Language* 84(4): 795–814.

—— and Lightfoot, David W. (2002). *The Language Organ: Linguistics as Cognitive Physiology*. Cambridge: Cambridge University Press.

Aoun, Youssef (1979). 'Is the Syllable or the Supersyllable a Constituent?' *MITWPL* 1: 140–8.

Arad, Maya (2003). 'Locality Constraints on the Interpretation of Roots: The Case of Hebrew Denominal Verbs.' *Natural Language and Linguistic Theory* 21: 737–78.

Archangeli, Diana, and Pulleyblank, Douglas (1994). *Grounded Phonology*. Cambridge, Mass.: MIT.

Aronoff, Mark (1976). *Word Formation in Generative Grammar*. Cambridge, Mass.: MIT.

—— Meir, Irit, Padden, Carol A., and Sandler, Wendy (2008). 'The Roots of Linguistic Organization in a New Language.' *Interaction Studies*, 9(1): 133–53.

Avery, Peter, and Idsardi, William J. (2001). 'Laryngeal Dimensions, Completion, and Enhancement.' In T. A. Hall (ed.), *Distinctive Feature Theory*. Berlin: Mouton de Gruyter, 41–71.

Baayen, R. Harald, Piepenbrock, Richard, and Gulikers, L. (1993). *The CELEX Lexical Database*. Philadelphia: Linguistic Data Consortium, University of Pennsylvania.

Bachrach, Asaf, and Katzir, Roni (2007). 'Right-Node Raising and Delayed Spellout.' MS, MIT.

—— and Wagner, Michael (2007). 'Syntactically Driven Cyclicity vs. Output–Output Correspondence: The Case of Adjunction in Diminutive Morphology,' MS, MIT and Cornell University.

Bagemihl, Bruce (1989). 'The Crossing Constraint and "Backwards languages".' *Natural Language and Linguistic Theory* 7(4): 481–529.

Baker, Mark C. (2008). 'The Macroparameter in a Microparametric World.' In T. Biberauer (ed.), *The Limits of Syntactic Variation*. Amsterdam: John Benjamins, 351–74.

Baković, Eric (2005). 'Antigemination, Assimilation, and the Determination of Identity.' *Phonology*, 22(3): 279–315.

Battistella, Edwin L. (1996). *The Logic of Markedness*. Oxford: Oxford University Press.

Belin, Pascal (2006). 'Voice Processing in Human and Non-human Primates.' *Philos. Trans. R. Soc. Lond. B. Biol. Sci.* 361: 2091–107.

Bender, B. (1968). 'Marshallese Phonology.' *Oceanic Linguistics* 7: 16–35.

Bermúdez-Otero, Ricardo (2010). 'Morphologically Conditioned Phonetics? Not Proven.' Paper presented at OnLI II, Belfast.

—— (forthcoming). *Stratal Optimality Theory*. Oxford: Oxford University Press.

Best, Catherine, Morrongiello, B., and Robson, R. (1981). 'Perceptual Equivalence of Acoustic Cues in Speech and Nonspeech Perception.' *Perception and Psychophysics* 29(3): 191–211.

Biro, Dora, and Matsuzawa, Tetsuro (1999). 'Numerical Ordering in a Chimpanzee (*Pan troglodytes*): Planning, Executing, and Monitoring. *Journal of Comparative Psychology* 113: 178–85.

Blaho, Sylvia (2008). 'The Syntax of Phonology: A Radically Substance-Free Approach.' Ph.D. thesis, Universitetet i Tromsø, Tromsø.

Blevins, Juliette (1995). 'The Syllable in Phonological Theory.' In J. A. Goldsmith (ed.), *The Handbook of Phonological Theory*. Oxford: Blackwell, 206–44.

—— (2003). 'The Independent Nature of Phonotactic Constraints: An Alternative to Syllable-Based Approaches.' In C. Féry and R. van de Vijver (eds.), *The Syllable in Optimality Theory*. Cambridge: Cambridge University Press, 375–403.

—— (2004). *Evolutionary Phonology*. Cambridge: Cambridge University Press.

—— and Garrett, Andrew (2004). 'The Evolution of Metathesis.' In B. Hayes, R. Kirchner, and D. Steriade (eds.), *Phonetically-Based Phonology*. Cambridge: Cambridge University Press, 117–56.

Bliese, Loren F. (1981). *A Generative Grammar of Afar*. Dallas: Summer Institute of Linguistics.

Bloomfield, Leonard (1934 [1970]). Review of W. Haver's *Handbuch der erklärenden Syntax*. In C. F. Hockett (ed.), *A Leonard Bloomfield Anthology*. Chicago: University of Chicago Press, 280–88.

Bobaljik, Jonathan (2000). 'The Ins and Outs of Contextual Allomorphy.' *University of Maryland Working Papers in Linguistics* 10: 35–71.

Boeckx, Cedric (2006). *Linguistic Minimalism*. Oxford: Oxford University Press.

——(2008). 'Elementary Syntactic Structures: A Minimalist Inquiry.' MS, Harvard University.

——(2010*a*). 'Defeating Lexicocentrism: Outline of *Elementary Syntactic Structures, Part a.*' MS, ICREA/Universitat Autònoma de Barcelona.

——(2010*b*). 'Linguistic Minimalism.' In B. Heine and H. Narrog (eds.), *The Oxford Handbook of Linguistic Analysis*. Oxford: Oxford University Press, 485–506.

——(2010*c*). 'What Principles and Parameters Got Wrong.' MS, ICREA/Universitat Autònoma de Barcelona.

——(forthcoming *a*). 'Approaching Parameters from Below.' In A. M. Di Sciullo and C. Boeckx (eds.), *Biolinguistic Approaches to Language Evolution and Variation* Oxford: Oxford University Press.

——(forthcoming *b*). 'Some Reflections on Darwin's Problem in the Context of Cartesian Biolinguistics.' In A. M. Di Sciullo and C. Aguero (eds.), *Biolinguistic Investigations*. Cambridge, Mass.: MIT.

——and Grohmann, Kleanthes K. (2007). The *Biolinguistics* Manifesto. *Biolinguistics* 1(1): 1–8.

——and Piattelli-Palmarini, Massimo (2005). 'Language as a Natural Object, Linguistics as a Natural Science.' *Linguistic Review* 22: 447–66.

Bolhuis, Johan J., Okanoya, Kazuo, and Scharff, Constance (2010). 'Twitter Evolution: Converging Mechanisms in Birdsong and Human Speech.' *Nature Reviews: Neuroscience* 11: 747–59.

Borer, Hagit (1984). *Parametric Syntax: Case Studies in Semitic and Romance Languages*. Dordrecht: Foris.

——(2009). 'Roots and Categories.' Paper presented at the 19th Colloquium on Generative Grammar, Vitoria-Gasteiz.

Bošković, Željko (2005). 'On the Locality of Left Branch Extraction and the Structure of NP.' *Studia Linguistica* 59: 1–45.

——and Lasnik, Howard (eds.) (2007). *Minimalist Syntax: The Essential Readings*. Oxford: Blackwell.

Brame, Michael (1972). 'On the Abstractness of Phonology: Maltese *'ain.*' In M. Brame (ed.), *Contributions to Generative Phonology*. Austin: University of Texas Press.

Brannon, E. M., and Terrace, H. S. (1998). 'Ordering of the Numerosities 1 to 9 by Monkeys.' *Science* 282: 746–49.

————(2000). 'Representation of the Numerosities 1–9 by Rhesus Macaques (*Macaca mulatta*).' *Journal of Experimental Psychology: Animal Behavior Processes*, 26(1): 31–49.

Brannon, E. M., Wusthoff, Courtney J., Gallistel, C.R., and Gibbon, John (2001). 'Numerical Subtraction in the Pigeon: Evidence for a Linear Subjective Number Scale.' *Psychological Science* 12: 238–43.

Brentari, Diane (1998). *A Prosodic Model of Sign Language Phonology*. Cambridge, Mass.: MIT.

Bresnan, Joan (1971). 'Sentence Stress and Syntactic Transformations.' *Language* 47: 257–81.

Brody, Michael, and Szabolcsi, Anna (2003). 'Overt Scope in Hungarian.' *Syntax* 6(1): 19–51.

Bromberger, Sylvain, and Halle, Morris (1989). 'Why Phonology is Different.' In A. Kasher (ed.), *The Chomskyan Turn*. Oxford: Blackwell, 56–77.

Brosch, Michael, Selezneva, Elena, Bucks, C., and Scheich, Henning (2004). 'Macaque Monkeys Discriminate Pitch Relationships.' *Cognition* 91: 259–72.

——, Selezneva, Elena, and Scheich, Henning (2005). 'Nonauditory Events of a Behavioral Procedure Activate Auditory Cortex of Highly Trained Monkeys.' *Journal of Neuroscience* 25(29): 6797–806.

Broselow, Ellen (1983). 'Salish Double Reduplications: Subjacency in Morphology.' *Natural Language and Linguistic Theory* 1(3): 317–46.

—— (1984). 'Default Consonants in Amharic Morphology.' *MITWPL* 7: 15–31.

Brown, Charles H., and Sinnott, Joan M. (2006). 'Cross-species Comparisons of Vocal Perception.' In S. Greenberg and W. A. Ainsworth (eds.), *Listening to Speech: An Auditory Perspective*. Mahwah, NJ: Lawrence Erlbaum Associates, 183–201.

Brown, J. C., and Golston, Chris (2004). 'The Evolution of Hierarchical Structure in Language.' In *Proceedings of BLS 30*, 13–22.

Brunelle, Marc (2008). 'Speaker Control in the Phonetic Implementation of Cham Registers.' Paper presented at the 3rd Conference on Tone and Intonation in Europe, Lisbon.

Budinger, Eike, and Heil, Peter (2006). 'Anatomy of the Auditory Cortex.' In S. Greenberg and W. A. Ainsworth (eds.), *Listening to Speech: An Auditory Perspective*. Mahwah, NJ: Lawrence Erlbaum Associates, 91–113.

Butler, Johnny (2007). 'The Structure of Temporality and Modality (or, Towards Deriving Something Like a Cinque Hierarchy).' In P. Pica (ed.), *Linguistic Variation Yearbook 2006*. Amsterdam: John Benjamins, 161–201.

Butterworth, Brian (1999). *What Counts: How Every Brain is Hardwired for Math*. New York: Free Press.

Byrne, Richard W. (2007). 'Clues to the Origin of the Human Mind from Primate Observational Field Data.' *Japanese Journal of Animal Psychology*, 57: 1–14.

Cairns, Charles (2009). 'Phonological Representations and the Vaux-Wolfe Proposal.' In E. Raimy and C. Cairns (eds.) *Contemporary views on Architecture and Representations in Phonological Theory*. Cambridge, Mass.: MIT, 145–64.

Cairns, P., Shillcock, R., Chater, N., and Levy, J. (1997). 'Bootstrapping Word Boundaries: A bottom-up Corpus-Based Approach to Speech Segmentation.' *Cognitive Psychology* 33: 111–53.

Calabrese, Andrea (1988). 'Towards a Theory of Phonological Alphabets.' Ph.D. thesis, MIT, Cambridge, Mass.

—— (1995). 'A Constraint-Based Theory of Phonological Markedness and Simplification Procedures.' *Linguistic Inquiry* 26: 373–463.

—— (2005). *Markedness and Economy in a Derivational Model of Phonology.* Berlin: Walter de Gruyter.

—— (2009). 'Markedness Theory versus Phonological Idiosyncrasies in a Realistic Model of Language.' In E. Raimy and C. Cairns (eds.), *Contemporary Views on Architecture and Representations in Phonological Theory.* 261–304. Cambridge, Mass.: MIT.

Carr, Philip (2006). 'Universal Grammar and Syntax/Phonology Parallelisms.' *Lingua* 166: 634–56.

Carstairs-McCarthy, Andrew (1999). *The Origins of Complex Language: An Inquiry into the Evolutionary Beginnings of Sentences, Syllables, and Truth.* Oxford: Oxford University Press.

Chambers, J. K., Trudgill, Peter, and Schilling-Estes, Natalie (eds.) (2002). *The Handbook of Language Variation and Change.* Oxford: Blackwell.

Cheney, Dorothy L., and Seyfarth, Robert M. (2007). *Baboon Metaphysics.* Chicago: University of Chicago Press.

Cho, Young-Mee Yu (1990). 'Syntax and Phrasing in Korean.' In S. Inkelas and D. Zec (eds.), *The Phonology-Syntax Connection.* Chicago: University of Chicago Press, 47–62.

Choi, J. (1992). 'Phonetic Underspecification and Target Interpolation: An Acoustic Study of Marshallese Vocalic Allophony.' *UCLA Working Papers in Phonetics* 82.

Chomsky, Noam (1957). *Syntactic Structures.* The Hague: Mouton.

—— (1959). 'A review of B. F. Skinner's *Verbal Behavior.*' *Language* 35(1): 26–58.

—— (1965). *Aspects of the Theory of Syntax.* Cambridge, Mass.: MIT.

—— (1967). 'Some General Properties of Phonological Rules.' *Language* 43(1): 102–28.

—— (1970). 'Remarks on Nominalization.' In R. Jacobs and P. Rosenbaum (eds.), *Readings in English Transformational Grammar.* Waltham, Mass.: Ginn, 184–221.

—— (1973). 'Conditions on Transformations.' In S. R. Anderson and P. Kiparsky (eds.), *A Festschrift for Morris Halle.* New York: Holt, Rinehart, and Winston, 232–86.

—— (1991). 'Some Notes on the Economy of Derivation.' In R. Freidin (ed.), *Principles and Parameters in Comparative Grammar.* Cambridge, Mass.: MIT, 417–54.

—— (1993). 'A Minimalist Program for Linguistic Theory.' In K. Hale and S. J. Keyser (eds.), *The View from Building 20: Essays in Honor of Sylvain Bromberger.* MIT, Cambridge, Mass.: MIT, 1–49.

—— (1995a). 'Bare Phrase Structure.' In G. Webelhuth (ed.), *Government and Binding Theory and the Minimalist Program.* Oxford: Blackwell, 383–439.

—— (1995b). *The Minimalist Program.* Cambridge, Mass.: MIT.

—— (2000). 'Minimalist Inquiries: The Framework.' In R. Martin, D. Michaels, and J. Uriagereka (eds.), *Step by Step: Essays on Minimalist Syntax in Honor of Howard Lasnik.* Cambridge, Mass.: MIT, 89–155.

Chomsky, Noam (2001). 'Derivation by Phase.' In M. Kenstowicz (ed.), *Ken Hale: A Life in Language*. Cambridge, Mass.: MIT, 1–52.

—— (2002). *On Nature and Language*. Cambridge: Cambridge University Press.

—— (2004). 'Beyond Explanatory Adequacy.' In A. Belletti (ed.), *Structures and Beyond: The Cartography of Syntactic Structures*. Oxford: Oxford University Press, 104–31.

—— (2005). 'Three Factors in Language Design.' *Linguistic Inquiry* 35(1), 1–22.

—— (2007). 'Approaching UG from Below.' In U. Sauerland and H. M. Gärtner (eds.), *Interfaces + Recursion = Language?* Berlin: Mouton de Gruyter, 1–29.

—— (2008). 'On Phases.' In C. Otero, R. Freidin, and M.-L. Zubizarreta (eds.), *Foundational Issues in Linguistic Theory: Essays in Honor of Jean-Roger Vergnaud*. Cambridge, Mass.: MIT, 133–66.

—— (2009). 'Opening Remarks.' In M. Piattelli-Palmarini, J. Uriagereka, and P. Salaburu (eds.), *Of Minds and Language*. Oxford: Oxford University Press, 13–43.

—— (2010). 'Some Simple Evo Devo Theses: How True Might They Be for Language?' In R. K. Larson, V. Déprez, and H. Yamakido (ed.), *The Evolution of Human Language: Biolinguistic Perspectives*. Cambridge: Cambridge University Press, 45–62.

—— and Halle, Morris (1968). '*The Sound Pattern of English*.' New York: Harper and Row.

—— ——, and Lukoff, Fred (1956). 'On Accent and Juncture in English.' In *For Roman Jakobson: Essays on the Occasion of his Sixtieth Birthday*. The Hague: Mouton, 65–80.

Christdas, Pratima (1988). 'The Phonology and Morphology of Tamil.' Ph.D. thesis, Cornell University, Ithaca, NY.

Cinque, Guglielmo (1993). 'A Null Theory of Phrase and Compound Stress.' *Linguistic Inquiry* 24: 239–97.

Citko, Barbara (2005). 'On the Nature of Merge: External Merge, Internal Merge, and Parallel Merge.' *Linguistic Inquiry* 36: 475–496.

Clements, George N. (1978). 'Tone and Syntax in Ewe.' In D. J. Napoli (ed.), *Elements of Tone, Stress, and Intonation*. Washington DC: Georgetown University Press. 21–99.

—— (1985). 'The Geometry of Phonological Features.' *Phonology Yearbook* 2: 225–52.

—— (1987). 'Phonological Feature Representation and the Description of Intrusive Stops.' In *Proceedings of CLS 23* 2: 29–50.

—— (2003). 'Feature Economy in Sound Systems.' *Phonology* 20: 287–333.

—— (2009). 'Does Sonority Have a Phonetic Basis?' In E. Raimy and C. Cairns (eds.), *Contemporary Views on Architecture and Representations in Phonological Theory*. Cambridge, Mass.: MIT, 165–76.

—— and Hume, Elizabeth (1995). 'The Internal Organization of Speech Sounds.' In J. A. Goldsmith (ed.), *The Handbook of Phonological Theory*. Oxford: Blackwell, 245–306.

Coen, Michael Harlan (2006). 'Multimodal Dynamics: Self-supervised Learning in Perceptual and Motor Systems.' Ph.D. thesis, MIT, Cambridge, Mass.

Coetzee, Andries W., and Pater, Joe (forthcoming). 'The Place of Variation in Phono-logical Theory.' In J. A. Goldsmith, J. Riggle, and A. C. Yu (eds.), *The Handbook of Phonological Theory. (2nd ed.)* Oxford: Blackwell.

Cohn, Abigail C. (1990). 'Phonetic and Phonological Rules of Nasalization.' *UCLA Working Papers in Phonetics 76.*

Cole, Jennifer (1995). 'The Cycle in Phonology.' In J. A. Goldsmith (ed.), *The Handbook of Phonological Theory.* Oxford: Blackwell, 70–113.

Compton, Richard, and Pittman, Christine (2007). 'Word-formation by Phase in Inuit.' MS, University of Toronto.

Conway, Christopher M., and Christiansen, Morten H. (2001). 'Sequential Learning in Non-human Primates.' *Trends in Cognitive Sciences* 5(12): 539–46.

Corina, David P., and Sagey, Elizabeth (1989). 'Are Phonological Hierarchies Universal? Evidence from American Sign Language.' In K. de Jong and Y. No (eds.), *Proceedings of the 6th Eastern States Conference on Linguistics*, 73–83.

Coseriu, Eugenio (1958). *Sincronía, diacronía e historia: el problema del cambio lingüístico.* Montevideo: Universidad de la Republica.

Côté, Marie-Hélène (2000). 'Consonant Cluster Phonotactics: A Perceptual Approach.' Ph.D. thesis, MIT, Cambridge, Mass.

Crain, Stephen, and Nakayama, Mineharu (1987). 'Structure Dependence in Children's Language.' *Language* 62: 522–543.

Davis, Henry, Matthewson, Lisa, and Rullmann, Hotze (2009). ' "Out of Control" Marking as Circumstantial Modality in St'at'imcets.' In L. Hogeweg, H. de Hoop, and A. Malchukov (eds.), *Cross-linguistic Semantics of Tense, Aspect, and Modality.* Amsterdam: John Benjamins, 205–44.

de Boer, Bart (2001). *The Origins of Vowel Systems.* Oxford: Oxford University Press.

Dediu, Dan, and Ladd, Robert D. (2007). 'Linguistic Tone is Related to the Popula-tion Frequency of the Adaptive Haplogroups of Two Brain Size Genes, ASPM and Microcephalin.' *Proceedings of the National Academy of Sciences* 104: 10944–9.

Dehaene, Stanislas (1997). *The Number Sense: How the Mind Creates Mathematics.* Oxford: Oxford University Press.

Dehaene-Lambertz, Ghislaine, Dupoux, E., and Gout, A. (2000). 'Electrophysiological Correlates of Phonological Processing: A Cross-linguistic Study.' *Journal of Cognitive Neuroscience* 12(4): 635–47.

de Lacy, Paul (2006). *Markedness: Reduction and Preservation in Phonology.* Cam-bridge: Cambridge University Press.

Dell, François, and Elmedlaoui, Mohammed (2002). *Syllables in Tashlhiyt Berber and in Moroccan Arabic.* Dordrecht: Kluwer.

Demuth, Katherine, and Mmusi, Sheila (1997). 'Presentational Focus and Thematic Structure.' *Journal of African Languages and Linguistics* 18: 1–19.

de Saussure, Ferdinand (1916). *Cours de Linguistique Générale.* Paris: Payot.

Devlin, Keith (2005). *The Math Instinct.* New York: Thunder's Mouth.

Di Sciullo, Anna Maria (2004). 'Morphological Phases.' In *Generative Grammar in a Broader Perspective: The 4th GLOW in Asia*, 113–37.

Di Sciullo, Anna Maria (2005). *Asymmetry in Morphology*. Cambridge, Mass.: MIT.

Dijkstra, Edsger W. (1959). 'A Note on Two problems in Connexion with Graphs.' *Numerische Mathematik* 1: 269–71.

Dobashi, Yoshihito (2003). 'Phonological Phrasing and Syntactic Derivation.' Ph.D. thesis, Cornell University, Ithaca, NY.

Doupe, Allison J., and Kuhl, Patricia K. (1999). 'Birdsong and Human Speech: Common Themes and Mechanisms.' *Annual Review of Neuroscience* 22: 567–631.

Dresher, Elan B. (2003). 'The Contrastive Hierarchy in Phonology.' *Toronto Working Papers in Linguistics* 20: 47–62.

——— (2009). *The Contrastive Hierarchy in Phonology*. Cambridge: Cambridge University Press.

Duanmu, San (2008). *Syllable Structure*. Oxford: Oxford University Press.

Dubinsky, Stanley, and Simango, Sylvester Ron (1996). 'Passive and Stative in Chichewa: Evidence for Modular Distinctions in Grammar.' *Language* 72: 749–81.

Dupoux, E., Kakehi, K., Hirose, Y., Pallier, C., and Mehler, J. (1999). 'Epenthetic Vowels in Japanese: A Perceptual Illusion?' *Journal of Experimental Psychology: Human Perception Performance* 25: 1568–78.

Eimas, P. D., Siqueland, E. D., Jusczyk, Peter W., and Vigorito, J. (1971). 'Speech Perception in Infants.' *Science*, 171: 303–6.

Elbert, T., Pantev, C., Wienbruch, C., Rockstroh, B., and Taub, E. (1995). 'Increased Cortical Representation of the Fingers of the Left Hand in String Players.' *Science* 270: 305–7.

Embick, David (2010). *Localism vs. Globalism in Morphology and Phonology*. Cambridge, Mass.: MIT.

——— and Noyer, Rolf (2001). 'Movement Operations After Syntax.' *Linguistic Inquiry* 32(4): 555–96.

Endress, Ansgar D., Carden, Sarah, Versace, Elisabetta, and Hauser, Marc D. (2009). 'The Apes' Edge: Positional Learning in Chimpanzees and Humans.' *Animal Cognition* 13(3): 483–95.

Epstein, Samuel David, Groat, Erich M., Kawashima, Ruriko, and Kitahara, Hisatsugu (1998). *A Derivational Approach to Syntactic Relations*. Oxford: Oxford University Press.

Everett, Daniel L., and Everett, Karen (1984). 'On the Relevance of Syllable Onsets to Stress Placement.' *Linguistic Inquiry* 15, 705–11.

Faarlund, Jan Terje (2008). 'A Mentalist Interpretation of Grammaticalization Theory.' In T. Eythórsson (ed.), *Grammatical Change and Linguistic Theory: The Rosendal Papers*. Amsterdam: John Benjamins, 221–44.

Fehér, Olga, Wang, Haibin, Saar, Sigal, Mitra, Partha P., and Tchernichovski, Ofer (2009). '*De novo* Establishment of Wild-Type Song Culture in the Zebra Finch.' *Nature* 459(7246): 564–8.

Feigenson, Lisa, and Halberda, Justin (2004). 'Infants Chunk Object Arrays into Sets of Individuals.' *Cognition* 91: 173–90.

Fitch, W. Tecumseh (2005). 'Dancing to Darwin's Tune.' *Nature* 438: 288.

——— (2010). *The Evolution of Language*. Cambridge: Cambridge University Press.

——, Hauser, Marc D., and Chomsky, Noam (2005). 'The Evolution of the Language Faculty: Clarifications and Implications.' *Cognition* 97(2): 179–210.

—— Huber, Ludwig, and Bugnyar, Thomas (2010). 'Social Cognition and the Evolution of Language: Constructing Cognitive Phylogenies.' *Neuron* 65: 795–814.

Fitzpatrick, Justin M. (2006). 'Sources of Multiple Reduplication in Salish and Beyond.' *MIT Working Papers on Endangered and Less Familiar Languages* 7: *Studies in Salishan*, 211–40.

Flack, Kathryn (2009). 'Constraints on Onsets and Codas of Words and Phrases.' *Phonology* 26: 269–302.

Fortuny, Jordi (2008). *The Emergence of Order in Syntax*. Amsterdam: John Benjamins.

—— and Gallego, Ángel J. (2009). 'Introduction: The Minimalist Program and the Concept of Universal Grammar.' *Catalan Journal of Linguistics* 8: 7–15.

Frampton, John (2009). *Distributed Reduplication*. Cambridge, Mass.: MIT.

Frascarelli, Mara (2007). 'Subjects, Topics, and the Interpretation of Referential *pro*.' *Natural Language and Linguistic Theory* 25(4): 691–734.

Freedman, D. J., Riesenhuber, M., Poggio, T., and Miller, E. K. (2001). 'Categorical Perception of Visual Stimuli in the Primate Prefrontal Cortex.' *Science* 291: 312–16.

Freidin, Robert (1999). 'Cyclicity and Minimalism.' In S. D. Epstein and N. Hornstein (eds.), *Working Minimalism*. Cambridge, Mass.: MIT, 95–126.

Frey, Scott H., Bogdanov, Sergei, Smith, Jolinda C., Watrous, Scott, and Breidenbach, Warren C. (2008). 'Chronically Deafferented Sensory Cortex Recovers a Grossly Typical Organization after Allogenic Hand Transplantation.' *Current Biology* 18: 1–5.

Fudge, E. C. (1969). 'Syllables.' *Journal of Linguistics* 5: 253–86.

Fujita, Koji (2007). 'Facing the Logical Problem of Language Evolution.' Review of Jenkins (2004), *Variation and Universals in Biolinguistics*. *English Linguistics* 24(1): 78–108.

—— (2009). 'A Prospect for Evolutionary Adequacy: Merge and the Evolution and Development of Human Language.' *Biolinguistics* 3(2–3): 138–53.

Fukui, Naoki (1995). 'The Principles and Parameters Approach: A Comparative Syntax of English and Japanese.' In M. Shibatani and T. Bynon (eds.), *Approaches to Language Typology*. Oxford: Oxford University Press, 327–72.

—— and Takano, Yuji (1998). 'Symmetry in Syntax: Merge and Demerge.' *Journal of East Asian Linguistics* 7: 27–86.

Gagnon, Michaël (2008). 'On Linearizing Subtractive Morphology.' MS, Concordia University.

—— and Piché, Maxime (2007). 'Principles of Linearization and Subtractive Morphology.' Paper presented at the CUNY Phonology Forum Conference on Precedence Relations, CUNY, 25–26 January.

Gallego, Ángel J. (2008). 'Phases and Variation: Exploring the Second Factor of the Faculty of Language.' MS, Universitat Autònoma de Barcelona.

Gallistel, C. R., and Gelman, Rochel (2005). 'Mathematical Cognition.' In K. Holyoak and R. Morrison (eds.), *The Cambridge Handbook of Thinking and Reasoning*. Cambridge: Cambridge University Press, 559–88.

Gambell, Timothy, and Yang, Charles (2005). 'Word Segmentation: Quick but Not Dirty.' MS, Yale University.

Garrett, Andrew, and Blevins, Juliette (2009). 'Morphophonological Analogy.' In S. Inkelas and K. Hanson (eds.), *The Nature of the Word: Studies in Honor of Paul Kiparsky*. Cambridge, Mass.: MIT, 527–45.

Gehring, W. J. (1998). *Master Control Genes in Development and Evolution: The Homeobox Story*. New Haven: Yale University Press.

Gelman, R., and Gallistel, C. R. (1978). *The Child's Understanding of Number*. Cambridge, Mass.: Harvard University Press.

Gentner, Timothy Q., Fenn, Kimberly M., Margoliash, Daniel, and Nusbaum, Howard C. (2006). 'Recursive Syntactic Pattern Learning by Songbirds.' *Nature* 440: 1204–7.

—— (2010). 'Simple Stimuli, Simple Strategies.' *PNAS* 107: E65.

Ghazanfar, Asif A., Chandrasekaran, Chandramouli, and Logothetis, Nikos K. (2008). 'Interactions Between the Superior Temporal Sulcus and Auditory Cortex Mediate Dynamic Face/Voice Integration in Rhesus Monkeys.' *Journal of Neuroscience* 28(17): 4457–69.

—— Maier, J. X., Hoffman, K. L., and Logothetis, Nikos K. (2005). 'Multisensory Integration of Dynamic Faces and Voices in Rhesus Monkey Auditory Cortex', *Journal of Neuroscience* 67: 580–94.

Ghini, Micro (1993). 'Phi Formation in Italian: A New Proposal.' *Toronto Working Papers in Linguistics* 12(2): 41–78.

Giegerich, Heinz (1992). *English Phonology*. Cambridge: Cambridge University Press.

Gil da Costa, Ricardo, Braun, Allen, Lopes, Marco, Hauser, Marc D., Carson, Richard E., Herscovitch, Peter, and Martin, Alex (2004). 'Toward an Evolutionary Perspective on Conceptual Representation: Species-Specific Calls Activate Visual and Affective Processing Systems in the Macaque.' *Proceedings of the National Academy of Sciences* 101(50): 17516–21.

Gnanadesikan, Amalia (2008). 'Syllables and Syllabaries: What Writing Systems Tell Us about Syllable Structure.' Paper presented at the CUNY Phonology Forum Conference on the Syllable.

Goldsmith, John A. (1976). 'Autosegmental Phonology.' Ph.D. thesis, MIT, Cambridge, Mass.

—— (forthcoming). 'The syllable.' In J. A. Goldsmith, J. Riggle, and A. C. Yu (eds.), *The Handbook of Phonological Theory*. 2nd edn. Oxford: Blackwell.

—— and Larson, Gary (1990). 'Local Modeling and Syllabification.' In *Proceedings of CLS 26 Parasession on the Syllable*, 129–41.

Golston, Chris (2007). 'Variables in Optimality Theory.' In S. Blaho, P. Bye, and M. Krämer (eds.), *Freedom of Analysis?* Berlin: Mouton de Gruyter, 345–72.

Gould, Stephen Jay (1976). 'In Defense of the Analog: A Commentary to N. Hotton.' In R. Masterson, W. Hodos, and H. Jerison (eds.), *Evolution, Brain, and Behavior: Persistent Problems*. New York: Wiley, 175–9.

Goyvaerts, Didier L. (1978). *Aspects of Post-SPE Phonology*. Ghent: E. Story-Scientia.

Greenberg, Joseph H. (1957). 'The Nature and Uses of Linguistic Typologies.' *International Journal of American Linguistics* 23: 68–77.

—— (1978). 'Typology and Cross-linguistic Generalization.' In J. H. Greenberg, C. A. Ferguson, and E. A. Moravcsik (eds.), *Universals of Human Language: Method and Theory*, Stanford: Stanford University Press, 33–59.

Greenfield, Patricia M. (1991). 'Language, Tools, and Brain: The Ontogeny and Phylogeny of Hierarchically Organized Sequential Behavior.' *Behavioral and Brain Sciences* 14: 531–95.

—— (1998). 'Language, Tools, and Brain Revisited.' *Behavioral and Brain Sciences* 21: 159–63.

—— Nelson, Karen, and Saltzmann, Elliot (1972). 'The Development of Rulebound Strategies for Manipulating Seriated Nesting Cups: A Parallel between Action and Grammar.' *Cognitive Psychology* 3: 291–310.

Guenther, Frank H., and Gjaja, Marin N. (1996). 'The Perceptual Magnet Effect as an Emergent Property of Neural Map Formation.' *Journal of the Acoustical Society of America* 100: 1111–21.

Gussmann, Edmund (1988). 'Review of Mohanan (1986), *The Theory of Lexical Phonology.*' *Journal of Linguistics* 24: 232–9.

—— (2002). *Phonology: Analysis and Theory.* Cambridge: Cambridge University Press.

Hale, Mark (2000). 'Marshallese Phonology, the Phonetics–Phonology Interface, and Historical Linguistics.' *The Linguistic Review* 17: 241–57.

—— (2007). *Historical Linguistics.* Oxford: Blackwell.

—— and Kissock, Madelyn (1998). 'Nonphonological Triggers for Renewed Access to Phonetic Perception.' In *Proceedings of GALA 1997*, 229–34.

—— and Reiss, Charles (2000*a*). 'Phonology as Cognition.' In N. Burton-Roberts, P. Carr, and G. Docherty (eds.), *Phonological Knowledge: Conceptual and Empirical Issues.* Oxford: Oxford University Press, 161–84.

—— —— (2000*b*). 'Substance Abuse and Dysfunctionalism: Current Trends in Phonology.' *Linguistic Inquiry* 31(1): 157–69.

—— —— (2008). *The Phonological Enterprise.* Oxford: Oxford University Press.

—— Kissock, Madelyn, and Reiss, Charles (2007). 'Microvariation, Variation, and the Features of Universal Grammar.' *Lingua* 117(4): 645–65.

Hall, Daniel Currie (2007). 'The Role and Representation of Contrast in Phonological Theory.' Ph.D. thesis, University of Toronto.

Halle, Morris (1959). *The Sound Pattern of Russian.* The Hague: Mouton.

—— (1992). 'Phonological Features.' *Natural Language and Linguistic Theory* 1: 91–105.

—— (2002). *From Memory to Speech and Back.* Berlin: Mouton de Gruyter.

—— (2002 [1978]). 'Knowledge Unlearned and Untaught: What Speakers Know about the Sounds of their Language.' In M. Halle, J. Bresnan, and G. A. Miller (eds.), *Linguistic Theory and Psychological Reality.* Cambridge, Mass.: MIT, 294–303. Repr. in Halle (2002).

—— (2005). 'Palatalization/Velar Softening: What It Is and What It Tells Us about the Nature of Language.' *Linguistic Inquiry* 36(1): 23–41.

Halle, Morris (2008). 'Reduplication.' In R. Freidin, C. Otero, and M.-L. Zubizarreta (eds.), *Foundational Issues in Linguistic Theory: Essays in Honor of Jean-Roger Vergnaud*. Cambridge, Mass.: MIT, 325–358.

—— and Marantz, Alec (1993). 'Distributed Morphology and the Pieces of Inflection.' In K. Hale and S. J. Keyser (eds.), *The View from Building 20: Essays in Honor of Sylvain Bromberger*. Cambridge, Mass.: MIT, 111–76.

—— and Vergnaud, Jean-Roger (1987). *An Essay on Stress*. Cambridge, Mass.: MIT.

Han, Chung-Hye, Lidz, Jeffrey, and Musolino, Julien (2007). 'V-raising and Grammar Competition in Korean: Evidence from Negation and Quantifier Scope.' *Linguistic Inquiry* 38(1): 1–47.

Hanks, Patrick (ed.) (1979). *Collins Dictionary of the English Language*. London: Collins.

Harley, Heidi (2009a). 'Roots and Locality.' Paper presented at Universität Stuttgart.

—— (2009b). 'Roots: Identity, Insertion, Idiosyncracies.' Paper presented at the Root Bound workshop, University of Southern California.

Harris, John (1994). *English Sound Structure*. Oxford: Blackwell.

—— (2004). 'Release of the Captive Coda: The Foot as a Domain of Phonetic Interpretation.' In J. Local, R. Ogden, and R. Temple (eds.), *Phonetic Interpretation: Papers in Laboratory Phonology 6*. Cambridge: Cambridge University Press, 103–29.

Haspelmath, Martin (1999). 'Optimality and Diachronic Adaptation.' *Zeitschrift für Sprachwissenschaft* 18(2): 180–205.

—— (2006). 'Against Markedness (and What to Replace It With).' *Journal of Linguistics* 42: 25–70.

Haugen, Einar (1956). 'The Syllable in Linguistic Description.' In M. Halle (ed.), *For Roman Jakobson: Essays on the Occasion of his Sixtieth Birthday*. The Hague: Mouton, 213–21.

Hauser, Marc D. (1996). *The Evolution of Communication*. Cambridge, Mass.: MIT.

—— and Glynn, David D. (2009). 'Can Free-Ranging Rhesus Monkeys (*Macaca mulatta*) Extract Artificially Created Rules Comprised of Natural Vocalizations?' *Journal of Comparative Psychology* 123: 161–7.

—— Carey, Susan, and Hauser, Lillian B. (2000). 'Spontaneous Number Representation in Semi-Free-Ranging Rhesus Monkeys.' In *Proceedings of the Royal Society: Biological Sciences* 267: 829–33.

—— Chomsky, Noam, and Fitch, W. Tecumseh (2002). 'The Faculty of Language: What Is It, Who Has It, and How Did It Evolve?' *Science* 298: 1569–79.

Hay, Jessica (2005). 'How Auditory Discontinuities and Linguistic Experience Affect the Perception of Speech and Non-speech in English- and Spanish-Speaking Listeners.' Ph.D. thesis, University of Texas, Austin.

Hayes, Bruce (1989). 'Compensatory Lengthening in Moraic Phonology.' *Linguistic Inquiry* 20: 253–306.

—— Kirchner, Robert, and Steriade, Donca (eds.) (2004). *Phonetically-Based Phonology*. Cambridge: Cambridge University Press.

—— and Steriade, Donca (2004). 'Introduction: The Phonetic Bases of Phonological Markedness. In B. Hayes, R. Kirchner, and D. Steriade (eds.), *Phonetically Based Phonology*. Cambridge: Cambridge University Press, 1–33.

Heinz, Jeffrey N. (2007). 'Inductive Learning of Phonotactic Patterns.' Ph.D. thesis, University of California, Los Angeles.

Hooper, Joan Bybee (1972). 'The Syllable in Phonological Theory.' *Language* 48(3): 525–40.

Hornstein, Norbert (2001). *Move! A Minimalist Theory of Construal*. Oxford: Blackwell.

—— (2005). 'What Do Labels Do? Some Thoughts on the Endocentric Roots of Recursion and Movement.' MS, University of Maryland.

—— (2009). *A Theory of Syntax: Minimal Operations and Universal Grammar*. Cambridge: Cambridge University Press.

—— and Boeckx, Cedric (2009). 'Approaching Universals from Below: I-universals in Light of a Minimalist Program for Linguistic Theory.' In M. H. Christiansen, C. Collins, and S. Edelman (eds.), *Language Universals*. Oxford: Oxford University Press, 79–98.

—— Nunes, Jairo, and Grohmann, Kleanthes K. (2005). *Understanding Minimalism*. Cambridge: Cambridge University Press.

Howard, Irwin (1972). 'A Directional Theory of Rule Application in Phonology.' Ph.D. thesis, MIT, Cambridge, Mass.

Hume, Elizabeth (2004). 'Deconstructing Markedness: A Predictability-Based Approach.' In *Proceedings of BLS 30*, 182–98.

Hyman, Larry (1975). *Phonology: Theory and Analysis*. New York: Holt, Rinehart, and Winston.

—— (1985). *A Theory of Phonological Weight*. Dordrecht: Foris.

—— (1990). 'Boundary Tonology and the Prosodic Hierarchy.' In S. Inkelas and D. Zec (eds.), *The Phonology–Syntax Connection*. Chicago: University of Chicago Press, 109–26.

—— (2008). 'Universals in Phonology.' *Linguistic Review* 25(1–2): 83–137.

—— and Valinande, Nzamba (1985). 'Globality in the Kinande Tone System.' In D. L. Goyvaerts (ed.), *African Linguistics: Essays in Memory of M.W.K. Semikenke*. Amsterdam: John Benjamins, 239–60.

Idsardi, William J. (2005). 'Poverty of the Stimulus Arguments in Phonology.' MS, University of Delaware.

—— and Raimy, Eric (forthcoming). 'Three Types of Linearization and the Temporal Aspects of Speech.' In T. Biberauer and I. Roberts (eds.), *Principles of Linearization*. Berlin: Mouton de Gruyter.

—— and Shorey, Rachel (2007). 'Unwinding Morphology.' Paper presented at the CUNY Phonology Forum Workshop on Precedence Relations, CUNY, 25–6 January.

Inkelas, Sharon (1990). *Prosodic Constituency in the Lexicon*. New York: Garland.

—— (1995). 'The Consequences of Optimization for Underspecification.' In *Proceedings of NELS 25*, 287–302.

—— and Zec, Draga (1995). 'Syntax–Phonology Interface.' In J. A. Goldsmith (ed.), *The Handbook of Phonological Theory*. Oxford: Blackwell, 535–49.

Ishihara, Shinichiro (2007). 'Major Phrase, Focus Intonation, Multiple Spell-out (MaP, FI, MSO).' *The Linguistic Review* 24: 137–67.

Itô, Junko, and Mester, Armin (2003). 'Lexical and Postlexical Phonology in Optimality Theory: Evidence from Japanese.' In C. Féry and R. van de Vijver (eds.), *The Syllable in Optimality Theory*, Cambridge: Cambridge University Press, 271–303.

—— (2007). 'The Onset of the Prosodic Word.' In S. Parker (ed.), *Phonological Argumentation: Essays on Evidence and Motivation*. London: Equinox.

Jackendoff, Ray, and Pinker, Steven (2005). 'The Nature of the Language Faculty and Its Implications for Evolution of Language (reply to Fitch, Hauser, and Chomsky).' *Cognition* 97(2): 211–25.

Jakobson, Roman (1927 [1962]*a*). 'The Concept of the Sound Law and the Teleological Criterion.' In *Selected Writings I: Phonological Studies*. The Hague: Mouton de Gruyter, 1–3.

—— (1931 [1962]*b*). 'Principes de phonologie historique.' In *Selected Writings I: Phonological Studies*. The Hague: Mouton de Gruyter, 202–20.

—— Fant, C. Gunnar M., and Halle, Morris (1952). *Preliminaries to Speech Analysis: The Distinctive Features and Their Correlates*. Cambridge, Mass.: MIT.

Jensen, J. T. (1977). *Yapese Reference Grammar*. Honolulu: University of Hawaii Press,

Jerne, Niels K. (1985). 'The Generative Grammar of the Immune System.' *Science* 229: 1057–9.

Jespersen, Otto (1904). *Lehrbuch der Phonetik*. Leipzig: Teubner.

Johnson, Douglas C. (1970). 'Formal Aspects of Phonological Representation.' Ph.D. thesis, University of California, Berkeley.

Johnson-Pynn, Julie, Fragaszy, Dorothy M., Hirsh, Elizabeth M., Brakke, Karen E., and Greenfield, Patricia M. (1999). 'Strategies Used to Combine Seriated Cups by Chimpanzees (*Pan troglodytes*), Bonobos (*Pan paniscus*), and Capuchins (*Cebus apella*).' *Journal of Comparative Psychology* 113(2): 137–48.

Jones, Daniel (1950). *The Pronunciation of English*. 3rd edition. Cambridge: Cambridge University Press.

Jun, Sun-Ah (1993). 'The Phonetics and Phonology of Korean Prosody.' Ph.D. thesis, Ohio State University, Columbus.

Jusczyk, Peter W., Houston, D. W., and Newsome, M. (1999). 'The Beginnings of Word Segmentation in English-Learning Infants.' *Cognitive Psychology* 39: 159–207.

Kahn, Daniel (1976). 'Syllable-Based Generalizations in English Phonology.' Ph.D. thesis, MIT, Cambridge, Mass.

Kahnemuyipour, Arsalan (2004). 'The Syntax of Sentential Stress.' Ph.D. thesis, University of Toronto, Toronto.

—— (2009). *The Syntax of Sentential Stress*. Oxford: Oxford University Press.

Kaisse, Ellen (1985). *Connected Speech: The Interaction of Syntax and Phonology*. Orlando: Academic Press.

—— and Hargus, Sharon (eds.) (1993). *Lexical Phonology and Morphology*. San Diego: Academic Press.

Kamali, Beste, and Samuels, Bridget (2008*a*). 'All Non-final Stress Suffixes in Turkish Are Not Created Equal.' Paper presented at the 2nd Mediterranean Syntax Meeting, Istanbul.

—— —— (2008*b*). 'The Syntax of Turkish Pre-stressing Suffixes.' Paper presented at the 3rd Conference on Tone and Intonation in Europe, Lisbon.

Kaplan, Ronald (1987 [1995]). 'Three Seductions of Computational Psycholinguistics.' In M. Dalrymple, R. Kaplan, J. Maxwell, and A. Zaenen (eds.), *Formal Issues in Lexical-Functional Grammar*, Calif. Stanford: CSLI.

Kaufman, E. L., Lord, M. W., Reese, T. W., and Volkmann, J. (1949). 'The Discrimination of Visual Number.' *American Journal of Psychology* 62: 498–525.

Kaye, Jonathan (1989). *Phonology: A Cognitive View*. Hillsdale, NJ: Erlbaum.

Kayne, Richard S. (1994). *The Antisymmetry of Syntax*. Cambridge, Mass.: MIT.

—— (2008). 'Antisymmetry and the Lexicon.' In J. van Craenenbroeck and J. Rooryck (eds.), *Linguistic Variation Yearbook*. Amsterdam: John Benjamins, viii. 1–31.

Kean, Mary-Louise (1974). 'The Strict Cycle in Phonology.' *Linguistic Inquiry*, 5: 179–203.

—— (1975). 'The Theory of Markedness in Generative Grammar.' Ph.D. thesis, MIT, Cambridge, Mass.

Keating, Patricia (1988). 'Underspecification in Phonetics.' *Phonology* 5: 275–92.

Kenstowicz, Michael (1994). *Phonology in Generative Grammar*. Oxford: Blackwell.

Kenyon, John Samuel, and Knott, Thomas Albert (1944). *A Pronouncing Dictionary of American English*. Springfield, Mass.: Merriam.

Kessler, Brett, and Treiman, Rebecca (1997). 'Syllable Structure and the Distribution of Phonemes in English Syllables.' *Journal of Memory and Language* 37: 295–311.

Kim, Yuni (2002). 'Phonological Features: Privative or Equipollent?' A.B. thesis, Harvard University.

Kiparsky, Paul (1968). *How Abstract is Phonology?* Bloomington: Indiana University Linguistics Club.

—— (1982). 'Lexical Phonology and Morphology.' In I. Yang (ed.), *Linguistics in the Morning Calm*. Seoul: Hanshin, 3–91.

—— (1985). 'Some Consequences of Lexical Phonology.' *Phonology Yearbook* 2: 85–138.

—— (2000). 'Opacity and Cyclicity.' *The Linguistic Review* 17, 351–65.

Kisseberth, Charles (1970). 'On the Functional Unity of Phonological Rules.' *Linguistic Inquiry* 1(3): 291–306.

Kitahara, Hisatsugu (2003). 'Acoustic Perception in Human Newborns and Cotton-top Tamarins—Recent Findings and their Implications.' *Reports of the Keio Institute of Cultural and Linguistic Studies* 35: 31–41.

Kluender, Keith R., Lotto, Andrew J., and Holt, Lori L. (2006). 'Contributions of Non-human Animal Models to Understanding Human Speech Perception.' In S. Greenberg and W. A. Ainsworth (eds.), *Listening to Speech: An Auditory Perspective*. Mahwah, NJ: Lawrence Erlbaum Associates, 203–20.

—— —— —— and Bloedel, S. L. (1998). 'Role of Experience for Language-Specific Functional Mappings of Vowel Sounds.' *Journal of the Acoustical Society of America*, 104: 3568–82.

Kratzer, Angelika (1996). 'Severing the External Argument from its Verb.' In J. Rooryck and L. Zaring (eds.), *Phrase structure and the Lexicon*. Dordrecht, Kluwer: 109–37.

Kreidler, Charles W. (2004). *The Pronunciation of English: A Course Book*. Malden, Mass.: Blackwell.

Kuhl, Patricia K. (1993). 'Innate Predispositions and the Effects of Experience in Speech Perception: The Native Language Magnet Theory.' In B. de Boysoon-Bardies, S. de Schonen, P. W. Jusczyk, P. MacNeilage, and J. Morton (eds.), *Developmental Neurocognition: Speech and Face Processing in the First Year of Life*. Norwell, Mass.: Kluwer Academic, 259–74.

—— (2000). 'Language, Mind, and the Brain: Experience Alterts Perception.' In M. S. Gazzaniga (ed.), *The New Cognitive Neurosciences*. Cambridge, Mass.: MIT, 99–115.

—— and Miller, James D. (1975). 'Speech Perception by the Chinchilla.' *Science* 190: 69–72.

Kuryłowicz, Jerzy (1948). 'Contribution à la théorie de la syllabe.' *Bulletin de la Société Polonaise de Linquistique* 8: 80–114.

Ladefoged, Peter (1967). *Three Areas of Experimental Phonetics*. London: Oxford University Press.

—— (2001). *Vowels and Consonants: An Introduction to the Sounds of Languages*. Malden, Mass.: Blackwell.

Lakatos, Imre (1970). 'Falsifications and the Methodology of Scientific Research Programs.' In I. Lakatos and A. Musgrave (eds.), *Criticism and the Growth of Knowledge*. Cambridge: Cambridge University Press, 91–195.

Lakoff, Goerge, and Nuñez, Rafael (2001). *Where Mathematics Comes From: How the Embodied Mind Brings Mathematics into Being*. New York: Basic Books.

Larson, Gary (1993). 'Dynamic Computational Models and the Representation of Phonological Information.' Ph.D. thesis, University of Chicago.

Lasnik, Howard (2006). 'Conceptions of the Cycle.' In L. Cheng and N. Corver (eds.), *Wh-movement: Moving On*. Cambridge, Mass.: MIT, 197–216.

—— and Lohndal, Terje (2010). 'Government-Binding/Principles and Parameters Theory.' *Wiley Interdisciplinary Reviews: Cognitive Science* 1: 40–50.

—— and Uriagereka, Juan (2002). 'On the Poverty of the Challenge.' *Linguistic Review* 19: 147–50.

—— —— and Boeckx, Cedric (2005). *A Course in Minimalist Syntax*. Oxford: Blackwell.

Lass, Roger (1976). 'Rules, Metarules, and the Shape of the Great Vowel Shift.' In R. Lass (ed.), *English Phonology and Phonological Theory*. Cambridge: Cambridge University Press, 51–102.

—— (1980). *On Explaining Language Change*. Cambridge: Cambridge University Press.

Leben, William (1973). 'Suprasegmental Phonology.' Ph.D. thesis, MIT, Cambridge, Mass.

Legate, Julie Anne (2003). 'Some Interface Properties of the Phase.' *Linguistic Inquiry* 34(3): 506–16.

—— and Yang, Charles D. (2002). 'Empirical Re-assessment of Stimulus Poverty Arguments.' *Linguistic Review* 19: 151–62.

Lenneberg, Eric H. (1967). *Biological Foundations of Language.* New York: Wiley.

Lepsius, Richard, and Whitney, William Dwight (1865). 'On the Relation of Vowels and Consonants.' *Journal of the American Oriental Society* 8: 357–73.

Levin, Juliette (1985). 'A Metrical Theory of Syllabicity.' Ph.D. thesis, MIT, Cambridge, Mass.

Lewontin, Richard C. (2000). *The Triple Helix: Gene, Organism, and Environment.* Cambridge, Mass.: Harvard University Press.

Liberman, Alvin (1982). 'On Finding that Speech is Special.' *American Psychologist* 37(2): 148–67.

Lightfoot, David W. (1979). *Principles of Diachronic Syntax.* Cambridge: Cambridge University Press.

—— (1999). *The Development of Language: Acquisition, Change and Evolution.* Oxford: Blackwell.

—— (2006). *How New Languages Emerge.* Cambridge: Cambridge University Press.

Lindau, Mona and Ladefoged, Peter (1986). 'Variability of Feature Specifications.' In J. Perkell and D. Klatt (eds.), *Invariance and Variability in Speech Processes.* Hillsdale, NJ: Lawrence Erlbaum, 464–78.

Lohndal, Terje (2009a). 'The Copula Cycle.' In E. van Gelderen (ed.), *Cyclical Change.* Amsterdam: John Benjamins, 209–42.

—— (2009b). 'Double Definiteness, Adjectives, and Parameters.' Paper presented at Universität Stuttgart.

—— and Samuels, Bridget (2010). 'The Edges of the Syntax–Phonology Interface.' MS, University of Maryland.

Lombardi, Linda (2002). 'Coronal Epenthesis and Markedness.' *Phonology* 19, 219–51.

Longobardi, Giuseppe (1994). 'References and Proper Names: A Theory of N-movement in Syntax and Logical Form.' *Linguistic Inquiry* 25(4): 609–55.

Lowenstamm, Jean (1981). 'On the Maximal Cluster Approach to Syllable Structure.' *Linguistic Inquiry* 12(4): 575–604.

Maddieson, Ian (1984). *Patterns of Sound.* Cambridge: Cambridge University Press.

Mailhot, Frédéric, and Reiss, Charles (2007). 'Computing Long-Distance Dependencies in Vowel Harmony.' *Biolinguistics* 1: 28–48.

Marantz, Alec (1982). 'Re Reduplication.' *Linguistic Inquiry* 13: 435–82.

—— (1997). 'No Escape from Syntax: Don't Try Morphological Analysis in the Privacy of Your Own Lexicon.' In A. Dimitriadis, L. Siegel, C. Surek-Clark, and A. Williams (eds.), *Proceedings of PLC 21*, 201–25.

—— (2001). 'Words.' MS, MIT, Cambridge, Mass.

—— (2008). 'Phases and Words.' In S.-H. Choe (ed.), *Phases in the Theory of Grammar.* Seoul: Dong In, 191–222.

—— (2010). 'Locality Domains for Contextual Allosemy in Words.' Paper presented in the MIT Linguistics Colloquium.

Marcus, Gary, Vijayan, S., Bandi Rao, S., and Vishton, P. M. (1999). 'Rule Learning by Seven-Month-Old Infants.' *Science* 283: 77–80.

Markman, E.M. (1990). 'Constraints Children Place on Word Meanings.' *Cognitive Science* 14: 57–77.

Martin, Roger, and Uriagereka, Juan (2000). 'Some Possible Foundations of the Minimalist Program.' In R. Martin, D. Michaels, and J. Uriagereka (eds.), *Step by Step: Essays on Minimalist Syntax in Honor of Howard Lasnik*. Cambridge, Mass.: MIT, 1–29.

Marvin, Tatjana (2002). 'Topics in the Stress and Syntax of Words.' Ph.D. thesis, MIT, Cambridge, Mass.

Mascaró, Joan (1976). 'Catalan Phonology and the Phonological Cycle.' Ph.D. thesis, MIT, Cambridge, Mass.

Maye, Jessica (2002). 'The Development of Developmental Speech Production Research: The Impact of Werker and Tees (1984).' *Infant Behavior and Development* 25: 140–43.

McCarthy, John J. (1979). 'Formal Problems in Semitic Phonology and Morphology.' Ph.D. thesis, MIT, Cambridge, Mass.

—— (1986). 'OCP Effects: Gemination and Antigemination.' *Linguistic Inquiry* 17: 207–63.

—— (2002). *A Thematic Guide to Optimality Theory*. Cambridge: Cambridge University Press.

—— and Prince, Alan (1996 [1986]). *Prosodic Morphology*. Technical Report 32, Rutgers University Center for Cognitive Science.

McGinnis, Martha (2001). 'Variation in the Phase Structure of Applicatives.' In *Linguistic Variation Yearbook*. Amsterdam: John Benjamins, i. 105–46.

McGurk, H. and MacDonald, J. (1976). 'Hearing Lips and Seeing Voices.' *Nature* 264: 746–48.

McMahon, April (2000). *Lexical Phonology and the History of English*. Cambridge: Cambridge University Press.

Merker, Björn (2000). 'Synchronous Chorussing and Human Origins.' In N. Wallin, B. Merker, and S. Brown (eds.), *The Origin of Music*. Cambridge, Mass.: MIT, 315–28.

Merriam-Webster (2004). *Merriam-Webster Online Dictionary*. <http://www.m-w.com/home.htm.>

Mesgarani, Nima, David, Stephen V., Fritz, Jonathan B., and Shamma, Shihab A. (2008). 'Phoneme Representation and Classification in Primary Auditory Cortex.' *Journal of the Acoustical Society of America* 123(2): 899–909.

Michaels, Jennifer (2007). 'Syntactically Conditioned Phonology—Causatives in Malayalam.' MS, MIT, Cambridge, Mass.

Mielke, Jeff (2008). *The Emergence of Distinctive Features*. Oxford: Oxford University Press.

Miller, George A. (1956). 'The Magical Number Seven, Plus or Minus Two: Some Limits on Our Capacity for Processing Information.' *Psychological Review* 63: 81–97.

Mithen, Steven (2005). *The Singing Neanderthals: The Origins of Music, Language, Mind, and Body*. Cambridge, Mass.: Harvard University Press.

Mobbs, Iain (2008). ' "Functionalism," the Design of the Language Faculty, and (Disharmonic) Typology.' MS, Cambridge University.

Mohanan, Karuvannur Puthanveettil (1982). 'Lexical Phonology.' Ph.D. thesis, MIT, Cambridge, Mass.

—— (1986). *The Theory of Lexical Phonology*. Dordrecht: D. Reidel.

—— (2000). 'The Theoretical Substance of the Optimality Formalism.' *Linguistic Review*, 17: 143–66.

Moravcsik, Edith A. (1978). 'Reduplicative Constructions'. In J. H. Greenberg (ed.), *Universals of Human Language*. Stanford: Stanford University Press, iii. 297–334.

Morén, Bruce (2007). 'Minimalist/Substance-free Feature Theory.' Handouts from the EGG summer school, Brno.

Murphy, Robin A., Mondragon, Esther, and Murphy, Victoria A. (2008). 'Rule Learning by Rats.' *Science* 319: 1524–52.

Mutaka, Ngessimo M. (1994). *The Lexical Tonology of Kinande*. Lincom Studies in African Linguistics 1. Munich and Newcastle: Lincom Europa.

Narita, Hiroki (2009a). 'Full interpretation of Optimal Labeling.' *Biolinguistics* 3(2–3): 213–54.

—— (2009b). 'Multiple Transfer in Service of Recursive Merge.' Paper Presented at GLOW XXXII, Nantes.

—— and Fujita, Koji (2010). 'A Naturalist Reconstruction of Minimalist and Evolutionary Biolinguistics.' *Biolinguistics* 4(4): 356–76.

—— and Samuels, Bridget (2009). 'The H-α Schema and Phonological Derivation by Phase.' MS, Harvard University and University of Maryland.

Neeleman, Ad, and van de Koot, Hans (2006). 'On Syntactic and Phonological Representations.' *Lingua* 116: 1524–52.

Nespor, Marina, and Vogel, Irene (1986). *Prosodic Phonology*. Dordrecht: Foris.

Nevins, Andrew I. (2004). 'Conditions on (Dis)harmony.' Ph.D. thesis, MIT, Cambridge, Mass.

—— (2010). 'Two Case Studies in Phonological Universals: A View from Artificial Grammars.' *Biolinguistics* 4(2): 218–33.

—— and Endress, Ansgar D. (2007). 'The Edge of Order: Analytic Bias in Ludlings.' *Harvard Working Papers in Linguistics* 12: 43–53.

—— and Vaux, Bert (2003). 'Metalinguistic, Shmetalinguistic: The Phonology of Shm-reduplication.' In *Proceedings of CLS 39*. Chicago: Chicago Linguistic Society, 702–21.

Newell, Heather (2008). 'Aspects of the Morphology and Phonology of Phases.' Ph.D. thesis, McGill University, Montreal, QC.

Newmeyer, Frederick (2005). *Possible and Probable Languages: A Generative Perspective on Linguistic Typology*. Oxford: Oxford University Press.

Newport, Elissa L., and Aslin, Richard N. (2004). 'Learning at a Distance I. Statistical Learning of Non-adjacent Dependencies.' *Cognitive Psychology* 48: 127–62.

Newport, Elissa L., Hauser, Marc D., Spaepen, Geertrui, and Aslin, Richard N. (2004). 'Learning at a Distance II. Statistical Learning of Non-adjacent Dependencies in a Non-human Primate.' *Cognitive Psychology* 49: 85–117.

Niyogi, Partha (2006). *The Computational Nature of Language Learning and Evolution.* Cambridge, Mass.: MIT.

—— and Berwick, Robert C. (1995). 'The Logical Problem of Language Change.' AI Memo 1516, MIT Artificial Intelligence Laboratory.

———— (1997). 'Evolutionary Consequences of Language Learning.' *Linguistics and Philosophy* 20: 697–719.

Nunes, Jairo (2004). *Linearization of Chains and Sideward Movement.* Cambridge, Mass.: MIT.

Odden, David (1987). 'Kimatuumbi Phrasal Phonology.' *Phonology* 4: 13–36.

—— (1988). 'Antiantigemination and the OCP.' *Linguistic Inquiry* 19: 451–75.

—— (1990). 'Syntax, Lexical Rules, and Postlexical Rules in Kimatuumbi.' In S. Inkelas and D. Zec. (eds.), *The Phonology–Syntax Connection.* Chicago: University of Chicago Press, 259–277.

—— (1991). 'Vowel Geometry.' *Phonology* 8: 261–89.

—— (1994). 'Adjacency Parameters in Phonology.' *Language* 70(2): 289–330.

—— (1996). *Kimatuumbi Phonology and Morphology.* Oxford: Oxford University Press.

—— (2003). 'Review of McCarthy (2002), *A Thematic Guide to Optimality Theory.*' *Phonology* 20: 163–7.

—— (forthcoming). 'Rules v. Constraints.' In J. A. Goldsmith, J. Riggle, and A. C. Yu (eds.), *The Handbook of Phonological Theory.* 2nd. edn. Oxford: Blackwell.

Ohala, John J. (1981). 'The Listener as a Source of Sound Change.' In *Papers from the CLS Parasession on Language and Behavior,* 178–203.

—— (1990). 'The Phonetics and Phonology of Aspects of Assimilation.' In J. Kingston and M. E. Beckman (eds.), *Papers in Laboratory Phonology I.* Cambridge: Cambridge University Press, 258–75.

—— (1992). 'Alternatives to the Sonority Hierarchy for Explaining Segmental Sequential Constraints.' In *Papers from the CLS Parasession on the Syllable,* 319–38.

—— and Kawasaki-Fukumori, Haruko (1997). 'Alternatives to the Sonority Hierarchy for Explaining Segmental Sequential Constraints.' In S. Eliasson and E. H. Jahr (eds.), *Language and its Ecology: Essays in Memory of Einar Haugen.* Berlin: Mouton de Gruyter, 343–65.

Ohshiba, Nobuaki (1997). 'Memorization of Serial Items by Japanese Monkeys, a Chimpanzee, and Humans.' *Japanese Psychological Research* 39: 236–52.

Ortony, Andrew (1993). *Metaphor and Thought.* Cambridge: Cambridge University Press.

Ott, Dennis (2008). 'On Noun Ph(r)ases.' MS. Harvard University.

—— (2009). 'The Evolution of I-Language: Lexicalization as the Key Evolutionary Novelty.' *Biolinguistics* 3(2): 255–69.

Oudeyer, Pierre-Yves (2006). *Self-Organization in the Evolution of Speech*. Oxford: Oxford University Press.

Padgett, Jaye (1995). 'Feature Classes.' In J. N. Beckman, L. Walsh Dickey, and S. Urbanczyk (eds.), *University of Massachusetts Occasional Papers: Papers in Optimality Theory* 18. Stanford: CSLI, 385–420.

Pak, Marjorie (2008). 'The Postsyntactic Derivation and its Phonological Reflexes.' Ph.D. thesis, University of Pennsylvania, Philadelphia.

Pascalis, Olivier, de Haan, M., and Nelson, Charles A. (2002). 'Is Face Processing Species-Specific During the First Year of Life.' *Science* 296: 1321–3.

Patel, Aniruddh (2008). *Language and Music*. Oxford: Oxford University Press.

—— and Iversen, J. R. (2006). 'A Non-human Animal Can Drum a Steady Beat on a Musical Instrument.' In *Proceedings of the 9th International Conference on Music Perception and Cognition*, 477.

—— —— Bregman, Micah R., and Schulz, Irena (2009). 'Experimental Evidence for Synchronization to a Musical Beat in a Nonhuman Animal.' *Current Biology* 19(10): 1–4.

Paul, Hermann (1880). *Prinzipien der Sprachgeschichte*. Halle: Max Niemeyer.

Payne, Katherine (2000). 'The Progressively Changing Songs of Humpback Whales: A Window on the Creative Process in a Wild Animal.' In N. Wallin, B. Merker, and S. Brown (eds.), *The Origins of Music*. Cambridge, Mass.: MIT, 135–50.

Pesetsky, David (1979). 'Russian Morphology and Lexical Theory.' MS, MIT.

Phillips, Colin (1999). 'Categories and Constituents in the Neuroscience of Language.' Paper presented at Keio University, Tokyo.

—— and Lau, Ellen (2004). 'Foundational Issues', Review of Jackendoff (2002). *Journal of Linguistics* 40: 571–91.

Piattelli-Palmarini, Massimo (1989). 'Evolution, Selection, and Cognition: from "Learning" to Parameter Setting in Biology and in the Study of Language.' *Cognition* 31: 1–44.

Pietroski, Paul (2005). *Events and Semantic Architecture*. Oxford: Oxford University Press.

Piggott, Glyne, and Newell, Heather (2006). 'Syllabification, Stress and Derivation by Phase in Ojibwa.' *McGill Working Papers in Linguistics* 20(1).

Pike, K. L. (1947). *Phonemics*. Ann Arbor: University of Michigan Press.

Pinker, Steven, and Jackendoff, Ray (2005). 'The Faculty of Language: What's Special about It?' *Cognition* 95: 201–36.

Poeppel, David (2005). 'The Interdisciplinary Study of Language and its Challenges.' *Jahrbuch des Wissenschaftkollegs zu Berlin*.

—— Idsardi, William J., and van Wassenhove, Virginie (2007). 'Speech Perception at the Interface of Neurobiology and Linguistics.' *Philos. Trans. R. Soc. Lond. B. Biol. Sci.* 363: 1071–86.

Polka, L., and Werker, J.F. (1994). 'Developmental Changes in Perception of Non-native Vowel Contrasts.' *Journal of Experimental Psychology: Human Perception and Performance* 20(2): 421–35.

Poser, William J. (1982). 'Why Cases of Syllabic Reduplication Are So Hard to Find.' MS, MIT.

——(2004). 'Phonological Writing and Phonological Representation.' Paper presented in the Harvard Linguistic Theory Colloquium.

Prince, Alan, and Smolensky, Paul (1993 [2004]). *Optimality Theory: Constraint Interaction in Generative Grammar.* Oxford: Blackwell.

Pritchett, B. (1984). 'The Mys-fuckin-sterious Behavior of S-stop Clusters in English Expletive Infixation.' MS, Harvard University.

Pulleyblank, Douglas (2006). 'Minimizing UG: Constraints upon Constraints.' In D. Baumer, D. Montero, and M. Scanlon (eds.), *Proceedings of WCCFL* 25, 15–39. Somerville, Mass.: Cascadilla.

Pullum, Geoffrey K., and Scholz, Barbara C. (2002). 'Empirical Assessment of Stimulus Poverty Arguments.' *Linguistic Review* 19(1–2): 9–50.

Pylkkänen, Liina (2002). 'Introducing Arguments.' Ph.D. thesis, MIT, Cambridge, Mass.

Pylyshyn, Zenon W. (2003). *Seeing and Visualizing: It's Not What You Think.* Cambridge, Mass.: MIT.

Radford, Andrew (2000). 'Children in Search of Perfection: Towards a Minimalist Model of Acquisition.' *Essex Research Reports in Linguistics* 34. Colchester: University of Essex.

Raimy, Eric (2000*a*). *The Phonology and Morphology of Reduplication.* Berlin: Mouton de Gruyter.

——(2000*b*). 'Remarks on Backcopying.' *Linguistic Inquiry* 31(3): 541–52.

——(2003). 'Asymmetry and Linearization in Phonology.' In A. M. Di Sciullo (eds.), *Asymmetry in Grammar.* Amsterdam: John Benjamins, ii. 129–46.

——(2005). 'Prosodic Residue in an A-Templatic World.' Paper presented in the Linguistics Colloquium, University of Delaware, 14 October.

——(2008). 'Preliminaries to Deriving Syllable Phenomena from Parallel Representations.' Paper presented at the CUNY Phonology Forum Conference on the Syllable.

——(2009). 'Deriving Reduplicative Templates in a Modular Fashion.' In E. Raimy and C. Cairns (eds.), *Contemporary Views on Architecture and Representations in Phonological Theory.* Cambridge, Mass.: MIT, 383–404.

Ramachandran, V.S., and Blakeslee, Sandra (1998). *Phantoms in the Brain: Probing the Mysteries of the Human Mind.* New York: William Morrow.

Ramus, Franck, Hauser, Marc D., Miller, Cory, Morris, Dylan, and Mehler, Jacques (2000). 'Language Discrimination by Human Newborns and by Cotton-top Tamarin Monkeys.' *Science* 288: 349–51.

Redford, Melissa A. (1999). 'An Articulatory Basis for the Syllable.' Ph.D. thesis, University of Texas, Austin.

——Chen, Chun Chi, and Miikkulainen, Risto (2001). 'Constrained Emergence of Universals and Variation in Syllable Systems.' *Language and Speech* 44(1): 27–56.

Reiss, Charles (2003*a*). 'Quantification in Structural Descriptions: Attested and Unattested Patterns.' *The Linguistic Review* 20: 305–38.

——(2003*b*). 'Towards a Theory of Fundamental Phonological Relations.' In A. M. Di Sciullo (ed.), *Asymmetry in Grammar*. Amsterdam: John Benjamins, ii. 214–38.

——(2008*a*). 'The OCP and NoBanana.' In B. Vaux and A. I. Nevins (eds.), *Rules, Constraints, and Phonological Phenomena*. Oxford: Oxford University Press, 252–301.

——(2008*b*). 'Search Algorithm Solves a Problem of Representational Ambiguity.' MS, Concordia University.

——and Simpson, Marc (2009). 'Reduplication as Iterated Projection.' Paper presented at GLOW XXXII, Nantes.

Remez, R., Rubin, P., Pisoni, D., and Carrell, T. (1981). 'Speech Perception Without Traditional Speech Cues.' *Science* 212: 947–50.

Rice, Curt (2005). 'Optimal Gaps in Optimal Paradigms.' *Catalan Journal of Linguistics* 4: 155–70.

Rice, Keren (2008). 'Review of de Lacy (2006), *Markedness: Reduction and Preservation in Phonology*.' *Phonology* 25: 361–71.

Richards, Marc (2004). 'Object Shift, Scrambling, and Symmetrical Syntax.' Ph.D. thesis, Cambridge University.

——(2008). 'Two kinds of Variation in a Minimalist System.' In F. Heck, G. Müller, and J. Trommer (eds.), *Varieties of Competition* in Linguistische Arbeits Berichte. Leipzig, Universität Leipzig, 133–62.

——(forthcoming). 'Deriving the Edge: What's in a Phase?' *Syntax*.

Richards, Norvin (2010). *Uttering Trees*. Cambridge, Mass.: MIT.

Rizzi, Luigi (1990). *Relativized Minimality*. Cambridge, Mass.: MIT.

——(2002). 'Locality and Left Periphery.' In A. Belletti (ed.), *Structures and Beyond: The Cartography of Syntactic Structures*. Oxford: Oxford University Press, 223–51.

Roberts, Ian (2007). *Diachronic Syntax*. Oxford: Oxford University Press.

——and Holmberg, Anders (2009). 'Introduction: Parameters in Minimalist Theory.' In T. Biberauer, A. Holmberg, I. Roberts, and M. Sheehan (eds.), *Parametric Variation: Null Subjects in Minimalist Theory*. Cambridge: Cambridge University Press. 1–57.

Robins, R.H. (1957). 'Vowel Nasality in Sundanese: A Phonological and Grammatical Study.' *Studies in Linguistics*, 87–103.

Rose, Sharon (1997). 'Theoretical Issues in Comparative Ethio-Semitic Phonology and Morphology.' Ph.D. thesis, McGill University, Montreal.

Saffran, J. R., and Thiessen, E. D. (2003). 'Pattern Induction by Infant Language Learners.' *Developmental Psychology* 39: 1926–8.

Sagey, Elizabeth (1990). *The Representation of Features and Relations in Nonlinear Phonology*. New York: Garland.

Saltzman, I. J., and Garner, W. R. (1948). 'Reaction Time as a Measure of Span of Attention.' *Journal of Psychology* 25: 227–41.

Sampson, Geoffrey (2005). *The 'Language Instinct' Debate*. London: Continuum.

Samuels, Bridget (2005). 'Phonological Representation in Akkadian Orthography.' Paper presented at the 3rd Harvard Undergraduate Linguistics Colloquium.

Samuels, Bridget (2009*a*). 'Structure and Specification in Harmony.' In A. Schardl, M. Walkow, and M. Abdurrahman (eds.) *Proceedings of NELS 38*. Amherst, Mass., GLSA, ii. 283–96.

——(2009*b*). 'The Structure of Phonological Theory.' Ph.D. thesis, Harvard University, Cambridge, Mass.

——(2009*c*). 'The Third Factor in Phonology.' *Biolinguistics* 3(2–3): 355–82.

——(2010*a*). 'From Syntax to Phonology: Phi and Phases.' Paper presented at the 18th Manchester Phonology Meeting.

——(2010*b*). 'Phonological Derivation by Phase: Evidence from Basque.' In *Proceedings of PLC 33*, Penn Working Papers in Linguistics 16.1: 166–75.

——(2010*c*). 'Phonological Forms: From Ferrets to Fingers.' Paper presented at the Language Design Conference, Montreal.

——(2010*d*). 'The Topology of Infixation and Reduplication.' *The Linguistic Review* 27(2): 131–76.

——(forthcoming *a*). 'Consequences of Phases for Morphophonology.' In Á. J. Gallego. (ed.), *Phases: Developing the Framework*, Berlin: Mouton de Gruyter.

——(forthcoming *b*). 'Phonological Forms: From Ferrets to Fingers.' In A. M. Di Sciullo (ed.), *Biological Explorations: Interfaces in Language Design*.

——Hauser, Marc D., and Boeckx, Cedric (forthcoming). 'Do Animals have Universal Grammar? A Case Study in Phonology.' In I. Roberts (ed.), *The Oxford Handbook of Universal Grammar*. Oxford: Oxford University Press.

Sandler, Wendy (2008*a*). 'The Emergence of Prosody and Syntax in a New Sign Language.' Paper presented at PSI2, Berlin.

——(2008*b*). 'Is Phonology Necessary for Language?' Paper presented at the First SignTyp Conference, Storrs, Conn.

——and Lillo-Martin, Diane (2005). *Sign Language and Linguistic Universals*. Cambridge: Cambridge University Press.

Sato, Yosuke (2008). 'Multiple Spell-out and Contraction at the Syntax–Phonology Interface.' MS, University of Arizona.

——(2009*a*). 'Nuclear Stress, Cyclicity, and Edge Sensitivity at the Syntax–Phonology Interface.' MS, National University of Singapore.

——(2009*b*). 'Spelling-out Prosodic Domains: A Multiple Spell-out Account.' In K. K. Grohmann (ed.), *InterPhases: Phase-theoretic Investigations of Linguistic Interfaces*. Oxford: Oxford University Press, 234–59.

Schachner, Adena, Brady, Timothy F., Pepperberg, Irene M., and Hauser, Marc D. (2009). 'Spontaneous Motor Entrainment to Music in Multiple Vocal Mimicking Species. *Current Biology* 19(10): 1–6.

Scheer, Tobias (2004). *A Lateral Theory of Phonology*. Berlin: Mouton de Gruyter.

——(2008*a*). 'Spell Out Your Sister' In *Proceedings of WCCFL* 27: 379–87.

——(2008*b*). 'Why the Prosodic Hierarchy is a Diacritic and Why the Interface Must be Direct.' In J. M. Hartmann, V. Hegedus, and H. van Riemsdijk (eds.), *The Sounds of Silence*. Amsterdam: North-Holland Elsevier, 145–92.

—— (forthcoming). *How Morpho-Syntax Talks to Phonology: A Survey of Extra-Phonological Information in Phonology Since Trubetzkoy's Grenzsignale*. Berlin: Mouton de Gruyter.

Schein, Barry (1997). 'Conjunction Reduction Redux.' MS, University of Southern California.

Schiering, René, Bickel, Balthasar, and Hildebrandt, Kristine A. (2010). 'The Prosodic Word is not Universal, but Emergent.' *Journal of Linguistics* 46: 657–709.

Schneider-Zioga, Patricia, and Vergnaud, Jean-Roger (2009). 'Feet and Their Combination.' Paper presented at the CUNY Phonology Forum Conference on the Foot.

Schusterman, Ronald J., and Kastak, David (1993). 'A California Sea Lion (*Zalophus californianus*) is Capable of Forming Equivalence Relations.' *Psychological Record* 43: 823–39.

Ségéral, Philippe, and Scheer, Tobias (2008). 'Positional Factors in Lenition and Fortition.' In J. Brandão de Carvalho, T. Scheer, and P. Ségéral (eds.), *Lenition and Fortition*. Berlin: Mouton de Gruyter. 131–72.

Seidl, Amanda (2000). 'Minimal Indirect Reference: A Theory of the Syntax–Phonology Interface.' Ph.D. thesis, University of Pennsylvania, Philadelphia.

—— (2001). *Minimal Indirect Reference: A Theory of the Syntax–Phonology Interface*. London: Routledge.

Selkirk, Elisabeth O. (1978). 'On Prosodic Structure and its Relation to Syntactic Structure.' In T. Fretheim (ed.), *Nordic Prosody*. Trondheim: TAPIR, ii. 111–40.

—— (1982). *The Syntax of Words*. Cambridge, Mass.: MIT.

—— (1984). *Phonology and Syntax: The Relation between Sound and Structure*. Cambridge, Mass.: MIT.

—— (1986). 'On Derived Domains in Sentence Phonology.' *Phonology* 3: 371–405.

Shattuck-Hufnagel, Stefanie (2008). 'The Syllable in Speech Production Planning.' Paper presented at the CUNY Phonology Forum Conference on the Syllable.

Shettleworth, Sara J. (2010). *Cognition, Evolution, and Behavior*. 2nd edn. Oxford: Oxford University Press.

Shiobara, Kayono (2009). 'A Phonological View of Phases.' In K. K. Grohmann (ed.), *InterPhases: Phase-Theoretic Investigations of Linguistic Interfaces*. Oxford: Oxford University Press, 182–201.

Siegel, Dorothy (1974). *Topics in English Morphology*. New York: Garland.

Slater, Peter J. B. (2000). 'Birdsong Repertoires: Their Origins and Use.' In N. Wallin, B. Merker, and S. Brown (eds.), *The Origins of Music*. Cambridge, Mass.: MIT, 49–64.

Smalley, W.A. (1968). *Manual of Articulatory Phonetics*. Ann Arbor: Cushing-Malloy.

Smith, Dinitia (1999). 'A Thinking Bird or Just Another Birdbrain?' *New York Times*, 9 October.

Sober, Elliott (1994). 'No Model, No Inference: A Bayesian Primer on the Grue Problem.' In D. Stalker (ed.), *Grue! The New Riddle of Induction*. Chicago: Open Court. 225–40.

Spelke, Elizabeth (2003). 'What Makes Us Smart? Core Knowledge and Natural Language.' In D. Gentner and S. Goldin-Meadow (eds.), *Language in Mind: Advances in the Study of Language and Thought*. Cambridge, Mass.: MIT, 277–311.

Sproat, Richard (1985). 'On Deriving the Lexicon.' Ph.D. thesis, MIT, Cambridge, Mass.

Steriade, Donca (1987). 'Redundant Values.' In *Proceedings of CLS* 23, 2: 339–62.

—— (1995). 'Underspecification and Markedness.' In J. A. Goldsmith (ed.), *The Handbook of Phonological Theory*. Oxford: Blackwell, 114–74.

—— (1999). 'Alternatives to Syllable-based Accounts of Consonantal Phonotactics.' MS, University of California, Los Angeles.

—— (2008). 'Metrical Evidence for an Interlude Theory of Weight.' Paper presented at the CUNY Phonology Forum Conference on the Syllable.

—— (2009). 'The Phonology of Perceptibility Effects: the P-Map and its Consequences for Constraint Organization.' In K. Hanson and S. Inkelas (eds.), *The Nature of the Word: Studies in Honor of Paul Kiparsky*. Cambridge, Mass.: MIT, 151–79.

Stokoe, William (1960). 'Sign Language Structure: An Outline of the Visual Communication of the American Deaf.' *Studies in Linguistics* 8.

Streeter, L. A. (1976). 'Kikuyu Labial and Apical Stop Discrimination.' *Journal of Phonetics* 4: 43–9.

Svenonius, Peter (2004). 'On the Edge.' In D. Adger, C. de Cat, and G. Tsoulas (eds.), *Peripheries: Syntactic Edges and their Effects*. Dordrecht: Kluwer, 259–87.

Swingley, Daniel (2005). 'Statistical Clustering and the Contents of the Infant Vocabulary.' *Cognitive Psychology* 50: 86–132.

Tallerman, Maggie (2006). 'Challenging the Syllabic Model of "Syntax-as-it-is".' *Lingua* 116(5): 689–709.

Taylor, Ryan C., Klein, Barrett A., Stein, Joey, and Ryan, Michael J. (2008). 'Faux Frogs: Multimodal Signalling and the Value of Robotics in Animal Behavior.' *Animal Behaviour* 76(3): 1089–97.

ten Cate, Carel, van Heijningen, Caroline A. A., and Zuidema, Willem (2010). 'Reply to Gentner et al.: As Simple As Possible, but Not Simpler.' *PNAS* 107: E66–E67.

Tincoff, Ruth, Hauser, Marc D., Tsao, Fritz, Spaepen, Geertrui, Ramus, Franck, and Mehler, Jacques (2005). 'The Role of Speech Rhythm in Language Discrimination: Further Tests with a Non-human Primate.' *Developmental Science* 8: 26–35.

Tokimoto, Naoko, and Okanoya, Kazuo (2004). 'Spontaneous Construction of "Chinese boxes" by Degus (*Octodon degu*): A Rudiment of Recursive Intelligence?' *Japanese Psychological Research* 46: 255–61.

Toro, José M., Trobalón, Josep B., and Sebastián-Galles, N. (2005). 'The Effects of Backward Speech and Speaker Variability in Language Discrimination by Rats.' *Journal of Experimental Psychology: Animal Behavior Processes* 31: 95–100.

Travis, Lisa (2010). *Inner Aspect: The Articulation of VP*. Dordrecht: Springer.

Tremblay, Kelly L., Kraus, Nina, Carrell, Thomas D., and McGee, Therese (1997). 'Central Auditory System Plasticity: Generalization to Novel Stimuli Following Listening Training.' *Journal of the Acoustical Society of America* 102(6): 3762–73.

Truckenbrodt, Hubert (1995). 'Phonological Phrases: Their Relation to Syntax, Focus, and Prominence.' Ph.D. thesis, MIT, Cambridge, Mass.

—— (1999). 'On the Relation between Syntactic Phrases and Phonological Phrases.' *Linguistic Inquiry* 30(2): 219–56.

—— (2007). 'The Syntax–Phonology Interface.' In P. de Lacy (ed.), *The Cambridge Handbook of Phonology*. Cambridge: Cambridge University Press, 435–56.

Uriagereka, Juan (1998). *Rhyme and Reason*. Cambridge, Mass.: MIT.

—— (1999). 'Multiple Spell-Out.' In S. D. Epstein and N. Hornstein (eds.), *Working Minimalism*. Cambridge, Mass.: MIT, 251–82.

—— (2007). 'Clarifying the Notion "Parameter".' *Biolinguistics* 1: 99–113.

van der Hulst, Harry (2005). 'Why Phonology is the Same.' In H. Broekhuis, N. Corver, R. Huybregts, U. Kleinherz, and J. Koster (eds.), *The Organization of Grammar*. Berlin: Mouton de Gruyter, 252–61.

—— (2007). 'The Phonological Mobile.' Paper presented at the CUNY Phonology Forum Conference on Precedence Relations.

—— and Ritter, Nancy (2003). 'Levels, Constraints, and Heads.' In A. M. Di Sciullo (ed.), *Asymmetry in Grammar*. Amsterdam: John Benjamins, ii. 147–88.

van Gelderen, Elly (2007). 'The Definiteness Cycle in Germanic.' *Journal of Germanic Linguistics* 19: 275–308.

—— (2008). 'Where Did Late Merge Go? Grammaticalization as Feature Economy.' *Studia Linguistica* 62: 287–300.

van Heijningen, Caroline A. A., de Visser, Jos, Zuidema, Willem, and ten Cate, Carel (2009). 'Simple Rules Can Explain Discrimination of Putative Recursive Syntactic Structures by a Songbird Species.' *PNAS* 106(48): 20538–43.

van Oostendorp, Marc, and van de Weijer, Jeroen (2005). 'Phonological Alphabets and the Structure of the Segment.' In M. van Oostendorp and J. van de Weijer (eds.), *The Internal Organization of Phonological Segments*. Berlin: Mouton de Gruyter, 1–25.

van Riemsdijk, Henk (2008). 'Identity Avoidance: OCP Effects in Swiss Relatives.' In R. Freidin, C. Otero, and M.-L. Zubizarreta (eds.), *Foundational Issues in Linguistic Theory: Essays in Honor of Jean-Roger Vergnaud*. Cambridge, Mass.: MIT, 227–50.

Vaux, Bert (2008). 'Why the Phonological Component Must be Serial and Rule-based.' In B. Vaux and A. I. Nevins (eds.), *Rules, Constraints, and Phonological Phenomena*. Oxford: Oxford University Press, 20–60.

—— (2009*a*). 'The Role of Features in a Symbolic Theory of Phonology.' In E. Raimy and C. Cairns (eds.), *Contemporary Views on Architecture and Representations in Phonological Theory*. Cambridge, Mass.: MIT, 75–98.

—— (2009*b*). 'The Syllable Appendix.' In E. Raimy and C. Cairns (eds.), *Contemporary Views on Architecture and Representations in Phonological Theory*. Cambridge, Mass.: MIT.

—— and Samuels, Bridget (2003). 'Consonant Epenthesis and Hypercorrection.' MS, Harvard University.

—— —— (2005). 'Laryngeal Markedness and Aspiration.' *Phonology* 22(4): 395–436.

Vennemann, Theo (1972). 'On the Theory of Syllabic Phonology.' *Linguistische Berichte* 18: 1–18.

—— (1988). *Preference Laws for Syllable Structure and the Explanation of Sound Change.* Berlin: Mouton de Gruyter.

Vercelli, Donata (2009). 'Language in an Epigenetic Framework.' In M. Piattelli-Palmarini, J. Uriagereka, and P. Salaburu (eds.), *Of Minds and Language.* Oxford: Oxford University Press, 97–107.

Vihman, M. M., Macken, M. A., Miller, R., Simmons, H., and Miller, J. (1985). 'From Babbling to Speech: A Re-assessment of the Continuity Issue.' *Language* 61: 397–445.

Wagner, Michael (2010). 'Prosody and Recursion in Coordinate Structures and Beyond.' *Natural Language and Linguistic Theory* 28: 183–237.

Walter, Mary Ann (2007). 'Repetition Avoidance in Human Language.' Ph.D. thesis, MIT, Cambridge, Mass.

Weikum, Whitney M., Vouloumanos, Athena, Navarra, Jordi, Soto-Franco, Salvador, Sebastián-Galles, Núria, and Werker, Janet F. (2007). 'Visual Language Discrimination in Infancy.' *Science* 316: 1159.

Weinreich, Uriel, Labov, William, and Herzog, Marvin I. (1968). 'Empirical Foundations for a Theory of Language Change.' In W. P. Lehmann (ed.), *Directions for Historical Linguistics: A Symposium.* Austin: University of Texas Press, 95–195.

Werker, J. F. and Tees, R. C. (1984). 'Cross-Language Speech Perception: Evidence for Perceptual Reorganization during the First Year of Life.' *Infant Behavior and Development* 7: 49–63.

—— and Vouloumanos, Athena (2000). 'Language: Who's Got Rhythm?' *Science* 288(5464): 280–1.

Williams, Heather, and Staples, Kirsten (1992). 'Syllable Chunking in Zebra Finch (*Taeniopygia guttata*) Song.' *Journal of Comparative Psychology* 106(3): 278–86.

Williams, L. (1974). '*Speech Perception and Production as a Function of Exposure to a Second Language.*' Ph.D. thesis, Harvard University, Cambridge, Mass.

Wilson, Colin (2003). 'Experimental Investigation of Phonological Naturalness.' In *Proceedings of WCCFL* 22, 533–46.

Wohlgemuth, Melville J., Sober, Samuel J., and Brainard, Michael S. (2010). 'Linked Control of Syllable Sequence and Phonology in Birdsong.' *Journal of Neuroscience* 30(39): 12936–49.

Wright, A. A., Rivera, J. J., Hulse, Stewart H., Shyan, M., and Neiworth, J. J. (2000). 'Music Perception and Octave Generalization in Rhesus Monkeys.' *Journal of Experimental Psychology: General* 129: 291–307.

Wright, Beverly A. (2006). 'Perceptual Learning of Temporally Based Auditory Skills Thought to be Deficient in Children with Specific Language Impairment.' In S. Greenberg and W. A. Ainsworth (eds.), *Listening to Speech: An Auditory Perspective.* Mahwah, NJ: Lawrence Erlbaum Associates, 303–314.

Yang, Charles D. (2002). *Knowledge and Learning in Natural Language.* Oxford: Oxford University Press.

—— (2004). 'Universal Grammar, Statistics, or Both.' *Trends in Cognitive Sciences* 8(10): 451–6.

Yip, Moira (1988). 'The Obligatory Contour Principle and Phonological Rules: A Loss of Identity.' *Linguistic Inquiry* 19: 65–100.

—— (2006a). 'Is There Such a Thing as Animal Phonology?' In *Wondering at the Natural Fecundity of Things: Studies in Honor of Alan Prince*, <http://repositories.cdlib.org/lrc/prince/15>, accessed 3 May 2011.

—— (2006b). 'The Search for Phonology in Other Species.' *Trends in Cognitive Sciences* 10(10): 442–5.

Yu, Alan C. L. (2007). *A Natural History of Infixation*. Oxford: Oxford University Press.

Zepeda, Ofelia (1983). *A Papago Grammar*. Tucson: University of Arizona Press.

Zoerner, Edward (1995). 'Coordination: The Syntax of & P.' Ph.D. thesis, University of California, Irvine.

Author Index

Language Index

Subject Index